J.R. BRADLEY

A FORGOTTEN LARIMORE BOY

C. WAYNE KILPATRICK

FLORENCE, ALABAMA

J.R. Bradley
A Forgotten Larimore Boy

Manufactured in the United States of America

Cataloging-in-Publication Data
Kilpatrick, C. Wayne (Charlie Wayne), 1943–
J.R. Bradley: A Forgotten Larimore Boy / by C. Wayne Kilpatrick
p. cm.
Includes index.
ISBN 978-1-7320483-3-1 (cloth)
1.Bradley, James R., 1846–1923. 2. Churches of Christ—Biography. 3.
Churches of Christ—Clergy—
Biography. I. Author. II. Title.
BX7077 .B7333 2019 286.63092—dc20
Library of Congress Control Number: 2019933603

Cover design by Brittany McGuire

For information:
C. Wayne Kilpatrick
432 Sky Park Rd.
Florence, AL 35634

To my beloved wife Brenda—
who kept admonishing me to finish this book and who
traveled with me many miles while researching the
material and places included in this volume

CONTENTS

FOREWORD

Hidden deeply within the chronicles of the all but forgotten past are ample descriptions of the life of a man of humble existence. Profoundly intrenched in the employ of the King of kings, this preacher went about doing good to all who were within his field of labor. His life was a demonstration of all things modest. This world's wealth was never his aim. Never society's clergyman with all his accolades, this mild-mannered parson set his ministry among the poor and the downtrodden.

James R. Bradley was born in the South during the years leading up to the Civil War. While still a teen, he was privy to the sounds of war being played out over forty miles away on Shiloh's bloody battlefield.

His life was changed in the late summer of 1869 when T.B. Larimore came to the region around his home preaching New Testament Christianity. Answering the gospel call, he humbly obeyed the Lord's will, being buried in the watery grave of baptism by the preacher's capable hands.

Within a decade he was sitting at the feet of his father in the gospel at Mars Hill College, near Florence, Alabama, with the likes of F.B. and F.D. Srygley. Future co-workers in the field, Thomas L. Weatherford, Felix L. Sowell, William B. McQuiddy, and others were those he surrounded himself with as he learned the way of the Lord more deeply. In the decades that followed these men co-labored with Bradley in the "hills and the hollars" to as many as would hasten to the call of Jesus.

Most of his evangelistic work was in the woodland counties of south-central Tennessee and North Alabama. J.R. Bradley was a church planter. A good number of the churches he started are still active to this day. He lived among the churches he planted. Each month involved weekly rotations of visiting fledgling church families in remote locations within a reasonable distance from his home.

His talents were multiple. J.R. was an enthusiastic singer and knew music well. Many were the times when in a protracted (extended) meeting, he led the singing while others did the preaching. But, most of the time people knew him for his preaching capabilities. He was described as a clear and forcible speaker, and one who delivered his sermons with zeal and earnestness that few surpassed. Further, it was noted that the spirit that he manifested was "love, gentleness, and kindness." He was said to have "a wonderful tact of gaining the attention of his hearers; and when gained, he tells the sweet story of the cross in such loving-kindness that he wins the hearts of many who hear him." With such impression it was easy to see how people were drawn to Jesus by his preaching.

J.R. and his wife Mary never had children of their own but devoted themselves to their children in the faith. That said, their roles differed significantly. Much should be pondered concerning the dutiful wife of a traveling preacher in those days. Hers was a life filled with great periods of extreme loneliness. Keeping the home fires burning, taking care of the farm, and maintaining her husband's duties as well as her own was Mary's way of life. For, after the farming activities of the spring and early summer were completed, the meetings began, and once again, her farmer-come-man of God was gone for weeks at a time.

As has been noted, the Bradleys led a most humble existence. This meant they were never wealthy. Often, they were neglected by their brethren. Perhaps this led to their numerous bouts with sickness, especially as they advanced in years. J.R. was of slight build, around one-hundred fifty pounds by his own estimation.

For over five decades J.R. labored in the vineyard of the Lord. In addition to his preaching, he was a capable writer. Several of his articles appeared in the pages of the *Gospel Advocate*, and occasionally in the Texas paper, *Firm Foundation*. But his greatest contributions in writing came in the way of his wonderful reports of his meeting work. For, in these the picture of his life has been drawn.

Wayne Kilpatrick has labored long to give the world the story you are about to read. Quickly you will see that it has been a labor of his great love for the man, the preacher, and his great, great uncle, James R. Bradley.

Scott Harp
July 2019

PREFACE

M any years of research have gone into the following sketch of a man, who was all but forgotten by Christians, and even his own family. I visited churches that J.R. helped to establish, and the members had never heard of him. But why should I be surprised? There are those who claim to be members of the Lord's Church, that are not even sure who established the New Testament Church. As far as the Bradley family was concerned, there was my grandmother and one niece that knew of J.R. Those of my mother's generation had never heard of J.R. Bradley.

It was needful—yes even imperative—that lives of devotion to the Lord's Kingdom, such as J.R.'s, be told. Younger generations need to know what they have. They need to know that men like J.R. sacrificed so much so we could be where we are today in the Churches of Christ. A generation, now in danger of squandering away the church, needs to appreciate the fact that men like J.R. went without proper clothing, proper medical attention many times, and constantly in need of financial means and made many other sacrifices to establish the Lord's work in so many places. It would be the greatest act of ungratefulness for J.R.'s generation of preaching brethren, who gave so much sacrificial devotion to help save the lost and dying world, if their stories remained in obscurity. We truly are standing on the shoulders of giants and J.R. was one of those giants.

PREFACE

For about twenty years this book has been a labor of love. I have consulted with many along this journey (many whose names I have forgotten) concerning places, community attitudes, and other information to gain insight into the times of J.R. Bradley. Without their help this book would be a different piece of literature.

I would like to acknowledge my brother-in-law Milton Chaney, who persuaded me to give up my job at TVA and become a student at International Bible College in 1972. That started me on my journey of learning that continues to this day. I love God's word and I love researching his church and writing about its history. Without this beginning, this book would never have been written.

I would like to acknowledge Juanita Davis who was the first to graciously consent to proofread the manuscript and make suggestions in grammar and style. Her expertise was invaluable. Lori Eastep gave the second proofing of the manuscript and aided in formatting and grammar. I owe her a big debt of gratitude.

Gratitude is expressed to a dear friend and brother in Christ, Scott Harp who gave advice in areas of preparation and offered some needed constructive criticism.

Tom Childers was brave enough to give the trial-layout and help call attention on his website, "Friends of the Restoration," to this work. I am indebted to him.

Frank Richey, another dear friend and author, has been and continues to be a great encouragement. He has been a great help for my research.

My grandmother Nellie Bradley, who died in 2004, and my great aunt Carrie Danley were the only two relatives that I knew persoanlly who had ever met J.R. Bradley. They confirmed that I was researching the correct J.R. Bradley.

There are many others who encouraged me in my work. Earl Kimbrough who has written several books and Larry Whitehead who edited the *Alabama Restoration Journal* were constant sources of inspiration. And two of the dearest and sweetest ladies—Hilda and Lavaga Logan—have been my biggest fans for many years.

It would have been impossible to complete this task without the support of my wife Brenda and family. She was like the old British historian Bede's scribe Cuthbert. As Bede was on his deathbed translating the final verses of the Gospel of John, Cuthbert kept saying, "Hurry sir. Time is running out." Brenda kept saying, "Hurry Wayne. You're not going to live forever."

Finally, I would like to express thanks to my colleagues at Heritage Christian University who helped make this book a reality.

This book is written to be used, hopefully, as a resource tool to encourage further research into local church histories and, perhaps, the lives of some of J.R.'s contemporaries.

C. Wayne Kilpatrick
January 2019

J.R. BRADLEY

A FORGOTTEN LARIMORE BOY

1

EARLY LIFE AND EDUCATION

The year of 1846 was significant in several ways. That was the year that California became a republic. That same year Elias Howe patented the sewing machine. It was the year that the second war with Mexico began. It was early in September of that year that Santa Anna returned from exile to organize the Mexican Army and go to war with the United States of America. In late September, General Zachary Taylor won the Battle of Monterrey, Mexico. However, the most significant thing of that year to the John Cruse Bradley family was the birth of their firstborn son.

On September 3, 1846 James R. Bradley was born on a farm located in a valley that ran along the banks of Agnew Creek, west of Pulaski, in Giles County, Tennessee. It was a cool, crisp autumn day with smoke rising from the chimneys of the tiny cabins that were scattered across the Weakley Creek and Agnew Creek valleys, and along the ridges which bordered them. The creek emptied into Weakley Creek not far from the Bradley cabin. John Cruse and Rebecca Warren Bradley (his parents) had settled here some two or three years before. Little did they know, at the time, that this newborn son would someday become a powerful force in the Kingdom of God. It was to this valley that a former Baptist preacher by the name of Wade Barrett came, just two months after J.R.'s birth, and held a brush arbor meeting in November of 1846. Before he left the valley, he established a congregation of fourteen members (*Bible Advocate*, January 1847, p. 20). This meeting was just up Weakley from the Bradley cabin. The Bradleys, having been associated with the Baptists, probably heard Barrett many times as he came to the valley.

By the time J.R. was a year old, his father moved them further up the valley to Dry Weakley Creek near present day Greenwood. That was 1847. It was there that John C. and one of J.R.'s uncles – "Shade East" — operated a wagon shop. "Shade East" was married to Rebecca Warren Bradley's sister Jincy. Rebecca and Jincy were daughters of Reuben R. Warren of Lawrence County, Tennessee. By February of 1853, Shade had moved his family to Arkansas (*Probate Minutes*, Lauderdale County, Alabama Book A, p. 353-354). These two men--John C. Bradley and Shade East-- also built wagons, as well as repaired them (*G.A.*, May 27, 1915, p. 532). The Bradleys were living there on Dry Weakley when their third child David Lafayette was born.

By 1850 John C. moved his family to the north central part of Lauderdale County, Alabama which was a wooded area known as Gist Town. This community was about two or three miles from modern day Iron City, Tennessee and on a ridge that ran along the eastern side of Shoal Creek and about two miles south of Wolf Creek (*Lauderdale County, Alabama 1850 Census*, December 22, 1850). While living in that Alabama community, Andrew Jackson, the third son of John C. and Rebecca, was born, on September 1, 1851. John Cruse's parents — James and Margaret Bradley, had moved to this community within the past ten years, as their youngest son was only ten years old and was born in Tennessee (*Lauderdale County, Alabama 1850 Census*, December 22, 1850). James had fought in the War of 1812 under Andrew Jackson at Pensacola and New Orleans (Tom Kanon, "Regimental Histories of Tennessee Units of the War of 1812," Tennessee State Library and Archives). He was given 80 acres of land for his service (*Record of Miscellaneous Military Grants*, vol.31, p. 496).

James A. having served under Andrew Jackson may explain why the name "Andrew Jackson" was popular in the Bradley families. Rebecca Warren Bradley's father, Reuben R. Warren, had moved his family to this neighborhood by August 6, 1851, because he purchased two parcels of land on that day – one from John R. Stutts and one from John and Margaret McDonald (*Land Records*, Lauderdale County, Alabama, Book 14, pp. 522-523). In April of 1852 Reuben had purchased forty acres of land from the United States government (*Land Certificate*, Number 15885, April 1, 1852). He sold John C. forty acres of land for fifty-eight dollars and ten cents on December 8, 1852 (*Deed Book*, Lauderdale County, Alabama, Book A-14, pp. 269-270). Reuben would die before January 7, 1853 (*Probate Records*, Lauderdale County, Alabama, Book A, pp. 353-355). It appears that Reuben Warren sold the land to John C. while he was expecting to die. Since there is no deed recorded showing that John C. had purchased land before buying the Warren land, apparently, he and his family were already living on the Warren farm. This may be what brought John C.'s family to Alabama from Weakly Creek. For a short time, J.R. lived among both sets of his grandparents near Gist Town. John C.'s family lived there among the families of Gist, Lawson, Hill, Cauhorn, McDonald and Rickman. These people were a close-knit group and many married within their own community. This is how J.R. would later meet his future bride.

J.R.'s Family had moved to Lawrence County, Tennessee by February 17, 1853 (*Probate Records*, Lauderdale County, Alabama, Book A, pp. 353-355) and by December 18, 1854, John C. bought 372.75 acres of land from Aaron Mayhew, for 350 dollars. For some unknown reason the deed was not recorded until January 12, 1857 (*Deed Book*, Lawrence County, Tennessee, January 12, 1857, p. 496). On November 13, 1856 John C. sold eighty-five acres of his farm to James Fondrin for two hundred and twenty-three dollars and twenty-five cents (*Lawrence County, Tennessee Deed Book M*, p. 497). It is apparent that John C. used his farm to make a living in various ways—by both farming part of it and selling part of it. The Bradley family remained on this farm throughout the Civil War.

To the north of the Bradley farm the beautiful Holly Creek intersected with Shoal Creek from the west. Holly Creek Valley ran north-westward for several miles to the place that would eventually become Collinwood, Tennessee. About a mile south, Wolf Creek entered on the east side of Shoal Creek. Wolf Creek Valley ran eastward toward the place where St. Joseph, Tennessee, would be established a few years later. It was in this fertile area that J.R. grew to manhood. The Bradley farm was always bustling with lots of activity, but most of it was work. There was an abundance of fertile farm land and much running water. This, perhaps, is what brought John C. and Rebecca to this particular part of Lawrence County. Later, when iron ore would be discovered, the Bradley family, along with their neighbors, would watch this peaceful valley turn into a virtual "mad house" called Iron City, Tennessee.

The only business in the valley, besides farming, was a mill owned by John Dickie Wade on Wolf Creek about two miles away and John C.'s wagon shop. Shortly after the Civil War the Wolf Creek School would be established not far up the road from the mill. Young J.R. made many trips to this mill to get the family's grain ground into meal and flour. The road that ran from Shoal Creek eastward along Wolf Creek was the main connection to Jackson's Military Road. They intersected at what is now known as St Joseph, Tennessee. This was J.R. Bradley's world for many years, but as the reader can see, he was moved around the area several times before reaching manhood. During these years he worked on the farm and helped his father build wagons. John C. Bradley was a wagon-maker by trade (U.S. Census of Lawrence County, Tennessee, 1860).

John C. and Rebecca had three children born to them on Weakly Creek and five were born while they lived near this valley (U.S. Census of Lawrence County, Tennessee, 1860). They had three daughters and five sons. Lucy A. Frances was the oldest child in the Bradley household and James R. (perhaps named after both grandfathers—James Bradley and Reuben Warren) was the oldest son. The next son after J.R. was David Lafayette (the great grandfather of this writer). J.R. and Lafayette would always be close to one another. It would be Lafayette who settled J.R.'s estate upon J.R.'s death (Carrie Danley, Lafayette's daughter).

During these years in the valley, young J.R. was so busy helping his father make a living for the family that there was no time for education. F.D. Srygley wrote of J.R.'s education:

> His education in younger days had been entirely neglected, and he was wholly without financial resources, and his only means of support was hard manual labor on the farm, as a renter or hireling (*Larimore and His Boys*, 1891, p. 159).

Farming would be his chief means of support throughout his entire life.

We know very few details of his youth except for the hard life he endured. J.R. grew up in a Primitive Baptist family. John C., his father, distilled whiskey and according to a family member, he bought a farm with 40 gallons of whiskey (Michael R. Bradley, Letter, Dec.12, 2009). Despite his whiskey making, he was a zealous member of the Primitive Baptist church (*G.A.*, Nov.10, 1904, p. 719). [A note of explanation is needed here: In those times corn was difficult to keep through the winter months because of spoilage and rats and mice eating it, thus it was made into whiskey which was used in place of money]. J.R. attended that Baptist church when he was too young to know what they taught. Later he did not attend any church on a regular basis until he was grown. Not much pertaining to entertainment was known by him, except from time to time a preacher would come into the valley and preach. On these occasions most of the valley folk would come and listen. Some came to hear the preacher give news from other communities. "Rowdies" came to look for mischief, and often found it. Others came out of concern for their souls. We do not know which of these brought young Bradley, but something brought him. It was at one of these meetings he attended at Wade's Chapel, the small church building located on John D. Wade's farm, that he obeyed the "Gospel call" and was baptized. It was in August of 1869 that he was baptized in the cool clear waters of Shoal Creek at Heffington's Bluff, which was just across the field from the church house, which later would be known as Antioch. T.B. Larimore did the honors. Wade had encouraged and helped organize a church here before the Civil War. John Taylor from Rock Creek, Alabama, had preached here many times (F. D. Srygley, *Larimore and His Boys*, p. 185). John D. Wade had been baptized in 1836 by Dr. William Henry Wharton of Tuscumbia, Alabama (*Bethelberry Church Record Book*). For some years the Church of Christ at Antioch (formerly Wade's Chapel, *Goodspeed's History of Tennessee*, p. 761) was one of only two churches of any kind in the vicinity, the other being the Primitive Baptist Church. Some years later the congregation on Wade's farm would move about a mile north to what is now known as Iron City, Tennessee. This congregation would always be referred to as J.R.'s home church. He would make many trips back to it and preach throughout his life. This little church was like a polar star to the community, partly because John D. Wade, the leading figure in the little congregation, was so well loved and respected by the people of the entire valley.

The valley folk endured much during the Civil War and the Bradley family was no exception. They heard the horrible cannons' roar for two days from the battlefield at Shiloh, which was more than forty miles away. J.R. recalled many years later how he and two younger brothers, on that fateful day of April 6, 1862, listened to the battle from a bluff-top near their house. He wrote:

> While I was but a small boy, I remember well that I, with my two younger brothers, was on a bluff in Lawrence County, Tenn., on the first day of this battle, and remained there nearly

all day, without dinner, listening to the roar of the cannon (*G.A.*, Nov. 21, 1907, p. 752).

The two brothers were David Lafayette and Andrew Jackson. It is tantalizing just to wonder which bluff was climbed by these young boys, so they could to listen to the deadly battle in the distance. Was it Heffington's Bluff or was it the one near the mouth of Holly Creek? Which other could it have been?

They were also terrorized by Tom Clark and his band of outlaws, who wore the Union uniform as a cover for all their horrendous crimes. J.R. knew of John D. Wade being robbed and hanged twice, only to be saved by his slave, Uncle Sandy. He knew John Boron, who was murdered near the mill on Wolf Creek in cold blood by Clark's gang. He heard of the terrible killings by the Clark gang in Dead Horse Hollow, just a mile or two from his home. The list of atrocities went on and on and became so terrible that General Dodge of the union Army ordered Tom Clark, and Elias Thrasher shot "if caught in an act of violence" (*Official Records*, Series I, Volume 49, Part1, pages 73-74).

During this terrible period, J.R. found little about which to rejoice. He did, however, make the best of this dark period and on March 31, 1864 he married Mary E. Lyles (*Marriage Records (1818-1923)*, Lawrence Co., Tennessee). He was seventeen and she was sixteen (*G.A.*, April 27, 1911, p. 495). She would be his companion for 47 years. Mary was from a neighboring farm, and like J.R., her farm life did not allow time for an education. This was still evident two years before her death when she signed a deed in Lincoln County, Tennessee on February 5, 1909, with just an "X" (*Deed Book*-1909, Lincoln Co., Tennessee, p. 339). J.R. and Mary never had any children, but they loved the children of their community and were loved back (Aunt Carrie Danley, J.R.'s niece, Interview, 1985). J.R.'s love for Mary was manifested, even after Mary had died, when he requested in his will to be buried beside Mary. His will stipulated as follows: "I request to be buried at Fayetteville, Tenn., beside my first wife! Mary E. Bradley" (*Will*

Book, no.7, p. 67, Lincoln Co., Tennessee). Even though J.R. had married Loula Emma Sloan after Mary died, his love for Mary remained the rest of his life.

Just a few months following J.R.'s baptism his grandfather James A. Bradley, near whom he had lived for most of his life, died. This was a blow that struck the family hard. His grandfather was a War of 1812 veteran who had served under Generals Andrew Jackson and John Coffee at New Orleans. His grandfather had been an encouragement to him. By that time in his life, J.R. and a Brother Smallwood had begun to preach in the nearby area of Antioch (F.D. Srygley, *Larimore and His Boys*, p185). By 1874 he had performed at least one wedding; which was rather comical as it was recorded in the *Florence Times*. The account read as follows:

> Married—Olive –Poole on Saturday, the 31st ult., in the public road, just beyond the Tennessee line, by Rev. Mr. Bradley, Mr. Olive and Miss Peel (Poole) both of Lauderdale County (*Florence Times*, February 1, 1874).

The weather must have been freezing cold on that January day. One can just imagine the scene as it unfolded. No doubt it was a day frozen in J.R.'s memory.

Sometime before 1878, J.R. and Mary had moved just south of Iron City to Lauderdale County, Alabama. The move was not more than two or three miles from their home places. Their home, at that time, was near present-day Gist Town, about three miles west of Greenhill. In the fall of 1878 they had relocated near Mars Hill College and close enough that J.R. could travel home each evening after classes. Shortly after moving, J.R. was saddened by the death of his grandmother Margaret Bradley, who died in November of that year. J.R. was about halfway through his first semester at Mars Hill when he received the sad news concerning his grandmother. School life was a struggle for the J.R. and Mary, but their trust in God never wavered. J.R. was a lucky man to have a woman like Mary, who was spiritually minded and not materially minded. She encouraged him in his schooling and never complained about not having the things she needed. He did whatever work could be found to do while at Mars Hill. Sometimes it was working on the farm as a farmhand. Sometimes he worked at odd jobs to support Mary and himself. They even took into their home at least one boarder (T.L. Weatherford of Limestone County, Alabama) to help them pay the bills. J.R. wrote upon Weatherford's death:

> He boarded with us at Mars Hill during the term of 1878. He assisted me in several meetings after we left school, and he was certainly a companionable man and a true yokefellow (*G.A.*, March 26, 1908, p. 197).

J.R. enrolled under Brother T.B. Larimore to learn how to preach more effectively. He and a friend of his had begun trying to preach soon after they were baptized in 1869. He and a Brother Smallwood began to preach in the nearby area of Antioch (F.D. Srygley, *Larimore and His Boys*, p. 185). This was probably George Smallwood, who was a member at Antioch, (*Bethelberry Church Book*) and was a preacher according to his obituary (*G.A.*, May 9, 1907, p. 303). J.R., however, wanted to do better so he began to think about school. Srygley remembered Bradley's coming to Mars Hill and wrote:

> J.R. Bradley, of Lauderdale County, Ala., was at Mars Hill in 1878-9. He was well along in years, and married when he entered school... In school he applied himself closely and attained a fair degree of proficiency in English grammar, logic, rhetoric, and general outline of history. He developed an easy and impressive delivery, acquired a correct knowledge of the doctrine of Christ and came to understand the leading doctrines of the different religious sects of modern times with tolerable accuracy (F.D. Srygley, *Larimore and His Boys*, p. 159).

Another source spoke of Bradley's educational efforts in much the same way as did Srygley. The *Fayetteville Observer* stated that he was "Educated after marriage under adverse conditions at Mars Hill under Eld. T.B. Larimore" (September 13, 1923). These accounts just accent the extreme poverty endured by J.R. and Mary while at Mars Hill and throughout their entire lives.

While a student at Mars Hill some of his classes were as follows: Mathematics was taught by Bro. E. C. Snow, a kind-hearted man who took great pride in his students and their recitations. He would help the students learn how to solve the most difficult problems (Lee Jackson, *G.A.*, Feb.4, 1909, p. 132). R. E. McKnight taught ancient history while J.R. was at Mars Hill. McKnight had been a student at Mars Hill and taught for one session after graduating. Lee Jackson described him as "strictly orthodox respecting the accepted records of history" (*G.A.*, Feb.4, 1909, p. 132). Srygley referred to Mars Hill as a school that loved to sing. He described the singing sessions in chapter XIV of *Larimore and His Boys*. Frank Tankersley, of Marshall County, Tennessee, was a student at Mars Hill, but upon graduation, he taught music. It was during this time (1879) that he taught J.R. and his friend, M. A. Beal, vocal music. Srygley said that he was a good leader of songs and an acceptable preacher (F.D. Srygley, *Larimore and His Boys*, p. 181). J.R. loved to sing, and he learned it at Mars Hill. Last, but not least, Larimore taught Bible. J. R's love and respect for Larimore would go to the grave with him.

While at Mars Hill, he began to preach at several mission points in Lauderdale and Colbert counties, Alabama, and Lawrence and Giles counties, Tennessee. He also preached in Limestone and perhaps Morgan Counties in Alabama, as is borne out by a report from R.W. Officer dated May 15, 1879. Officer reported that Murrell Askew and J.R. Bradley were with him in Limestone County, Alabama. The report was as follows:

On the 4th Lord's day in April I met with a congregation of brethren at New Hope Baptist church; we were closed out; a

large congregation moved to the grove—we had three added.
Bro Askew and Bro. Bradley were there with gospel harness
all on. Last Lord's day [May 11th] I met with the brethren at
Cedar Plains, in Morgan Co., Ala. One added (*G.A.*, June 12,
1879, p. 370).

The above report contained the first mention of J.R. in the pages
of the *Gospel Advocate*.

J.R. had somehow meet Officer and Askew. These men had both
withdrawn from the Baptist church over doctrinal issues and immediately began preaching the New Testament pattern. That was
the reason for their problems in the Baptist church—they had begun teaching the Bible and not Baptist doctrine. They became
valuable assets in the New Testament church. Maybe J.R. identi-
fied with these men, since he had been raised as a Baptist himself.
Upon leaving Mars Hill, J.R.'s first preaching points were congregations that had transformed from Baptists to New Testament
Christianity—such as the Union Grove and Salem congregations
in Lauderdale County, Alabama. They had been transformed by
Murrell Askew.

As a student at Mars Hill he made some life-long acquaintants
with men like F.D. and F.B. Srygley, J.C. McQuiddy, Wm. B.
McQuiddy, M.A. Beal, Lee Jackson, John T. Underwood, T.L.
Weatherford, W.J. Hudspeth and others. He would work in meetings alongside these men. After leaving for the summer, from
Mars Hill, J.R. worked with W.J. Hudspeth of Prescott, Arkansas,
until school began in the fall. A brother C.J. Herren wrote of one
such meeting:

> I am certain you are anxious to hear from all good Congrega-
> tions and meetings; therefore, I will give you a short history of
> one [meeting] commenced at Antioch, 10 miles south of this
> place (West Point) on the 3rd Saturday in August last, con-
> ducted by Bro. J.R. Bradley, Bro. W.J. Hudspeth, and others.
> Myself and my wife and daughter were in attendance the first
> two days and witnessed the largest congregation (said to be)

that ever met at that church. All appeared to be interested, giving undivided attention. With good dinner on the ground, the meeting continued five or six days and resulted in eleven who made the good confession and were added to the church (*G.A.*, September 18, 1879, p. 602-603).

Another meeting for Bradley and Hudspeth was in Lauderdale County, Alabama, during the month of September of that year. This meeting took place at a newly established congregation of the Church of Christ at Union Grove which was originally known as the Union Grove Baptist Church. Murrell Askew, a former Baptist preacher converted almost the entire Baptist congregation in September of 1875 when he withdrew from the Indian Creek Association (*G A.*, May 11, 1876, p. 454). J.R. reported on the meeting held by him and Hudspeth as follows:

Bro. Hudspeth and I commenced preaching at a place in Alabama, Lauderdale county, called Union Grove, which was some two or three years ago, entirely a Baptist congregation. The result, of this meeting, was 25 additions. I left Bro. H., there on Wednesday –went to my uncle's [house] on the Tennessee River, preached Thursday; my uncle who is above 60 years old confessed and was baptized –had one addition last night at Salem, Ala. We praise the good Lord for it all (*G.A.*, September 18, 1879, p. 603).

This is the first reference by anyone, except Askew's reports, on the work after the initial establishment of the Church at that place. J.R. would return for other engagements. His reference to his uncle is intriguing because J.R. will refer to him one more time later, yet never names him. No doubt this was Terry Bradley, James A. Bradley's older brother, who was listed as a doctor in the 1850 census. His land lay just west of the mouth of Bluewater Creek. At the present (2019), a large part of his original holdings is under Wilson Lake (*Family Maps of Lauderdale County, Alabama*, by Greg A. Boyd, 2006, pp. 277-279). The summer of '79

14

had begun J.R.'s preaching career, while attending Mars Hill College.

F.D. Srygley wrote the following about J.R.'s and Hudspeth's work for that summer:

> Bro. Hudspeth, who labored with Bro. J.R. Bradley including three Lord's days –the fifth in August and first two in September–reports 79 accessions as the result of their united labors. Bro. Hudspeth has had many successful meetings since he left school in June, the result of which is not included in the above report. Bro. Bradley, with whom I spent many pleasant hours here in '78, has done much effective preaching since July 1st besides the joint labor with Bro. Hudspeth. These brethren are worthy laborers in the vineyard of the Lord (*G.A.*, October 9, 1879, p. 646).

Srygley could have used different things to praise Mars Hill but he wrote the following:

> While there are many things connected with the College of which I might speak in commendation of the Institution, I shall content myself with a brief statement of the labor and success of the young men whom I have met (*G.A.*, October 9, 1879, p. 646).

J.R. and his preaching companion, Hudspeth, continued to preach after returning to school in the fall. Brother M.D. Small wrote the following report about Bradley and Hudspeth having preached near Waynesboro, Tennessee, on the 25th and 26th of October. The letter read as follows:

> On the last Saturday in October brethren W.J. Hudspeth and J.R. Bradley, both students of Mars Hill, paid us a visit near Waynesboro for the purpose of holding a meeting of a week's duration, but as the people were busily engaged in sowing wheat, gathering their crops & c., it was thought best not to protract it longer than Sunday evening. They have made good

impressions on the minds of the people, and I have seldom witnessed such earnestness in presenting the truth of the gospel; tears flowed from young and old, but none had the moral courage to obey that form of doctrine that was once delivered to the saints; the people are honest in their convictions, but they have been sucking the paps of sectarianism so long, it is hard to get them to drink, or even taste of the pure, sincere milk of the word. It will take time to unbias the minds of the people, but most of the fault lies at our own door; we are not zealous enough (*G.A.,* November 20, 1879, p. front page of that issue).

This meeting was near present day Wayne's Furness. Other meetings followed that fall.

During the month of November, Larimore was highlighting the school by reporting on the labors of some of the students and he gave a report on J.R., in which he said that J.R. had two additions because of his preaching on the last Sunday in October ((*G.A.,* November 20, 1879, p. front page of that issue)). Larimore did not say where this took place.

During the fall session of 1879, someone organized the students in the Bible Department into writing an appeal to *Gospel Advocate,* trying to get churches to encourage new students to come to Mars Hill College. It seems that Larimore had considered closing the school down if more students and funds could not be found.

We do not know who got the appeal written, but J.R.'s name was the first on the list which may suggest that he was the one responsible for the appeal. It was stated in the appeal:

> Our appeal is for more students. Have you sons and daughters to send to school? Then "few places more closely approximate perfect freedom from every temptation to idleness, extravagance, or any other species of vice.... You may rest assured that the constant aim of the President of Mars Hill College and his associate professors is, and ever will be, to make thorough, practical scholars, and earnest devout Christians—to refine,

elevate, ennoble, and save, by educating those committed to their care as to render them eminently qualified for the purest circles of society, the highest spheres of usefulness, and the noblest deeds of life—especially to encourage them to so live as to be honorable, successful, and happy through life, and to be permitted, having borne the cross faithfully here a little while, to wear the crown blissfully "over there' for ever more."

Unless there is a large increase of students the first of next term, which begins first Monday in January '80, there is a probability that the school will close next June never to be revived. Brethren, will you let this school, which has done so much for the cause of Christ, go down for the want of patronage? Will you sit with hands folded and see it die? As prices have been reduced, rendering it within the power of all to attend, will you generously respond by making one united effort to prevail on all you can, to become students of Mars Hill College? Our prayers shall go up for the success of the school and we believe God will hear us, and that Mars' Hill College will live many years and continue to send out devoted Christians to break the bread of life to a perishing world. If our prayers, tears, and labors, will save the school, while we live it never, never, no never, shall go down. We appeal to a grateful people, hoping and praying that they will generously respond.

With hearts full of love for the cause of Christ, we express these sentiments voluntarily without being requested by Bro. Larimore or any of his of his associate teachers to do so. We have been prompted to make this appeal by a sense of duty, and with the hope that we may contribute to the prosperity of the cause of Christ and to the temporal and eternal welfare of our fellow travelers to the tomb. We wish it distinctly understood that this is purely an offering of love from the hearts and hands of children who know and appreciate the worth of their *alma mater*, and who actuated by the principles which that mother has instilled in their bosoms, are determined to sustain her till her death (*G.A.*, November 27, 1879, p. 757).

There were twenty-six names attached to this appeal, with J.R.'s name at the head of the list. Srygley used this same list of names as the core of his biographical sketches in his book—*Larimore and His Boys*. J.R. left Mars Hill on May 13, 1880, having completed his course of studies at that institution. This must have been a bitter-sweet time for him. He had finished his studies that prepared him to do the thing he desired most—to preach; but he was leaving behind friends at Mars Hill that perhaps he would never see again on this earth. He loved those friends and the teachers, especially Larimore; however, his circle of friends was about to grow even larger—very much larger.

2

ALABAMA DAYS

F.D. Srygley wrote of the nine or ten years after J.R. was graduated from Mars Hill:

> On leaving school, he settled in Giles county (sic), Tenn., where he still resides [1889]. He has preached constantly and very successfully in Giles, Lawrence, Maury and Wayne counties, Tenn., and Lauderdale, Colbert and Limestone counties, Ala. He has baptized hundreds of people and has been instrumental in establishing many strong country churches in his field of labor (F. D. Srygley, *Larimore and His Boys*, 1891, p. 159).

After Mars Hill College, he did not move immediately to Giles County, Tennessee, as Srygley seems to have indicated. Instead he moved a little eastward to Salem in Lauderdale County, Alabama. He would work much nearer to his old home place, on what was known as the Wolf Creek Road, near the Wolf Creek School. This was in the direction of the newly settled community of St. Joseph, Tennessee. St. Joseph was situated on Jackson's Military Road and had been established in 1872, by German Catholic immigrants who had fled the ravages of the Franco-Prussian War back in Europe. St. Joseph had a post office and it was from this post office that Bradley would send reports to the *Gospel Advocate* during the next year. He made his presence known at St. Joseph by preaching wherever he could get a hearing. Even though the Catholic opposition was strong, he did not grow weary. His persistence saw the Church of Christ established at St. Joseph.

He began to preach quite regularly at Antioch, his old home church. It was located about one mile south of present-day Iron City, Tennessee, about a mile from where J.R. grew to manhood, and about 400 yards due east of John Dickie Wade's house. It was here, some years before, that J.R. had accepted the Gospel call and was baptized into Christ in nearby Shoal Creek. J.R. had a helper sometimes in his preaching in this region. One of his friends was William B. McQuiddy of Farmington, Marshall County, Tennessee, who had married John D. Wade's daughter, Chappell Wade. William B. McQuiddy, a Mars Hill classmate, was his preaching companion. McQuiddy wrote of one of these preaching efforts as follows:

> Bro. Bradley and I closed yesterday a meeting with his home congregation, Antioch. We preached thirteen discourses having large and attentive audiences most of the time. Two were added; may they always serve the Lord. If my health will permit, I desire to labor sometime with Bro. B. (Wm. B. McQuiddy, *Gospel Advocate*, August 26, 1880, p. 557).

J.R. Bradley and M.A. Beal held a meeting at Brush Creek, near Killen, Alabama, just prior to the Antioch meeting. J.R. reported twelve additions (*Gospel Advocate*, August 26, 1880, p. 256). Bradley did the preaching and Beal was the song leader. They worked several meetings in this way.

One can see from the early efforts that J.R. wasted no time in his evangelizing. Some unknown writer wrote the following about Bradley's first field of labor:

Bro. J.R. Bradley, recently a pupil at Mars Hill is laboring with
success in Lauderdale county, Alabama, and adjoining counties of Tennessee. He is a very earnest workman, and those
with, and among whom he labors seem to esteem him highly
'for his work's sake" (*Gospel Advocate*, June 17, 1880, p. 398).

He continued to preach in the southern part of Lawrence County,
Tennessee, but he was branching further northward also. He was
being drawn toward Lawrenceburg and eastward. This move
would come later, but he did begin to visit some mission points
in the northern part of the county.

Bradley described one such mission point in a letter to the *Gospel Advocate* dated March 1, 1880:

Last Saturday night (Feb. 28th) I met with a loving little band
of Christians at (or near) Sykes' Factory; commenced preaching at seven o'clock; preached about half an hour, when we
commenced to sing, "Am I a soldier of the cross?" Two ladies,
considering themselves not soldiers, made the good confession and went the "same hour of the night; and obeyed that
"form of doctrine," While standing on the banks of the creek
—lanterns burning—this little band singing "Am I a Soldier of
the Cross?"—it dark- all seemingly "hushed to rest:" who could
help but have the mind go back to the "jail"—Paul and Silas—
the jailor, and obedience on the part of all, not withstanding
the opposition which surrounded them? I delivered three discourses to little band, had good attention and interest
manifested by all. The good seed was sown here, first, by Bro.
Spivey. This little band worships in a little house, donated to
the Lord's work by our friend, Mr. Gibbs, who is not a member
of Christ's body, but has knowledge of his duty, and is working
for the Lord. This good man has a good wife, and two loving
daughters, who are all members of the little band. I never in
life have met a congregation which was as small, as much surrounded with opposition that had members so live; working,
talking, singing, praying, all seemed to be "fighting the good
fight of faith," and all this in Lawrence county, Tenn., about
one and a half miles west of Lawrenceburg (sic). May God be

with them and all who are fighting for our King (*G.A.*, March 11, 1880, p. 171).

This little congregation eventually became the Salem Church of Christ at Lawrenceburg and is still a solid congregation. It was J.R. Bradley and W.R. Spivey who organized that little band into a church. Lipscomb wrote of this work:

> There were 27 additions at Sykes' Ferry near Lawrenceburg, Tenn., at a meeting conducted by W.B. McQuiddy and J.R. Bradley. The little band now numbers forty-nine and manifests much zeal. They have taken steps to build a new and more commodious house in which to worship. (*G.A.*, September 16, 1880, p. 604).

Another congregation called Salem got some of Bradley's attention, but it was in Lauderdale County, Alabama. This congregation had been a Baptist Church but became a New Testament church under the preaching of Murrell Askew in 1876. J.R. had done some preaching at Salem as early as September of 1879. On July 14, 1880, Bradley wrote:

> Last Friday before starting to my appointment at Salem, Ala., I baptized an old gentleman, who according to his own statement is about 83 years of age. Went on to my appointment at Salem where I preached Saturday and Sunday and on Sunday, baptized five persons (*G.A.*, July 22, 1880, p. 447).

In October Bradley would return with his friend Wm. B. McQuiddy, and they would hold a meeting of five days (*G.A.*, Oct. 28, 1880, p. 696).

It seems that J.R. had established a circuit of preaching points by this time in 1880. In his letter of July 14, he left Salem on Sunday afternoon and preached at his uncle's house on the Tennessee River that evening. From there he went to Brush Creek, near present day Killen, and preached in a grove, being prevented from preaching in the building that had been built for all religious groups. The Methodists had commandeered the building (*G.A.*, July 22, 1880, p. 447). These other preaching points such as Brush Creek and his uncle's house on the river may help explain why Bradley left McQuiddy at Salem to finish out the meeting by himself.

William Comer wrote about the same events J.R. had described:

> I can inform you that Bros. J.R. Bradley (and) W.B. McQuiddy commenced a protracted meeting at Salem church, Lauderdale county, Ala., Saturday before the 2nd Lord's day of this month and continued up to Wednesday following with eight accessions, two from the C.P. church, the balance from the world, all by confession and baptism (*G.A.*, October 28, 1880, p. 696).

By the end of 1880, J.R. Bradley had moved to Comer, Alabama, between Elgin Cross Roads and Lexington in Lauderdale County. Salem was located at Comer. The community took its name from William Comer, who was a charter member at Salem. The families of William Comer and R.T. Lanier had transitioned from Separatist Baptist to the Church of Christ at Salem. Salem was one of two rural Lauderdale county churches that were growing rapidly. Comer wrote of this congregation: "We have a good Bible class and meet almost every Lord's day, investigate and partake of the emblems and are trying to advance the God's cause" (*G.A.*, October 28, 1880, p. 696). The other congregation on J.R.'s circuit was Union Grove. Both churches had been established by Murrell Askew as Baptist churches and had been converted by him to churches of Christ after he left the Baptists. Both would become a part of Bradley's circuit in 1881.

J.R. felt compelled to send a lengthy letter to David Lipscomb at the *Advocate*. This letter would appear in *Advocate* in May 5, 1881. He began by saying:

As I have said nothing through your pages in a good long time and thinking in all probability that the brethren – especially my old classmates at and of Mars Hill Bible College – would like to hear of myself and labors –I thought by your permission to give the outlines: (*G.A.*, May 5, 1881, p. 280).

With these opening lines he expresses his purpose for writing the letter. To fill in a gap on his work for his classmates at Mars Hill was his main intention, but the letter also served another purpose. That was to inform the readers of the *Advocate* his intentions for 1881. Bradley was always busy at either preaching or at farming.

J.R. wrote that he and McQuiddy had ended their protracted meetings in the fall of 1880 (*G.A.*, May 5, 1881, p. 280). Late fall was the time when protracted efforts in the southeastern states normally ended because of the weather. They usually began in late July and ran through October. The reason they started so late in the year in the rural regions was that farming demanded most of the farm families' time until the crops were "laid by," Most of the preachers, such as Bradley, were farmers also. This explains why Bradley would ask for meetings to begin in July or August and end in October.

He wrote of his winter's work as follows:

I have preached every Saturday and Sunday, except two appointments, which were disappointed on account of sickness and high water. I preached the first Sunday in the month for our home congregation, at Salem, Ala. The brethren here are doing moderately good work in the vineyard of the Lord. We have a few good old faithful brethren here who are determined to do the work. The second Sunday I am at Rural Hill, Giles County. This is an old congregation and I have been informed that they do not meet regularly in winter. This does not speak well for them, but we hope to hear better things of them next winter. The third Sunday I go to Union Grove, Ala. Here is a good place to get a large crowd on preaching days, but the brethren do not meet only when they have preaching.

They say that their Lord's Day work is always "spoiled" by one of the brethren who believes and contends that the Lord has not made it binding upon us to meet every first day. Such an excuse will not please the Lord in the Day of Judgment. No, never. The fourth Sunday I go to Sikes' Factory, near Lawrenceburg, Tenn. Here we have some members who are as good as I ever saw. They are but few, and surrounded by strong opposition (*G.A.* May 5, 1881, p. 280).

Bradley gives a good insight into each of these congregations, as well as revealing his work habits during the long winter months. He further wrote of the Sykes' Factory work.

Last Sunday [April 28] being the fourth I was there, and preached Saturday night and Sunday. One young lady came forward, made the confession, and was baptized, "the same hour of the night." This young lady has had to obey the gospel while earthly friends and relatives were begging and pleading her to join "their church," But no, she took the Lord's plan, and we hope will ever prove faithful (*G.A.* May 5, 1881, p. 280).

It seems that J.R. was rather partial to this little band at Syke's Factory. This is the second time he has given a rather lengthy report on what transpired at this place.

Bradley also mentions Center Point as being his fifth Sunday appointment. He wrote as follows: "The fifth Sunday I am with the brethren at Centre (sic) Point, a new congregation near the line between Lawrence and Giles counties. They seem to be in good order" (*G.A.* May 5, 1881, p. 280).

This Center Point was east of Lawrenceburg being near the Greenwood community and very near Lawrence-Giles county line. There is a later community called Center Point is on Rabbit Trail Road about four or five-miles southeast of Leoma, Tennessee and about five or six miles west of the county line. This Center Point is not to be confused with the Center Point that J.R. had mentioned in his report.

He closed his letter by telling about his work on his new place of residence (this was located near Comer, Lauderdale County, Alabama). He said: "The time that I am at home, I am trying to settle my new place." He further stated that he had "a great deal of hard work" (*G.A.* May 5, 1881, p. 280). He also gave statistics on his work, from the time he left Mars Hill, at the end of 1879, until April 1881. This was to let his former classmates know of his work. This was apparently what most of "Larimore's Boys" did. Bradley said that he had "tried" to preach 375 discourses [sermons], had 250 additions, and baptized 135. He stated in his own modest words: "It looks as if I might have done better, but this is all. Please let me hear from my scattered schoolmates" (Ibid). J.R. typically underestimated the good that he did, as was seen in this report. With this letter we have a good summary of his work for the winter months of 1880 and the early months of 1881.

He wrote a letter to *Gospel Advocate* on May 25th, 1881 and reported on his work at Sykes' Factory. He wrote: "Two additions at Sykes' Factory last (4th) Sunday. The brethren there will soon have a house of worship, tendered by Mr. Sykes. Some say "the Campbellites and locusts are going to take the country" (*G.A.* June 2, 1881, p. 347).

Again, one can see Bradley's fondness for the Sykes' Factory work showing through. On July 25th he wrote: "Four additions at Sykes' Factory, last Sunday. I preached in the new church house while there. The name of the church is "Bellview," so named by old mother Sykes (*G.A.* August 4, 1881, p. 491).

By the end of July, Bradley and another former class mate from Mars Hill — F.C. Sowell, held a meeting near West Point in Lawrence County, Tennessee. A brother C. J. Harris reported this effort as follows:

> Permit me to publish through the Advocate, the results of a six days' meeting, held in a Beech Grove, near West Point, Lawrence County, Tenn.; conducted by Bro J.R. Bradley and F.C. Sowell, two noble and faithful workers; students of Mars Hill

College, which fact is enough to recommend them to any congregation of the Christian order. Meeting closed last Thursday, after nine good faithful soldiers of Christ having marched up and not being afraid of much water, waded in and were buried with Christ in baptism, arose and came out rejoicing. One other sister would have done the same, had not her brother prevented by severe threats. I pray the Lord to pardon the brother for this, perhaps unthoughted wickedness, and protect and support the sister in her trials and difficulties (*G.A.* Aug. 4, 1881).

This was Bradley's first extended meeting of 1881.

The next meeting conducted by J.R. was with his preaching companion from the previous year, William B. McQuiddy. The meeting was held at Rural Hill in Giles County, Tennessee. A.J. Neal writes from Rural Hill:

Our protracted meeting commenced at Rural Hill on the 2nd Lord's Day in August. The meeting was conducted my J.R. Bradley and W.B. McQuiddy for four days, six accessions. T.B. Larimore preached four very able discourses and baptized one, and one reclaimed, eight in all. Several took membership; we have a very interesting Lord's day school, fifty or sixty names on the roll. To the Lord be praise (*G.A.* Sept. 1, 1881, p. 550).

Bradley had spoken about their being lax on their attendance in the winter months, in a previous article (*G.A.*, May 5, 1881, p. 280). It is hard to believe after this meeting that the members would be so weak in their duty toward the Lord.

His next reported meeting was at his local congregation of Salem. His home was still at Comer and that was his adopted home congregation. The meeting began on August 27, 1881 and continued for six days. The meeting was conducted by Bradley and W.B. McQuiddy. Seven were baptized and three others confessed Christ and postponed their baptism until Brother T.B. Larimore would come on the second Sunday in September. Two had been baptized a month earlier when F.C. Sowell preached at Salem, while Bradley was away in a meeting (*G.A.*, Sept. 8, 1881, p. 567).

Bradley next reported of a meeting that he held at Cool Springs, near Pulaski, Tennessee:

> I have just closed a very interesting meeting at Cool Springs, Giles county, Tenn., commenced Saturday before the second Sunday in this month continued six days with seven confessions and baptisms. The little band of brothers and sisters here are strong in the love of the Lord. Bros. Waldron and Nance were with me a part of the time (*G.A.*, September 29, 1881, p. 611).

The Brother Nance to whom J.R. referred was Martin M. (M.M.) Nance who had established the Cool Springs congregation. He had built the building with his own hands and had been their regular preacher since its establishment. His house, which he also built, was across the road from the church building. Both houses are still standing today (2019). More important, however, the spiritual building he established at that place is still there. Bradley would preach many times at Cool Springs throughout the rest of his life.

His preaching companion, Wm. B. McQuiddy, wrote of another meeting that Bradley and McQuiddy held at Union Grove in Lauderdale County, Alabama. This Union Grove would become the North Carolina Church of Christ in the early 1900's. McQuiddy wrote:

> Bro. J.R. Bradley and the writer closed last night a six days meeting with the congregation at Union Grove, Lauderdale county, Ala. Nine were added to the church and the church seemed greatly encouraged and strengthened. May they ever abound in zeal and knowledge of the truth (*G.A.*, Sept. 29, 1881, p. 611).

North Carolina (Union Grove) had been established by Murrell Askew sometime after the Civil War.

On October 12th, J.R. received the sad news that the five-year-old son of one of his good friends had shot himself accidentally and died immediately. The little boy was the son of Joseph and Mary Gibbs. Bradley wrote the following just minutes after he received the news:

> Our hearts were made sad this evening by the sudden death of dear little Charlie Gibbs; having a few minutes ago, accidentally shot and killed himself. He was playing with an old pistol, which had been used as a plaything for the children for a long time, and which had not been loaded, as any one knew of for years. This is the third son of Mr. Joseph and sister Mary Gibbs. Oh, how we all sympathize with the father, mother, brothers and sisters of dear little Charlie. Charlie was a nice, healthy, promising little boy. Dear fathers and mothers take warning from this, and do not let the little ones have such things for toys... (*G.A.* Oct. 20, 1881, p. 662).

You can understand Bradley's concern for the safety of little children. Remember that he and his wife were childless, and they loved all children. The death of little Charlie Gibbs awoke these strong emotions within J.R. He now turned his attention back to his protracted meeting schedule.

Along with the letter about little Charlie Gibbs' death J.R. sent a report on his labors for past two or three weeks. His report read as follows:

> I am on my way to Belleview, have been in Marshall and Giles counties, in the company of Bros. McQuiddy, Dixon, and others. I closed a meeting last Tuesday night at Beech Grove in Marshall county, Tenn., with one addition, one reclaimed, and one took membership Wednesday, and Thursday nights. I preached at Roberson Fork, Giles county with four confessions and baptisms. These are all good live congregations (*G.A.* Oct. 20, 1881, p. 662).

On November 10, 1881, *Gospel Advocate* printed a report, written by a Brother G.C. Thigpen of Comer, about a meeting at Brush Creek, near Killen, Alabama. Thigpen wrote:

The brethren at Brush Creek, (a Methodist house) have just closed an interesting meeting of five days; resulting in five additions, four by confession and baptism, and one from the Baptists. Bro. J.R. Bradley did the preaching and did it well. During the five days he preached nine sermons and left the people of this vicinity without excuse. Twelve months ago, sectarianism locked the very doors against the very man (Bro. Bradley) which has been so kindly thrown open during this meeting. And let me say, that the people of this community have the thanks and prayers of the brethren for their hospitality (*G.A.* Nov 10, 1881, p. 711).

You may recall that first meeting to which Bro. Thigpen referred. Bradley had just mentioned it in passing, in a report about the Salem congregation (*G.A.* July 22, 1880, p. 477). He wrote of this incident as follows:

Went from there [Salem] to my uncle's [house] on the Tennessee River, preached there Sunday evening — went from there to Brush Creek, Ala., and being compelled by the Methodist, had to go to the grove. This Brush Creek house was built by all for a free house (*G.A.* July 22, 1880, p. 477).

This demonstrates Bradley's persistence. He never gave up on a community. This work would become the Beech Grove Church of Christ which would later move into Killen and become the Killen church of Christ and it still is a faithful congregation in 2019. Thigpen continued in his report and gave us an insight into Bradley's style of preaching. He described his preaching as follows:

He shunned not to declare all the counsel of God and did it in so mild and kind way that none took offense: but all could see the truth. Sectarianism is strong here, though not so strong as it was one year ago (*G.A.* July 22, 1880, p. 477).

It was through Bradley's kind yet persistent manner that the work at Brush Creek was firmly established and continues to this day.

His next meeting was at Cool Springs, Giles County, Tennessee. He preached four times and had one conversion from the Methodists. He then went to a Methodist church called Hagen's Chapel. He preached twice with no additions, but he said that he had "a good hearing" (*G.A.* Oct. 27, 1881, p. 678). Hagen's Chapel was another Giles County community. One can see Bradley being slowly drawn more and more northward into Tennessee. While on one of his preaching tours of Giles County, he had made the acquaintance of Marmaduke Clifton and his wife Sarah. Bradley had baptized them on September 24, 1880. This was probably in the Rural Hill area, since Bradley was preaching there monthly. He reported Marmaduke Clifton's death through the pages of the *Advocate*, (Nov. 24, 1881, p. 749). This was J.R.'s last communication for the year 1881. He would typically stay close to home and preach during the winter months and begin his crops in the spring.

His first correspondence for 1882 appeared in the *Advocate*, in the form of a Bible question on June 7, 1882. More than likely he wrote the letter of inquiry sometime in May. His question was:

Who are the two Adams spoken of in 1 Corinthians XV: 45? Was Adam in the garden the first man, and was Christ "the Lord from heaven," the second? One man, with whom I conversed, contends differently (*G.A.*, June 8, 1881, p. 360).

Either Lipscomb or E.G. Sewell answered with one sentence: "Certainly, Adam in Eden was the first and Christ the second" (*G.A.*, June 8, 1881, p. 360). This shows Bradley's insight into the scriptures, yet his cautiousness to be correct in his dealings with others. This was commendable of him to have wanted to teach the truth as near correctly as he could.

Either in this same correspondence, or in another written within a day or two, he wrote about another problem some brethren were having in some of the congregations. To give the problem its context, we shall give the letter in full:

> Dear Editors and Readers of the *Gospel Advocate*: Is it detrimental to the cause we love, and for which we plead, to read from the pages of the *Gospel Advocate* or A.C. Review [American Christian Review], or any other good religious paper in our Sunday schools? I think not. It appears to me, that if the reading of these good articles around our firesides, in our family, to our friends, and those by whom we are surrounded, and with whom we associate, would be edifying, that it would be so in our Sunday schools. Now, I know some of our Sunday-school workers who do this, and I think they do no wrong. But at the same time, these good brethren will (or some of them) fight even the idea of "Lesson Leaves," Is this not "straining at a gnat and swallowing a camel?" These brethren contend that the "Lesson Leaves," is man's work. Whose work is it when any of them, without the lesson leaf, propound questions, give light, etc.? [Signed] J.R. Bradley (*G.A.*, June 8, 1882, p. 360).

Elisha G. Sewell gave an answer to Bradley's letter and his answer agreed with Bradley's own deduction. J.R. had found himself in the middle of the Sunday School Literature controversy. This would eventually escalate into a division of some of our brethren as to whether Sunday School Literature was Biblical or not. J.R.'s letter was one of the earliest reports on this problem to be published in the *Advocate*.

In this letter J.R. demonstrates the good use of logic taught him at Mars Hill College. Srygley had commented about Bradley's grasp of logic and other subjects while a student at Mars Hill. Srygley wrote in his book on Larimore: "In school he [Bradley] applied himself closely and attained a fair degree of proficiency in English grammar, logic, rhetoric, and general outline of history" (F.D. Srygley, *Larimore And His Boys*, 1889, p. 159). J.R.

would use his logic in several debates and his preaching for many years to come.

His first report of his speaking engagements for 1882 was in the Advocate for August 17th. He had just returned to Comer, Alabama, from his regular 5th Sunday appointment at Center Point in Lawrence County, Tennessee. He wrote of this new little band of Christians: (I)...preached two discourses, one Saturday night and one Sunday, 5th Sunday in July, had four confessions and Baptisms. The brethren and sisters there seem to be pressing for the mark. They are talking of building a new house of worship. May the Lord help them (*G.A.* Aug. 17, 1882, p. 504).

We really do not know what became of this work. In 1954, E. O. Coffman and G.F. Gibbs published a history of churches of Christ in Lawrence County, Tennessee. In this work they named all the old congregations and they never mention Center Point (Coffman and Gibbs, *Churches of Christ, Lawrence County, Tennessee*, 1954, pp. 7-8).

This leads us to believe that after Bradley moved further eastward, the congregation either died or merged with another nearby congregation. It is also possible that it became part of the Greenwood Congregation, later established by Bradley and McQuiddy.

The above report turns out to be the last report sent by J.R. while living in Alabama. He was being drawn more and more back to Tennessee, the state of his birth. He would continue to preach in Alabama often. He would even move back to Alabama for a brief period later in his career.

3

BACK HOME TO TENNESSEE

Even though J.R. had preached many times in Tennessee, up to this point in time he was still living in Alabama. By the middle of August 1882, J.R. had moved to Lynnville, Tennessee. He was now in the middle of the old congregations that Wade Barrett had established more than a half a century earlier. Many of these churches had formerly been Baptist churches and had been converted or transformed by Wade Barrett, who a half century earlier, had left the Baptist church in the same manner R.W. Officer and Murrell Askew had left. He wasted no time holding meetings for some of the old Barrett congregations. The last August issue of 1882 for the *Advocate* shows J.R. still encountering some problems with some of the churches for which he worked. He had a difficulty, it seems, with elders overstepping the scriptural bounds and causing trouble in some of the churches. He also took issue with some articles that he had read, either in the Advocate or the American Christian Review, concerning elders withdrawing from members without "referring the matter to the congregation" (*G.A.* Aug. 31, 1882, p. 551). He cites 1 Corinthians 5:4-5 and 1 Timothy 5:20 to show that elders do wrong by not including the whole church in the matter of withdrawing from an unrepentant brother or sister. The answer came back from either Lipscomb or Sewell that elders are to include the congregation in this kind of matter. I must be quite related to J.R., because this has always been my understanding of God's word concerning the duties of elders. It seems that J.R. was usually in line with the thinking of David Lipscomb and Elisha Sewell, but sometimes he would verbalize his differences with them.

In his first communication to the *Advocate* concerning his work around the Lynnville area he wrote of his past few weeks' work:

> I will give the meetings and results of Bro. W. B. McQuiddy and myself: At Robertson Fork, Marshall County, Tenn., commencing Saturday before second Sunday in August, and continued five days; five additions. Campbell's Station, Maury County, Tenn., commencing Saturday before the third Sunday, lasting five days; only one addition, and an agreement for the brethren to again keep house for the Lord. Rural Hill, commencing Saturday before fourth Sunday in this month continued seven days; six additions. And also, of nights would preach at Reed's academy; two additions there. I had one at Belleview [Syke's Factory] last (fourth) Sunday at a regular appointment (*G.A.*, Oct. 5, 1882, p. 630).

He reported 15 baptisms in all for his labors during the month of August. From Lawrenceburg, he traveled to Iron City to his home congregation and heard Wm. B. McQuiddy, F.D. Srygley and a Brother Goodwin in a meeting at Bradley's home congregation of Antioch. He stayed for a day or two and returned to Lynnville. He reported four additions up to the day he left for home (Ibid). Before the Antioch meeting ended a total of twelve additions were made (*G.A.* Nov. 23, 1882, p. 741). He would now begin a new schedule of work for the next several months.

As J.R. was establishing his new circuit of labor in Middle Tennessee, his Alabama work was becoming less and less. Eventually his labor would all be in Tennessee, with a few exceptions for an occasional meeting in Alabama.

Now that J.R. was working in a former Baptist stronghold, it seems that some of those old Baptist questions began to raise their ugly heads. He wrote the *Advocate* with a list of problems and questions that he had encountered. He asked if Baptists taught the things he listed or if they were just fables. In the question he had nine commonly taught points of doctrine by Baptists and further commented:

> And many more such might be given, which things are said to be taught by Baptists; and if taught, they form the faith of everyone that believed them. Now, is such faith gospel faith? If so, they are all right with their former baptism; if not, their baptism is no baptism. It does seem to me, dear brethren that you or I must show these things (if so taught) do not form the faith of these people, before we can say that they have gospel faith (*G.A.* Oct. 26, 1882, p. 675).

Sewell gave a rather lengthy answer, but finally concluded that: When we present the Gospel plainly, telling the people exactly what the Lord requires to make Christians, and ask Christians to unite with us upon the Bible, and they come to do so, claiming they have done these things, we can do nothing but to receive them (*G.A.* Oct. 26, 1882, p. 675).

Sewell further stated that the "gospel as given in the New Testament is so plain that people may read, understand and obey independently of these errors" (*G.A.* Oct. 26, 1882, p. 675). J.R. apparently accepted Sewell's answer, because he never brought it up in the pages of the *Advocate* again. His new field of labor presented him with many new challenges and rewards. He worked hard during the protracted season. Sometimes he required the aid of others in these efforts.

W.B. McQuiddy reports on his own work and tells of co-laboring some of the time with Bradley. He wrote: "Though not incessantly engaged the past summer and present fall in evangelistic work, I have not been wholly idle. Assisted Bro. J.R. Bradley in three meetings, in which were thirteen added: ... All these meetings were short, from three to six days long..." (*G.A.*, Nov. 23, 1882, p. 740).

McQuiddy and Bradley's friendship and partnership in the kingdom of God was a long lasting one. These two men would work as friends and co-laborers until death intervened. It is worthy of note that both Bradley and McQuiddy were both prone to illness very often in the winter months.

J.R.'s last report for November 1882 was a succinct. J.R. wrote:

> I delivered a series of discourses at Smyrna, Maury County, Tenn., commencing Saturday before the fifth Sunday in October; had good interest manifested all the time, and there were two restored, but none confessed. The congregation at this place, has been somewhat divided for some years, but there are some noble members here. I preached last Sunday and night, at Cool Springs, six miles south of Pulaski, had one to confess and be baptized, also united in marriage, Mr. J.D. Hannah and Miss Estelle J. Nance. We pray our father's blessing upon the newly married couple (*G.A.*, Nov. 23, 1882, p. 741).

The Estelle J. Nance mentioned in the above excerpt was Brother M.M. Nance's daughter. He was the one who established Cool Springs and was one of its elders until his death.

The last communication for the year of 1882 was written in December but was not actually published until January 4, 1883. It would be an appeal on behalf of a very dear friend of his near Lawrenceburg, Tennessee. Joseph Gibbs, whom J.R. had befriended when he began preaching at Sykes' Factory in Lawrence County, Tennessee, had already endured one tragedy a little more than a year before. You may recall that on October 12, 1881, little Charlie Gibbs accidentally shot and killed himself. This was Joseph Gibbs' five-year-old son. Tragedy struck again on December 17, 1882. The house of Joseph Gibbs and family burned to the ground and with it nearly everything they owned. J.R. wrote the following about this event:

Although Mr. Gibbs is not a member of the church, he has done more to establish the cause there than any member belonging to Belleview congregation. I mean by giving money, encouragement, feeding preachers, and reading the Bible to the people, circulating books and tracts; and at one time, when the congregation had no house of worship, Mr. Gibbs bought a school house, moved it on his own land and gave it to the brethren. And then, there proved to be a deficiency in the deed to his land, and so he lost land, money (about seven hundred dollars which he had paid on the place, if I remember correctly) and all, and the congregation lost its house (*G.A.*, Jan. 4, 1883, p. 7).

One can see from this that this man was a strong and determined man; he just was not a Christian at this time. That, however, would eventually change. It is strange that sometimes the world has more of a giving heart than do some members of the church. Joseph Gibbs gave more than any other person toward the expense, even though he was a poor man. Bradley asked the brethren to help this family. He explained that the brethren were "poor factory hands, and hence are not able to do much for this family" (*G.A.*, Jan. 4, 1883, p. 7). E.G. Sewell put a footnote to this letter by saying that the family was worthy of help. Bradley said that if the brethren knew of the worthiness of these good people, and the enemies they have made by standing up for our cause, they surely would send them a little help (*G.A.*, Jan. 4, 1883, p. 7).There were many people like Joseph Gibbs, who helped the spread of the gospel long before they became Christians. This was the case in nearly every community throughout the south. Because of Mr. Gibbs' encouragement, his wife and two daughters became members in the earliest days of the work at Belleview, and later he would obey also.

Along with this request on behalf of the Gibbs family, J.R. had reported three marriages that he had performed during December 1882, but Lipscomb and Sewell did not print them until

February 1, 1883. This was due to the format of the Advocate. There was a section in the paper from time to time entitled "Married," The editors would wait until there were a certain number of marriages to report before printing them. This delayed Bradley's report nearly two months. He reported having performed weddings for the following couples: R.N. Thornberry to Sallie Nix on December 14, 1882, both Christians; and R.S. Compton and Jennie Braden on December 21, 1882. In January Bradley reported performing the marriage of J.A. Keiser and Alpha Braden, January 18, 1883. Bradley made the following comments about the last two weddings:

> Messrs. Compton and Keiser are both members of the Christian Church and are worthy young brethren. The young ladies, to whom they are united for life, are worthy young women, but are Methodists. Hope the boys will do some preaching in the name of Christ (*G.A.* Feb. 1, 1883, p. 70).

With this report, the final touch was placed upon 1882 for J.R. and the first glimpse was seen for 1883.

In April 1883, Bradley wrote an article for the *Advocate*, entitled "Excuses," (*G.A.*, April 11, 1883, p. 235). In this article he used *Luke 14:15-24* as the basis for his writing. He pointed to the excuses that people make for not attending their duties as a Christian. Bradley had heard a lot of excuses from people he taught in Tennessee and Alabama. He was especially upset at the brethren who used their jobs as an excuse for not coming to worship. He had a lot of patience with everyone except those who misused the Bible for their own purposes.

The misuse of the scriptures by other brethren evoked the wrath of his pen again in July of 1883. He wrote an article on "The Sabbath and Lord's Day" (*G.A.* July 25, 1883, p. 466). Some brethren worked throughout the week and used Sunday as a family day and did not attend worship services. He wrote the following:

There are things over which we have not control, daily occurring, that keep us from attending the service on every first
day; such as sickness, and the like. But for a brother to be in
town all day Saturday, dressed in what ought to be his Sunday-
go-to meeting clothes, and then stay at home Sunday, having
no excuse, only to entertain company, walk over the farm, salt
the stock, play with the children, etc., assumes a fearful responsibility. I, how many little boys and girls are brought up
to manhood and womanhood by such parents, and then lead
such lives of disobedience and waywardness, as will damn
their souls (*G.A.* July 25, 1883, p. 466).

In this article one can see this distress over laxity toward attendance at worship services and over young people being reared to
do the same. He would preach as it should be and leave it up to
the individuals to choose obedience or disobedience.

He began his concentration on the season of protracted meetings in late July. By the first Lord's Day in August, he held a
meeting in co-operation with Brethren W.H. Dixon and E.S.B.
Waldron. This meeting was held at Wilson Hill, Marshal County,
Tennessee. This congregation had been established by Barton W.
Stone in the 1830's. A brother N.W. Fowler reported this meeting, which ended with sixteen baptisms (*G.A.* Aug. 25, 1883, p.
552). Bradley would preach many more times at Wilson Hill
through-out his preaching career. He also would work in many
meetings with Brother W. H. Dixon. This was his first week long
meeting of the season.

On September 8, he began a meeting at his old home congregation, Antioch, near Iron City, Tennessee. This meeting lasted
until September 13 and ended with eleven additions. He was
aided part of the time by Brother Willie Morton. Bradley said that
Morton "did good preaching" (*G.A.*, Dec. 12, 1883, p. 787). From
Antioch, they went to a new church house at Chapel Hill, near
Lexington, Alabama, in Lauderdale County. The meeting house
was built by brother James McPeters. Bradley said that Professor
A.D. Ray was "an excellent teacher "and taught there. He also said

that Professor Ray and his daughters greatly aided the meeting with their good singing. J.R. said that Ray's daughters "are fine singers," The meeting continued through Wednesday, September 19, 1883. There was only one addition during this effort. This Lexington work would struggle to survive until the early 1900's, when it finally would get on firm footing.

From Lexington, Morton returned home and J.R. went to the waters of Chisholm Creek and preached in a new schoolhouse located in Lawrence County, Tennessee. He began on Saturday, 22nd of September and preached until September 26th, which was on Wednesday. He had four baptisms. It was at this place that Bradley first met Brother Hardin of Wayne County, Tennessee. J.R. said that Hardin was preaching without any compensation and doing a 'good work in our Master in these parts...' Following this J.R. wrote: "What a shame!" J.R. could sympathize with other poor ministers. From this point he began to make his way homeward (*G.A.*, Dec. 12, 1883, p. 787).

Bradley wrote of his journey homeward as follows:

> We started homeward, called at Belleview, (Sykes' factory) preached once. Stayed all night at Mr. Joseph Gibbs. This family is still suffering from being burned out. I greatly fear that one reason why our brethren and sisters do not respond more liberally in this and other like case, is because such people are so poor; because such giving, or giving to such people, will not enhance the esteem and praise of men. Maybe I am wrong, but something is the matter. I see and know of them giving largely to persons who already have good means (*G.A.*, Dec. 12, 1883, p. 787).

You can see that J.R.'s heart went out to the distressed and had little patience with brethren who did not give properly. He would back his feelings by sending $5.00 to the Gibbs family. By October 9th, L.D. Smith reported that J.R. had sent this amount of money (*G.A.*, Oct. 24, 1883, p. 803). Five dollars may not seem like a lot of money to us in 2019, but in the 1880's it could buy two or three acres of land in some locations of the country. Remember also, that J.R. was giving out of poverty and not out of abundance. He set a good example to the people of his day and this example still lives on today. May we all take note and follow his pattern.

At this point in time, he traveled back home to be greeted by his best friend and wife, Mary. He had left Lawrenceburg on the morning of September 28 and traveled all day to arrive home in the late evening of the same day. He rested all day on the 29th, which was a Saturday. Early on the next morning, Sunday 30th, he drove about five miles north of his home to Campbellsville. On this Lord's Day, his old Mars Hill friend, J.C. McQuiddy, began a meeting. J.R. remained at Campbellsville for most of the meeting but had to leave on October 5 for Wilson Hill in Marshall County, Tennessee. He only preached on the 6th and 7th of October. He had one baptism (*G.A.* Dec. 12, 1883, p. 787). This gives us an insight into what a week at home with J.R. Bradley was like. You can understand why he often became gravely ill during the winter months.

As though J.R. did not have enough to do, he was challenged to a debate with a Universalist by the name of Dr. W.E. McCord. McCord was from Kentucky. The debate was held at Smyrna, Maury County, Tennessee, on October 27th and 28th. There were two propositions discussed. On the 27th, the proposition was: "Do the Scriptures teach that the punishment of those who do not obey God is endless?" Bradley affirmed, and Dr. McCord denied. J.R. Robbins of Lynnville, Tennessee, reported the of the debate to the *Advocate* (*G.A.* Dec. 12, 1883, p. 786). Robbins wrote:

> Though Bradley is almost entirely inexperienced in debating, we think in this he was a "grand success," The doctor said he had been preaching about twenty years and had been engaged in three discussions; while Bro. Bradley had only been preaching about five years. Hence McCord so far as experience is concerned, had decidedly the advantage of Bro. Bradley (*G.A.* Dec. 12, 1883, p. 786).

Robbins' article concluded by saying the debate went off pleas-
antly: "Some expressed regret because it came up, but afterwards
the same persons said they thought it was a good thing. The brethren and sisters at Smyrna, as a general thing, were well pleased
with Bro. Bradley's efforts, and think the debate will do good." So,
Bradley's first debate was counted as a success. This debate's closing ended Bradley's extended work for 1883. He would do local
preaching during the winter months, when his health allowed.

His first report of 1884 was the obituary of Sarah Jones, a member at Robertson Fork's Church of Christ. Her death came on
January 11, 1884. Bradley reported that her husband was not a
member of the Lord's Church, but Bradley expressed his hope
that he would soon obey (*GA*. Mar. 19, 1884, p. 184). His next
report was also an obituary. This obituary was different from any
other that J.R. had reported. It was the account of the death of
one of his Mars Hill classmates and former co-workers, M.A. Beal.
J.R. wrote:

> I loved Bro. Beal; and now my eyes fail to be dried, because I
> know we shall never meet again on the plain of earth. Shall I
> say it? Bro. Beal is dead! I will also say that he was a good man,
> a Christian, a brave soldier. Bro. Beal was a good, plain, logical
> preacher. He was a deep thinker. Bro. Beal was a fine singer.
> It is to him and his worthy name I shall ever feel thankful for
> what I know about vocal music. I am sure that I have never
> enjoyed my preaching brethren any more, in our labors to-
> gether in the vineyard of the Lord, (according to the time I
> was with him,) than Bro M.A. Beal (*G.A.* Mar. 26, 1884, p.
> 195).

It was Beal that worked with J.R. in the first meeting at Brush
Creek, near Killen, Alabama. He led the singing while Bradley
preached.

F.D. Srygley wrote of Beal: "M.A. Beal was the gentle-spirited
and sweet-voiced songster of the memorable class of 1878...He

unquestionably had remarkable gifts for music... (F.D. Srygley, *Larimore and His Boys*" 1889, p. 161).

J.R. would miss his dear friend and would make an appeal on behalf of Beal's widow. He requested his brethren to aid her financially. Beal had died in the night of March 4, 1884. He was 39 years of age. He was buried near his home at Lyles Station, Hickman County, Tennessee (*G.A.*, March 26, 1884, p. 195). Brethren heeded J.R.'s call for them to help Beal's wife and two little boys. Brethren from Texas and Tennessee began sending money to aid the Beal family (*G.A.*, May 7, 1884, p. 299). This aid would continue to trickle in for some time, thanks to J.R.'s efforts.

His next correspondence with the Advocate would be an article on "Grumbling," He wrote of those who complained or grumbled at any kind of physical work for the church that might cost time and money. Some complained about using new songs in worship, while some complained of using old songs. Some grumbled about Sunday school and said that the church was "getting too much like the denominations" (*G.A.*, April 2, 1884, p. 225). He ended by saying: "Now brethren, I suggest that we quit so much grumbling, and come up like men and Christians, and learn to do any and everything that God has commanded" (*G.A.*, April 2, 1884, p. 225). It seems that Bradley, just as we still do today, had heard a lot of grumbling from his brethren.

His next correspondence was in the form of a question about 1 Peter 4:18. The question was: "Do we have three characters - the righteous, the ungodly and the sinner - in 1 Peter IV: 18?" The answer came back from the Advocate that the Greek text contained all three words and that they should be understood as three characters. This again shows that J.R. was trying to study deeper into the Word of God. This correspondence was written the last of March and appeared in the *Advocate* in May (*G.A.* May 7, 1884, p. 291).

By the end of May, he was challenging a Brother H.L. Walling over an article that he had published in the Advocate, (April 23, 1884). In this article Walling had said that he and his brethren around the McMinnville and Spencer Area had been preaching error "in regard to the purification of the heart by faith," Walling had said: "I have seen my error, and have repented, and I will in future preach what the apostles teach." As was customary with J.R., he was a straight shooter with Walling. He outright accused Walling of misapplying the scriptures. He ended by writing the following:

> Now, in conclusion, let me say, I cannot yet believe that our dear brother has been fully converted from the truth. He speaks of faith giving the power to become the children of God. That is all I claim it does. But in what way faith gives the power to this become God's children is a different thing (*G.A.*, May 28, 1884, p. 340).

J.R. ended with a bit of poetry to illustrate the "how" faith gives the power to become the children of God.

Also found on another page of the same issue of the Advocate, J.R. asks another perplexing question. He wrote the following:

> Within the bounds of my labor, we have two churches within a half mile of each other – a Christian and a Cumberland. The Cumberland brethren agree to have their Sunday – school in the evening when there is preaching at the Cumberland church, so that we can go to preaching and Sunday – school at both places. Now would we do anything but right, to be to them, as they propose to be with us (*G.A.*, May 28, 1884 p. 339)?

This letter had been written by J.R. on May 19. The answer was attached to the bottom of J.R.'s question by Lipscomb or Sewell. The conclusion was that Christians should never make worship on the Lord's Day seem secondary to anything else. But it further stated:

It is the duty of the church to meet on the Lord's Day to worship God. It is the duty of all the Christians to meet on every Lord's Day. If they can meet as well with the proposed arrangement as otherwise, there is no harm in doing so. But the point is, the Lord's Day worship must be treated and regarded as the most important service of the day. My observation has been that to put it at any other hour than one regarded as the chief of the day, is to assign it a secondary position. But this is not necessarily so (*G.A.*, May 28, 1884 p. 339)

We do not know how J.R. received the answer. He never brought it up again. We do not know if the Christian – Cumberland arrangement was carried through. We do know that in most of the territory in which Bradley preached, the Cumberland Presbyterian church is almost non-existent.

On May 28, 1884, Bradley wrote of having preached in a new area. He stated that "None of our brethren have ever been there before." He also reports the deaths of two members at Robertson's Fork – F.W. Hill and H. J Griffis. It is unfortunate for us that J.R. did not name the new location where he had preached on Sunday, May 28, 1884 (*G.A.*, June 18, 1884, p. 363).

In this same issue of the *Advocate* H.L. Walling attempted to answer J.R.'s challenge on Walling's first article. He accused Bradley of mixing "things that should not be mixed" (*G.A.*, June 18, 1884, p. 392). J.R. seems to have dropped the challenge and never mentions it again in the *Gospel Advocate*. Walling on the other hand brings up the subject at least once more and then drops the subject himself. It seems that the problem J.R. and Walling had was one of semantics. They were not too far apart on what seemed to him a misuse or misunderstanding of scripture.

A similar problem evoked another article from the pen of J.R. titled: "A Seeming Contradiction," Some of the preachers who preached at times on J.R.'s circuit had been teaching that John 14:2 contradicted Matt. 25:34. John said that Jesus went "to prepare a place for you." Matthew shows that Jesus said, "Inherit the kingdom prepared for you from the foundation of the world."

Some preachers were saying that this was a contradiction. Was it a "prepared place" or was it a "kingdom prepared?" J.R. contended that it was the point in time in which each statement was made that was the key to understanding the seeming contradiction. He concluded there was no contradiction (*G.A.* June 25, 1884, p. 404). He was never challenged for his conclusion, at least in the pages of the *Advocate*. You may notice that Bradley was writing more articles than usual for the *Advocate*. We do not know how a farmer – preacher had enough time to write more, but several factors could contribute to this. He may have been confined to home more because of his health or his wife's health. He, however, does not mention this in his reports. 1884 could have been a very rainy spring, thus hindering his field work. What we do know is that he had turned into a writer as well as a farmer and preacher.

By the latter part of June, J.R. was answering Walling again. Brother Walling had made a second installment to *Gospel Advocate* to accuse J.R. of "mixing things that should not be mixed." In Walling's former article, he had said that Bradley did "...mix things that should not be mixed..." (*G.A.* July 2, 1884, p. 418) J.R. responded by saying:

> Brother Walling, I have a suggestion for you which I hope you will receive kindly. It is this: You have become so frightened at the errors of Babylon, and in your flight from these errors, you have gone a little beyond Jerusalem (*G.A.* July 2, 1884, p. 418).

Bradley ended his article by saying:

> Brother Walling, I think we have said enough. I am tired of so much war in the camps. I tell you, I do believe that some of the discussions in the *Advocate* are doing a great injury; especially so, when such little matters are the thing disputed about (*G.A.* July 2, 1884, p. 418).

J.R. did not completely close the door to Walling but made it clear that any further debating the issue was futile. He must have known that Walling would try to get the last word. He tried later in the year to do just that. Even though J.R. had challenged Walling's original conclusion, he never imagined that the argumentation back and forth would have occurred. He did not like useless conflict. The only reason he objected to Walling's writings, in the first place, was because he was afraid that division would occur in the Lord's church. The unity of the church was foremost in his mind.

While Walling's final response was forthcoming, a note of levity occurred. On July 16, 1884, Lipscomb would relate, through the pages of the *Advocate*, a very funny anecdote which he, perhaps, thought J.R. would enjoy. Lipscomb reflected upon an amusing story that J.R. had told some weeks earlier. Lipscomb wrote: "As an offset to Bro. Bradley's church, that could only sing, "Am I a soldier of the Cross," J.D. Wells tells of a young preacher, who in his zeal for singing class, forgot the Lord's supper at a meeting" (*G.A.*, July 16, 1884, p. 459).

J.R. always loved a funny story or joke. Lee Jackson, one of J.R.'s old friends and classmates at Mars Hill, wrote some years later about a funny story that J.R. would tell about one of his acquaintances. He related the story in the *Gospel Advocate*, as follows:

> Brother J.R. Bradley used to tell a little story in his jolly good-natured manner, which I have not forgotten, and I would like to know if he now remembers it. Somewhere he had known a man who had built a new house, and after building it he found it necessary to cut down some tall trees which stood too close for safety in time of storms. The man had a coon dog that he called "Trailer," This dog was so eager to run under a falling tree that it was necessary to hold him to keep him from getting crippled or killed. So, when a tree was ready to fall, Bro. Bradley's man would call the dog and hold him until the tree was

on the ground. At length the man cut a tall tree and failed to notice that he was felling so that it would fall toward the house and strike his stove and dining rooms. When this tree started to break from its stump, Mr. Jones called his dog; but seeing that the tree was falling on his home, he became excited and failed to get hold of him. The dog ran toward the falling tree; but when it struck the stove room and broke it with a great crash, it scared the dog so badly that he tucked his tail and ran in the other direction, howling for all he was worth. As he was running away, Jones looked after him and exclaimed, in a disconsolate drawl: "Trailer, you are the biggest simpleton that I ever saw!" Bradley could tell this so that it was really amusing, the point in his mind being that Jones failed to see his own folly in cutting a tree on his own house, and that, therefore, he had no just grounds for calling the dog a 'simpleton'" (*G.A.*, Feb. 4, 1909, p. 133).

Walling finally responded as the readers of the *Advocate* probably expected. J.R. knew there would be a response. He also knew that answering was to no avail. He began his last response by saying:

> My dear Brother: On reading your last criticism on my reply to you, I at once decided that you would be alright, as soon as you had time to reflect and settle down; but a number of my brethren say that an answer is demanded. I therefore proceed to try clear the mist away. I am no metaphysician; neither do I propose a treatise on metaphysics. The dictionary and the Bible are my only treasure, upon which to draw, to drive away the fog rising down in the mountains (*G.A.*, Aug. 6, 1884, p. 498).

Walling opened this correspondence with a rather sarcastic air and ends it much the same way. His closing remarks were: "My brother is opposed to war over small matters. Who started this war?" (*G.A.*, Aug. 6, 1884, p. 498).

Neither Walling nor Bradley had the final work in the disagreement. It was David Lipscomb who put the finishing touch to the debate. He wrote an answer because some brother finally asked: "Which is Right," Under a heading with the same title Lipscomb wrote: "We think there is not much difference, if they used terms in the same sense without referring to what they have said, we submit this" (*G.A.*, Aug. 27, 1884, p. 550).

Lipscomb then uses Peter's sermon on Pentecost to illustrate his reasoning. He stated the following to prove his point concerning the people in Acts chapter 2:

> What has brought about the change of mind, feeling and purpose in these people? The belief that he (Jesus) is the Son of God produced that change. Bro. Walling does not doubt or deny this. Bro. Bradley maintains it. Where in then do they differ? Simply as to whether a heart in this condition ought to be called a purified heart. The only difference is as to the propriety of applying the terms pure and purified, to a heart in this condition. They do not differ as to the facts or the results of these facts. It is only this, Bro. Bradley thinks the term pure or purified may be applied to the heart at this stage as indicative of its correct thinking, feeling, impulses, before it takes steps to free itself from the guilt of sin. Brother Walling thinks it ought not to be applied until it has taken those steps which frees it from the guilt of sins heretofore committed...We think in the sense in which each uses the term pure or purified, that each is right (*G.A.*, Aug. 27, 1884, p. 550).

Lipscomb's short article seemed to have satisfied everyone. Neither Walling nor J.R. responds to the solution given by Lipscomb. Thus, ends this debate between Bradley and Walling.

Peace was not long for J.R., however. He was challenged about the article he had written which had been published in the *Gospel Advocate* of April 2, 1884. J.R. had written his article on "Grumbling" to encourage the brethren not to get stalled in their work for the Lord by being sidetracked and begin to complain and grumble. He then gave an example of a church that had apparently done that very thing. This is where he told the story to which Lipscomb referred in the above account. The church had only learned the one song: "Am I a Soldier of the Cross," Bradley's point was that this church should concentrate on learning new songs and not do other things of lesser importance and ignore learning to sing praises to God (*G.A.*, April 2, 1884, p. 218).

A friend of Walling's, J.E. Wells, challenged Bradley's motive. He wrote as follows:

> If I am not mistaken, grumbling is rather infectious, and Bro. Bradley is rather threatened with the same disease...is it not strange that some who claim to be Christians, and preachers of the gospel, are always watching an opportunity to expose someone's errors instead of correcting their own mistakes? They usually strike at some good old congregation which has been doing the best it could, and if not doing the best, it ought to be preacher's effort to stir up their pure minds by way of remembrance (*G.A.* Aug. 27, 1884, p. 554).

Wells seemed almost angry toward J.R. in this short article. The anger is so evident in his writing that David Lipscomb wrote a footnote to Wells' complaint and published it immediately under Wells' article.

Lipscomb wrote as follows, to stop another debate:

> Two wrongs don't make a right. This old congregation may have done the best it was able, and still be blameworthy. We are frequently responsible for our lack of ability. The lack of ability in most cases, and certainly in this one arises from failure to cultivate, exercise and use the faculties God has given us. And to encourage in the proper cultivation and use of our faculties, was what we understood Bro. Bradley's article to aim at. To mention things that thus occur, as examples to encourage in the practice, cultivation and use of our faculties is right. Many say they can't do this or that, the meaning of which is they have not tried to use their faculties, have not cultivated them. No man can do anything without educating himself by practice in the work (*G.A.* Aug. 27, 1884, p. 554).

This seemed to have accomplished what Lipscomb set out to do. Wells never responded, and Bradley never brings it up in his future correspondence. Lipscomb and Bradley both seemed to be on the same track when it understood of Biblical teaching.

One is left to wonder just what had sent Wells into such fury against Bradley. When J.R. mentioned the "One Song Church" could it have been Wells' home church, the Weakly Creek Church of Christ? Whatever it was, it really touched off Wells. An interesting note: The Weakly Creek congregation, at first, had been established in November of 1846 by Wade Barrett (*Bible Advocate*, Jan. 1847; Dec. 1847; and Mar. 1848). It had ceased meeting sometime before 1880 and was reestablished by J.R. and his friend Wm. B. McQuiddy. If Wells ever harbored any ill will toward Bradley after this, it must not have lasted long. In July 1890, J.R. Bradley held a gospel meeting at Green Wood (recently changed name from Weakley Creek) which began on the third Sunday of July 1890 (*G.A.*, Aug. 13, 1890, p. 531). He reported: "Had good attendance all the time, but no good done, I fear." J.R. held several more meetings on Weakly Creek, as can be found in the old Greenwood record books.

A passing comment on J.D. Wells is needed. It appears that he was an elder at Greenwood at sometime and was, also, the preacher for a short time. There are still families of Wells around Greenwood in 2019. This little outburst by Wells upon J.R. shows just how volatile our brethren could be sometimes, and yet later, love one another and even show appreciation toward each other. This demonstrates, also, the self-control J.R. must have had to never bring this up in the *Advocate,* even though it had been through its pages that Wells had attacked him.

On the third Saturday (August 16, 1884) of August, J.R. wrote a report of a meeting that he held at Wilson Hill in Marshall County, Tennessee. The meeting began on August 9th and continued through the 15th. T.W. Brents preached on Sunday and J.R. did the rest of the meeting. J.R. preached two sermons per day throughout the remainder of the meeting and reported six additions: four baptisms and two restorations. He concluded by saying: "We have a good Sunday school here" (*G.A.*, Sept. 3, 1884, p. 555). Wilson Hill was now part of J.R.'s scheduled preaching points.

From Wilson Hill, J.R. held a meeting at Beech Grove, also in Marshall County, Tennessee. The meeting began on the third Lord's Day of August and embraced the fourth Sunday. W. S. Morton and T.W. Brents helped Bradley in this meeting. J.R. reported the following:

> Had good interest all the time. Had eleven noble souls to join the army of the Lord. They have the best singing of any congregation I know. Dr. Brents, of Lewisburg, delivered our first sermon on the third Lord's Day. His subject was: "Types and Shadows." The venerable Dr. Brents is a deep searcher (*G.A.* Sept. 3, 1884, p. 563).

By now, it may be observed that J.R. Bradley was slowly moving eastward in his field of labor.

His western-most points of evangelism were Campbell's Station, Maury County; Lynnville, Giles County; and Roberson Forks, in Marshall County, Tennessee. He reported on their regularly scheduled meeting. This meeting was conducted by J.C. McQuiddy, Bradley's old Mars Hill school-mate. Bradley wrote the following report:

> Bro. J.C. McQuiddy has just closed a very good meeting at Roberson's Fork, had twenty-one additions. Had a prayer meeting every morning at ten o'clock during the meeting, which resulted in great good to the church. Many of the young men took part in these exercises, that were never known to pray in public before. The congregation is splendidly worked up. Bro. McQuiddy's lady was with him, she is a fine lady (*G.A.*, Oct. 1, 1884, p. 627).

J.R. wrote this report to the *Advocate* on September 22, 1884. He had about a week's break from meetings before he began his next appointment.

His next appointment was on the first Lord's Day of October. J.R. returned to Smyrna, a very troubled congregation in Maury County, Tennessee. He had preached there as early as October of 1882. He had written that "the congregation at this place has been somewhat divided for some years, but there are some noble members here" (*G.A.*, Nov. 23, 1882, p. 741). Bradley wrote of this third meeting:

> Have just closed a meeting at Smyrna, Maury County, Tenn., embracing first and second Lord's day in this month. Had a good meeting for the place. Some old difficulties hanging over the people of this community which is a great offset to the power of a little man like me. Young Bro. Sewell preached twice and Bro Derryberry once during the meeting; had five additions. I have been going there almost three years, and my first additions were at this meeting, owing to this trouble (*G.A.*, Oct. 22, 1884, p. 683).

This report shows that J.R. did not give up on people, even though they had problems. He just worked patiently with them to help them.

It seemed that a lot of the churches in southern-middle Tennessee had problems of some sort. Robertson's Fork was no exception. J.R. wrote that the congregation had decided to cancel a lot of their subscriptions to "the old subscription paper doings" (the *Advocate* excepted, of course [writer's own comment]). Bradley said that was done to 'keep up weekly contributions." He further added: "And I hope that all the brethren in my entire field will "follow suit," The sooner we go to work according to the Lord's rule, the better for us" (*G.A.*, Jan. 7, 1885, p. 10).

The brethren had been in the habit of subscribing to Methodists' and Baptists' journals, as well as to some liberal brotherhood journals. Bradley thought that these were injurious to the cause of the Lord, in his field of labor. He was also disturbed that the brethren were losing money in the ordering of denominational materials. One case in point was that of a brother N.J. Walker, who had ordered a Study Bible from one of the publications, sent his two dollars, as advertised, for the book. He received, instead of a Study Bible, a bill saying that he would have to send three more dollars to the publisher before receiving the Bible (*G.A.*, Jan. 7, 1885, p. 10).

J.R. also included his field of labor for 1885 in the above report. He reported that he would labor with Wilson Hill, Smyrna, Campbell's Station and Robertson's Fork. These would be his regular Sunday appointments. He would hold several meetings, in addition to his regular preaching points. Sometime in December 29, 1884, he changed his address from Lynnville, Giles County, Tennessee to Cornersville, Marshall County, Tennessee. It was published in the first issue of the *Advocate* for January (Jan. 7, 1885, p. 7). For some reason unknown to the writer, J.R. changed his address again. This time it was Roberson's Fork, Marshall County, Tennessee (*G.A.*, Feb 4, 1885, p. 61). The county lines of Giles and Marshall had been moved back and forth a time or two. J.R. may not have moved at all, however, his address could have changed; or he could have moved a mile or so east to be nearer to Roberson's Fork, since that was one of his regular preaching points and the address was uncertain to J.R. Whatever the explanation, it is certain that J.R.'s address changed to Roberson's Fork. This was also Bradley's home congregation for the year 1885.

In his first report, written in 1885, he says that he "promises to do all he can for the *Advocate*" (*G.A.*, Feb 4, 1885, p. 61). This underscores what we have already said about Bradley excluding the *Gospel Advocate* from the list of dropped papers, at Roberson's Fork. He wrote of two weddings he performed: "Married on December 25, 1884; Mr. Willie Gower to Miss Mary Keiser. Also, on January 29, 1885; Mr. M.J. Walker to Miss Sallie Colvett. All are members at the church at Roberson's Fork, except one. Ceremonies by the writer" (*G.A.*, Feb. 18, 1885, p. 135).

During these winter months, J.R.'s wife was sick for most of the winter. In late February he wrote to the *Advocate*, saying that Mary's health "is some better of late" (Mar. 4, 1885, p. 103). He also reported that his home church, Roberson's Fork, had met every Lord's Day throughout the winter. He said that this is a "new thing in the history of this, a congregation fifty years of age." Either Lipscomb or Sewell wrote a footnote saying that, "We are glad to hear this, and hope this congregation may continue in the good and right way "(Ibid).

This causes one to wonder if Roberson's Fork ever met regularly, even when Wade Barrett was alive, or if they fell into this pattern after Barrett's death in December of 1870. J.R.'s expression: "I am told is a new thing in the history of this, a congregation fifty years of age," causes us to believe that they had never met every Sunday. There is a possible explanation to this problem. In the earlier days of the nineteenth century a congregation on Sunday would meet at one location, where the preacher was preaching, and the next Sunday they would relocate to a nearby location where the preacher was preaching. Barrett's congregations were located near enough to do just that. Roberson's Fork was only about two miles from Elk Ridge, and Lynnville was only about four miles away. Across a couple ridges Campbell's Station was located. Thus, in about a five- or six-mile radius, there were four congregations that had been established by Wade Barrett, and he preached for all of them, in a circuit, until his death, December 10, 1870. Once Barrett had died the people of each community had no "polar star" in the person of a preacher, until J.R. Bradley came to that area in August 1882 (*G.A.* Oct. 5, 1882, p. 630). J.R.'s arrival was only twelve years after the venerable Barrett had died. J.R. began working Barrett's old circuit with the same congregations. It may be that this laxity in meeting regularly was due to the above occurrences. Whatever the cause, J.R. would not rest until he had helped those churches to correct their ways, and it seems that he had achieved that at Roberson's Fork Church of Christ. They remained faithful in their worship to the

Lord while JR continued to work with them. Today (2019) they are still a very vibrant congregation. Those old problems are long forgotten. They are still a shining star among the hills and valleys of Western Marshall County, Tennessee.

J.R. continued throughout the spring and summer on his preaching circuit. He worked during the week on his farm and attended to his "preacher" duties, such as marriages and funerals. These were the kind of things a country preacher such as J.R. would always have to do. As summer ended and the crops were "laid by," folks began wanting a "meeting," This began a very hectic season for J.R. He would pack his clothes, saddle his horse, kiss Mary, and then leave, sometimes for weeks. 1885 was no different. During the summer the letters began to come to J.R., and the requests for meetings dictated his schedule for the remainder of the year.

J.R.'s first meeting for the season was in late July at Antioch in Lawrence County, Tennessee. This was where Bradley grew to manhood. It was in the cool waters of Shoal Creek, flowing just a few hundred yards from the Antioch building, that J.R. and Mary had been baptized in August of 1869 by T. B Larimore. This was really his home congregation. He would see some old friends for the last time upon this earth. Mary would accompany him to Antioch. This was also the community where Mary's childhood was spent. She visited friends and family during the meeting. There was one damper on the meeting, however. John Dickey Wade, the spiritual father of the church at Antioch, was getting frail from old age and could not attend regularly. He would die from injuries he sustained in an accident at his mill on November 15 of that year (John D. Wade's Tombstone, Antioch cemetery, Iron City, Tennessee). The meeting would go on as planned. Wade would enjoy the last meeting he would ever be able to attend.

J.R. preached for nine days. He baptized five and had one restoration. Bradley wrote: "The church at Antioch has gone down, somewhat but the failure I am sure is not the Lord's. We may have the best of preaching and yet fail to keep up the work for the lord and all is a failure" (*G.A.* Aug. 12, 1885, p. 503).

This "gone down somewhat" was due, no doubt, to the fact that Wade, who had been the stabilizing force at Antioch, had been ill for a long period. After the meeting, the Bradley's returned home to Roberson's Fork. Upon arrival, J.R. would take care of chores and rest a little. He would use this time to prepare for his next meeting.

The next meeting would start on Saturday, Aug 8, 1885. The meeting was on Globe Creek (later became Wilson Hill) in Marshall County, Tennessee. J.R. met up with his old friend, Wm. B. McQuiddy. They would conduct the meeting as co-laborers. Bro. Robert P. Richardson sent the following to the *Advocate*:

> I will report our meeting which began Saturday before the 2nd Lord's day and continued eight days. Bro. W. B. McQuiddy and J.R. Bradley preached for us. Twelve added to the church, seven by confession and baptism, one from the Baptists, four reclaimed. Generally large audiences and good interest (*G.A.* Aug. 29, 1885, p. 535).

J.R. was pleased with the meeting for two reasons. First, and most important, was the number of souls placed in a "right" relationship with God. Secondly, he was always overjoyed to work with Wm. McQuiddy. Their friendship was forged on the anvil of hard work and study at Mars Hill College. This was a lifelong friendship for these two "soldiers of the cross,"

His next meeting would be a joint effort with Bro. W. H. Dixon. They began a meeting at Philadelphia, Lincoln County Tennessee, on the third Sunday (August 16, 1885). Dixon wrote to the Advocate about a problem that had arisen at Philadelphia over the Lord's Supper. He described the problem as follows:

> The position is taken by a good brother that we are not commanded to meet upon the first day of the week to break bread as is taught by the brethren. That to meet in the day to take

the supper is wrong. That the supper was instituted at night; hence is not a supper taken any other time than in the evening or at night (*G.A.*, Sept. 9, 1885, p. 571).

This is a problem of the sort with which J.R. had been concerned when he had persuaded the brethren at Robertson's Fork to drop their subscriptions to all denominational journals and publications. This brother had been reading the *Evangelists*, which was a Methodists' publication. The brother, according to Dixon, leaned "to the idea that it (the Lord's Supper) should be taken in an upper room" and maybe only "one time a year" (*G.A.*, Sept. 9, 1885, p. 571). Neither Lipscomb nor Sewell responded.

It is necessary to deviate chronologically to give the outcome to this problem and the answer from the *Advocate*. The problem began to move from congregation to congregation with the brother who started it. He made his next appearance at Campbell's Station where Bradley and E.G. Sewell began an eight-day meeting. It began on September 13th and continued through September 20th, resulting in eleven baptisms and three restorations. Sewell wrote of Bradley:

> Bro. J.R. Bradley, their regular monthly preacher, was with us nearly all the time, and rendered much assistance in the meeting and we enjoyed his hearty co-operation, and that of the brethren also.... All seemed greatly encouraged by the meeting, and we hope much permanent good was accomplished there (*G.A.* Nov. 4, 1885, p. 696).

Sewell, however, omitted to address or even mention the problem that came up with a visiting brother. This was the same brother who had brought up the Lord's Supper, and its proper time to be taken, with Dixon and Bradley at Philadelphia. He had asked Sewell the same question. J.R. was found asking Sewell in the Advocate to give an answer to this problem. By May of 1886, Bradley is reminding Sewell that he had promised to answer this in the Advocate. Sewell obliges in the May 19 issue of 1886, on the front page (*G.A.* May 19, 1886). The answer came under the title 'What Time of Day?" Bradley had pointed out to Sewell that the promise was made during the meeting at Campbell's Station.

J.R. further stated that it was not a matter of "contrariness" with the brother, but a matter of "faith" with him. He said that the brother would "not become offended at what you may in kindness write." Sewell devotes the entire front page of this issue to answering the problem (Ibid). Sewell's answer was thorough and well stated; so much so, that it seemed to be enough. That was all that was written on that subject by Sewell and it never had to be addressed in the *Advocate* again.

To the reader, you must keep in mind that to fully treat the problem about the time of the Lord's Supper that we had to jump ahead into May of 1886. We now continue with the proper chronology of J.R. Bradley's life and labors.

J.R.'s next meeting for the year of 1885 was conducted at Smyrna, Maury County, Tennessee. It began on September 6th and continued through September 13th, which was on a Sunday. J.R.'s old Mars Hill classmate, Wm. B. McQuiddy worked with him in that meeting. It was McQuiddy who reported the following:

> The meeting at Smyrna, Maury County, Tennessee, conducted by Bro. J.R. Bradley and the writer, continued eight days, closing on Sunday night, the thirteenth inst. and resulted in sixteen additions to the church, eight from the world, five reclaimed and three from the Baptists. This is one point in Bro. Bradley's field of labor. The brethren say this it the best meeting they have had for many years (*G.A.* Sept. 23, 1885, p. 599).

From Smyrna, J.R. had just six days to return home and take care of farm duties and try to get rested for the next meeting.

On September 20, 1885, an eight-day meeting began at Campbell's Station. This meeting was partially addressed earlier in answering the question on the proper time for the Lord's Supper. E. G. Sewell would be the principal speaker, but Bradley would help in many ways, including doing some of the speaking. As has already been reported, eleven baptisms and three restorations were the results of the meeting. Sewell had remarked that J.R. was there for the meeting "nearly all the time" (*G.A.* Nov. 4, 1885, p. 696). The reason J.R. was not there all the time was that his congregation at Robertson's Fork began their meeting on September 26, causing Bradley to have to absent himself from Campbell's Station on the last Saturday and Sunday of their meeting.

J.R. reported that the Robertson's Fork meeting continued until October 3rd, making it an eight-day meeting, also. He wrote of the meeting as follows:

> [The meeting resulted] in 25 additions, 17 baptized, 4 reclaimed, 2 from the Baptists, and 2 took membership. Church much revived. Bro. W.H. Dixon of Petersburg preached for us. One added at Campbell's Sta., since the meeting there (*G.A.* Oct. 21, 1885, p. 667).

Bradley also wrote in this report that he was building a house at Reuben, Lincoln Co., and that he would move soon (Ibid). This meant that he would be moving further east and closing his work, for most part, in Giles County.

4

EARLY LINCOLN COUNTY WORK

J.R. and Mary moved into their new house in December. That would be a big Christmas gift from J.R. to Mary. He reported the move in the *Advocate,* for January 13, 1886. Prior to this, Bradley had bought two and a half acres of land on little Bradshaw Creek from J.H. Wright. The land was situated on the Pulaski-Fayetteville Road, where it crossed little Bradshaw Creek. The deed was dated August 26, 1885 (Lincoln County, Tennessee, 1885, Deed Book, p 70). He paid twenty-five dollars for the land. No doubt, this was the best land deal that J.R. would ever make in his entire life.

Before this move, however, he would send two more reports for 1885. He wrote on November 5 concerning his work for the month of October. His report read as follows:

> Since my last report, I have baptized seven. Five at "Nights (probably "Knights") of Honor" hall, where I have been preaching on fourth Sunday nights after preaching at Roberson (sic) Fork at eleven o'clock. One at Philadelphia, Lincoln County; one at Gipsonville, Giles County, which is a Baptist church. We also had one wanderer to come back at this place, who had wandered from Bethel congregation. Preached

seven times at this place (Gipsonville). A good hearing all the time (*G.A.* Nov. 11, 1885, p. 715).

His very last report for the year was a very short one. He wrote that one person was baptized at Campbell's Station and one was restored. This had all taken place since the meeting with E. G. Sewell in September (*G.A.* Dec. 2, 1885, p. 763). He would spend much of his time working on his new house at Reuben. Some of the brethren would aid him in preparation and moving sometime in December. This would close his work for the year of 1885, and this also closes his work at Roberson Fork and Campbell's Station. He, however, would continue to work with Smyrna and Wilson Hill for the next year.

There is one sad note that should be entered here and that is the death of John Dickie Wade. He died on November 15, 1885, after being mangled by some machinery at his mill. He was almost like a father to J.R. and may be considered a spiritual father to him, as well as Larimore was. It was Wade's example in the community in which J.R. had spent his childhood that caused many people to know what Christianity was all about. If anyone at Antioch ever encouraged J.R. to attend Mars Hill and preach, Wade would have been his strongest encourager, both morally and financially. That was the kind of man John D. Wade was: an encourager to all good people. Larimore described him as:

> He was a devoted friend of mine. One of the best friends of the needy I have ever known. He read the Bible and the *Advocate*, he seemed to care for no other paper, no other book (*G.A.*, May 26, 1886, p. 331).

J.R. found it easy to love Wade and his family. This is perhaps the reason he and W. B. McQuiddy were such great friends. McQuiddy had married John Dickie's daughter, Chappel Wade. The kind influence that Wade had exerted was well known throughout his community and Bradley was led by his example of having a soft spot for the downtrodden and the needy. J.R. would practice this example the rest of his life.

He began his new year's work by sending a rather lengthy report to the Advocate. It was written from his new address, Reuben, Lincoln County, Tennessee and dated Jan. 1, 1886. You can see and feel his joy as he proudly announced:

> We are in our new house though it is not completed. We will have a good and comfortable little house.... Some of the brethren of this congregation (Philadelphia) have helped us very much in getting our house as near done as it is. Had it not been so we would not have been living in it now (*G.A.* Jan. 13, 1886, p. 27).

This was probably the best house that J.R. and Mary had ever lived in. It was, for sure, the first new house they had ever owned.

The little village of Reuben was a lazy little farming community, nestled among the mountainous hills of Giles, Marshall, and Lincoln Counties of Tennessee. J.R. described it as follows: "This Reuben is a growing little village, in a rich, though mountainous country, about half way between Pulaski and Fayetteville" (*G.A.* Jan. 13, 1886, p. 27). He further wrote that his home, which was located at Reuben was near the corner where Lincoln, Giles, and Marshall Counties intersected, or to put it in J.R.'s words: "near the corners of Marshall, Giles, and Lincoln."

J.R. also included in the report that his scheduled weekly work for '86 was to be at the following congregations: Beech Grove and Wilson Hill in Marshall County; Smyrna in Maury County; Bunker Hill in Giles County; and Philadelphia in Lincoln County (*G.A.* Jan. 13, 1886, p. 27). One may recall that Philadelphia was the congregation where the brother began the strange teachings about the time at which the Lord's Supper should be observed. This did not hinder J.R. from moving near Philadelphia, when he moved to Reuben, and preaching for the brethren there on a regular basis. It seems that the brother who taught such things still had not accepted the truth on the matter and Philadelphia was not living up to its name as a place of "brotherly love," J.R. had placed himself in the middle of this controversy and he would need help in bringing "love" and "harmony" back to that church.

His next correspondence with the Advocate was addressed to E. G. Sewell, who had been approached by the troubled brother, while in the meeting with Bradley at Campbell's Station in September of the previous year. This correspondence of Bradley's had been touched upon when the meeting with Sewell had been previously discussed earlier in this sketch. In his letter, J.R. wrote:

> Dear Brother – while at Campbell's Station last fall, in a conversation with you, in regard to a certain brother and his views, regarding the "time of day" to partake of the Lord's Supper, I remember that you promised to give us an article in the Advocate on the subject (*G.A.* May 19, 1886, Title page).

It seems that the brother had pressed J.R. for help in understanding the truth on the subject. J.R. either did not know how to answer the brother or wanted Sewell's or Lipscomb's input before he gave a final answer. He wanted the brethren at the *Advocate* to know that he did not believe that the brother was being contentious, but rather wanted to understand the truth in the matter.

J.R. wrote the following to defend the brother's motive:

> The brother is a good and worthy man, and certainly will not become offended, at what you may in kindness write. The brother said to me recently, "Bro. B. this is not a matter of contrariness with me, but of faith." I believe he told me the truth. His faith is, "that since Jesus instituted the supper at night, or in the "eve" and since Paul in 1st Cor. XI: speaks of "the same night in which he was betrayed, etc., therefore we ought to observe this ordinance at the same (*G.A.* May 19, 1886, p. 305).

His letter was almost in a scolding tone toward Sewell, and even Lipscomb, as editor of the Advocate, for having not written on the subject. Bradley wrote: "Now Bro. Sewell, or Bro Lipscomb, we don't care which protracted meeting will soon be on hand, and hence you will not probably have time to notice this" (*G.A.* May 19, 1886, Title page). Knowing Bradley's love and respect for the editors at *Gospel Advocate*, it may be that he was saying that "when you have the time from your meetings, please answer this."

J.R. mentioned another problem with the brother at Philadelphia. He also believed that the brethren should "wash feet as stated in the 13th chapter of John. J.R. pleads with Sewell and/or Lipscomb to respond in the *Advocate* so that the cause at Philadelphia would no longer be "languishing," He wrote: "Please, dear brethren, as Bro. Sewell has come back (to Nashville) now, attend to this and oblige us all, in these parts at least" (*G.A.* May 19, 1886, p. 305).

Sewell answers with an explanation that he had been so busy with meetings that it had slipped his mind to respond. His answer takes up almost the entire front page of the May 19 *Advocate*. Everything was apparently set right. J.R. seemed satisfied with Sewell's lengthy answer. We do not know how the 'good" brother at Philadelphia received the answer, but one would hope that he received it well. Bradley would devote the rest of spring and summer to preaching on his regular circuit and farming. He would also use this time to plan his fall schedule of meetings.

His first reported meetings were joint efforts with Bro. J.H. Morton and W. H. Dixon. The first was at Gnat Grove, Lincoln County, Tennessee, and the second was at Gum Springs, Lincoln County. The meeting at Gnat Grove began on August 1, 1886 and was reported by J.H. Morton. The next meeting was at Gum Springs and it began on the second Lord's Day, August 8, 1886. Morton reported ten baptisms combined for the two meetings (*G.A.* Sept. 1, 1886, p. 555). J.R. never reported these two meetings. It seemed that he was satisfied with Morton's report. J.R.

seemed to love the meetings that were joint efforts with his other preaching brethren. Remember that he and Wm. B. McQuiddy began to work together while students at Mars Hill.

It was during one of J.R.'s next meetings that he was expecting McQuiddy to join him in the preaching. First, he would hold a meeting at a Baptist church, called New Hope, in Lincoln County, which was near Reuben, J.R.'s home. He converted four in this meeting. This meeting was the last week of August. His next meeting was held at Haywood Academy, near Brick Church, Tennessee. It began on September 4th and continued through the 11th. In his first report (*G.A.*, Sept. 15, 1886, p. 586), he wrote that ten had confessed and been baptized. This meeting had apparently unexpectedly been extended an extra day. J.R. in the report to the Advocate of the 15th of September had written that he had promised to begin a meeting at Greenwood on Weakly Creek in Giles County on the following Saturday. That would have been the 11, as J.R. had written in his first report on September 7. It was not uncommon for preachers to extend a meeting past the beginning day of their next meeting, if the response was good enough. Apparently, it was good enough, as Bradley wrote the largest crowd was on the 11th, the last night of that meeting. No doubt he had notified the brethren at Green Wood concerning the delay.

He began the meeting at Greenwood on September 12, 1886, which was the second Sunday of the month. Bradley had written on the 7th that he expected Wm. B. McQuiddy to help him in this meeting. He wrote:

> It afforded me much pleasure to be with these good brethren and sisters. They now have a good house of worship. Bro. Wm B. McQuiddy and I started the interest that resulted in this house and congregation. We expected him at this meeting, but he could not reach us (*G.A.* Oct. 6, 1886, p. 638).

For some reason McQuiddy could not come to Greenwood and aid in the meeting. One observation should be made in relation to this report. J.R. indicated that he and W.B. McQuiddy were responsible for getting the building built and the congregation established. He wrote: "Wm. B. McQuiddy and I started the interest that resulted in this house and congregation" (*G.A.* Oct. 6, 1886, p. 638). This sounds like these two men started the congregation at Greenwood. There is, however, another possible explanation. We know that Barrett had reported of having established the Weakly Creek work in November of 1846 (Wade Barrett, *Bible Advocate*, Jan. 1847). It may be that McQuiddy and Bradley re-organized the work at Greenwood, which is the same as Weakley Creek. Whatever the explanation, Bradley had a special fondness for the Greenwood brethren.

He wrote a lengthy description of the Greenwood meeting, thus showing the special place they had in his heart. He very seldom went into such detail about his meetings. He wrote:

> Embracing the 2nd and 3rd Sundays of this month [September] I was with the brethren at Greenwood in Giles, county. The Baptist association was in session within about one mile of our meeting, and for the three days in our commencement we gave way for them, only preached at night. After the association, the rain began and for two days and nights we could do but little. The brethren contended that we must continue over Sunday (3rd Lord 's Day) (sic) which we did. Our audiences grew to be much better size. The interest became to be better, and before we closed we had good audiences and good interest. Four confessions and baptisms the last day for the meeting (*G.A.* Oct. 6, 1886, p. 638).

One might wonder why the brethren at Greenwood and J.R. had yielded their day time services for the first three days to the Baptist association. If you keep in mind what the real purpose of those Gospel meetings really was, then you could understand the brethren's actions at Greenwood. The meeting was designed to reach out and convert those who were not members of the church. If they had met during the day while the Baptist association was in session, they would have defeated their purpose. They were in no way putting the association meeting on equal standing with the Gospel meeting.

J.R. had written this letter on September 24, 1886, and it was postmarked- McDowell's Mill, Tennessee. J.R. had not moved but his address had changed. The post office at Reuben, his home post office, had closed as Reuben and had been renamed McDowell's Mill on February 9, 1886. (This is taken from "Post Offices of Lincoln County," Library in Fayetteville, Tennessee). This report was his last to the *Gospel Advocate* for the year 1886. His work continued with his regularly scheduled monthly appointments throughout the remainder of the year.

The year 1887 began with a new schedule of Bradley's labors for that year, as far as his monthly circuit was concerned. His schedule was printed in the March 16th issue of the *Advocate* on page 174. It read as follows:

> My work for this year is first Sundays at the Academy near Mr. Sheb Marsh in Giles. Second at Gum Springs in Lincoln county, (and to places where they direct); third at Philadelphia, Lincoln; fourth at Roberson (sic) Fork in Giles (and to places where they direct). Also, I preach in the evenings of the first at Diana in Giles (*G.A.* Mar. 16, 1887, p. 174).

The above academy mentioned by Bradley was Haywood Academy, near Brick church, Tennessee. That community was situated about four miles west of Cornersville, Marshall County, Tennessee, and on the Lewisburg-Pulaski Road. It was in Giles County. The Lewisburg-Pulaski road is better known today (2019), as US Highway 31A. You may remember that J.R. had established this work at the academy the preceding September.

In the above report, he had mentioned the work at Diana, Tennessee. He was scheduled to preach there every first Sunday evening. He had gathered a few disciples at this place and had organized them into the church at Diana. Diana was located near Reuben and McDowell's Mill, where J.R. made his home. Diana, however, was in Giles County. He gave us a very good description of the work at that place. He wrote:

> We have some noble workers at this place. Dear old sister Trigg lives here. She is one that can rightfully be called faithful and true. She has been a member a long time, and though right in midst of strong opposition (Methodist) she has kept on reading her Bible, and praying until the light has begun to shine, and her influence realized. She told the writer "that she had prayed and hoped for a number of years that her dear children might see the true gospel light as she saw it, and now her prayers were being granted," Two of her boys (Bro. John and David, and also Bro. John's wife, Sister Mary) have taken their stand firmly on the Bible. Bro. John has seated a nice little cabin for us, on his own place and there we have our evening meetings. Pray for us (*G.A.*, March 15, 1887, p. 174).

J.R. has given us a description of the establishment of Diana Church of Christ. Today it is known throughout the southeastern United States for the popular "Diana Singings," The Diana Singing is conducted on the second Friday and Saturday of June and on the second Friday and Saturday of September of each year. This little congregation is a bright and shining star throughout the South. J.R. would work with the brethren at the place in meetings, and sometimes, as part of his monthly circuit, throughout the rest of his life.

In April he was called upon to help in a funeral of a friend of his. The friend was Brother B. W. White, who had preached the Gospel for many years. Bradley said that Bro. White would often speak of "an old yokefellow" in the Gospel by the name of Cone. That "old yokefellow" would be G.W. Cone, who did a tremendous amount of work in Middle Tennessee, and especially in Williamson, Bedford, and Rutherford Counties. White had moved to Giles County some years before. He made his home there until his death. As J.R. had been working in Giles County for much of his career, up to this time, he met Bro. White and learned to love and appreciate him as a fellow laborer in the King-dom of God. This obituary was published May 4, 1887, in the Advocate on page 287. J.R. expressed his desire that Bro. White's children would follow their father's and mother's footsteps in the Lord. J.R. expressed this same kind of sentiment at the end of many obituaries that he had written. His soul was on fire for the lost and wanted everyone to obey the Lord and be saved.

In June Bradley would write to the *Advocate*, reporting the fol-lowing:

> Two confessions and baptisms at Molino last Lord's day (June 12). Our Gum Springs brethren are co-operating in the work there this year. Protracted meeting there (Molino) will com-mence second Lord's day (Aug. 14) in August. We hope and pray for much good to be done there (*G.A.* June 22, 1887, p. 387).

> Molino was one of the preaching points that had been estab-lished by J.R. as part of his evangelistic work. He would preach there many times. He further states of his summer's work: "One confession at Marsh Academy, not long ago. Also, one confession first Lord's day night (June 5); this month at the house of Dr. Harwood, where we preach occasionally" (*G.A.* June 22, 1887, p. 387).

The above locations were on J.R.'s regular work schedule. Re-member that part of his regular circuit was to start new works or build new ones already in existence. Gum Springs and Roberson Fork were involved with Bradley in planting and building new works, as well as his working with them in their local congrega-tions some of the time.

In the above report, J.R. also gives a partial list of extended or protracted meetings in which he will participate during late sum-mer and early fall. They were as follows:

Third Lords day in July (17th) and week following, at a school-house called Rabbit Hill; fourth Lord's day (24th) at or near Diana. Bro. W.H. Dixon will help us here. Do not know how long we will continue. Fifth Lord's day (31st) in Giles County, at school-house on Blue Creek, if we are not hindered by our sectarian friends. Second Lord's day (14th) in August, at Molino; fourth (28th) in August, at Roberson's Fork (sic). Bro. Dixon is to help us there (*G.A.* June 22, 1887, p. 387).

This was just a sample of what kind of work schedule J.R. Bradley had when the protracted meeting season arrived. He reported two more baptisms since his last note on June 22 in the *Advocate*. This report of the two baptisms was written in the early part of July.

His next report was written on August 7, 1887 and published ten days later in the *Advocate*. He held a meeting at Blue Creek schoolhouse in Giles County, beginning on July 29 and ending on August 5, with twenty baptisms and two more to be baptized later. J.R. wrote concerning the congregation at Blue Creek:

This is a community of as much prejudice as any place I ever saw, I think. This school-house was built by the people of the community, (our brethren bearing a large part,) with the understanding that preachers of all religious bodies should preach there, but when our time came, "a fly got into the lock" immediately. They tried to stop us, first by running a prayer-meeting on Lord's day nights and when they failed in this, Cumberlands and Methodists all united, and set up a big meeting, (or tried) against us. But we had a crowded house all the time.

The Roberson Fork brethren co-operated in this meeting. It was close to Roberson Fork Church. Oh, what a grand old time of rejoicing it was! We are in a meeting now at Marsh Academy, will report when through (*G.A.* Aug. 17, 1887, p. 527).

This work at Blue Creek is another church that can be added to the list of churches established by J.R. Bradley. This is one reason

Srygley wrote: "He has baptized hundreds of people and has been instrumental in establishing many strong country churches in his field of labor" (Srygley, F.D. *Larimore and His Boys*, p. 159).

In J.R.'s foregoing report he mentioned that he was engaged in a meeting at Marsh Academy. That meeting had begun on August 5th and ended on August 11th. It ended with three baptisms because of the meeting and one of the two from Blue Creek, who confessed, but postponed baptism until later. W.H. Dixon aided Bradley in the meeting at Marsh Academy. Denominational opposition showed its head in this community also. Bradley said that "they did all they could to hinder, it seemed, but we had a fine hearing all the time, thank God" (*G.A.* Aug. 21, 1887, p. 531). This meeting had begun and ended at an odd time of the week, beginning on Friday and ending on Thursday of the following week. Maybe this meeting began and ended to accommodate J.R.'s next meeting. That would give him a couple of days to a give attention to farm chores and maybe even rest a little.

He began his next meeting on the following Sunday, August 19th, with sixteen baptisms— one from the Baptists, one from the Methodists, and one who confessed but postponed their baptism. The meeting was held in the Baptist church. J.R. wrote: "Our Baptists friends have been very kind to us indeed, have loaned us their house till Christmas. We had very good attendance and attention all through the meeting. Our brethren here are going to make an effort to build soon" (*G.A.*, Aug. 31, 1887, p. 555). J.R. believed that much good could be accomplished at Molino with the "proper efforts," He would be proven correct upon this belief with a year or two more work. T.C. Little of Fayetteville was with Bradley on the first night of the meeting and preached also. His sermon topic was "Heart-felt Religion." J.R. said that Little "preached a fine sermon" (*G.A.*, Aug. 31, 1887, p. 555). He continued to ask for the prayers of the brethren in the good work of the Lord. J.R. did not return home form Molino, as Molino was several miles from home. From here it was just about as close to his next meeting and he only had one day to travel. He wrote a report for the Advocate, bid his friends farewell at Molino, and traveled the rest of the day to the Southern part of Giles County for his appointment.

He arrived at Shoals Bluff community by dark. He rested that night and began his meeting at that place on the next morning, August 21st. Later Bradley wrote a report on that meeting and the congregation at Shoals Bluff. He wrote with joy and expectation as he penned these words:

> Commenced preaching at Shoals Bluff, Giles county, Tenn., on the third Sunday (21st) this month, continued till Monday after the 4th Lord's day (29th) and closed with nineteen confessions and baptisms, twelve restored and two took membership, which are thirty-three additions to that congregation. One dear old man, 84 years old, confessed and was baptized causing great joy to all. This congregation is doubtless greatly strengthened. Eight years ago, Bro. W.T. Hudspeth, of Arkansas, and I, held a meeting with these good people of God, and I believe added forty-seven to the congregation. Oh, what a grand treat! To (sic) be permitted to be with them again. We hope and pray that our elders and workers there will keep the good work going. 'Feed the flock' is an injunction too much disregarded. Hope it will not be so in this case (*G.A.* Sept. 7, 1887, p. 562).

J.R. had closed the meeting at Shoals Bluff on August 29th and he traveled on Tuesday (30th) and wrote this report on Wednesday (31st). Clearly, he had no time to rest. It appears that J.R. did not get home on August 30, because his report was sent from Robertson Fork on August 31, and not from McDowell's Mill, his home post office. It could be that he and the Robertson Fork brethren were discussing plans for the meeting, about to begin, at their new work - Odd Fellow's Hall. J.R. had preached there and established this work and it was sponsored by Robertson Fork Church of Christ. He began the meeting on September 3, which was on a Saturday, and continued it through Thursday,

September 8, 1887. The results were seven baptisms, two from the Baptists, one from the Methodists, and one took membership at that place. There were eleven additions in all at Odd Fellow's Hall during this meeting. W.H. Dixon came and preached some with J.R., from Monday through Wednesday. It must be remembered that usually, during these type meetings, two services per day were common, thus J.R. would welcome the relief in some of the preaching from his friend (*G.A.* Sept. 21, 1887, p. 606).

From Odd-Fellows Hall, Bradley traveled to Molino and preached on Sunday night. Two were baptized. Bradley wrote of this congregation: "The brethren at this place have begun to gather up the means with which to build a house of worship. Two hundred dollars already subscribed. Don't think we will have any trouble raising six or seven hundred. Our Gum Springs brethren are co-operating in this work (*G.A.* Sept. 21, 1887, p. 606).

Upon leaving Molino, J.R. and W. J. Dixon would co-operate in the next meeting, which was at Gum Spring (*G.A.* Sept. 21, 1887, p. 606). The meeting would go from September 10, a Saturday, to September 16, which was on a Friday (*G.A.,* Sept. 28, 1887, p. 610). J.R. reported six baptisms – one to take place the following morning. Gum Spring was the sponsor of the work at Molino. Bradley had established that work with the support of Gum Spring. The brethren at Gum Spring sent Bradley to preach an evening service at Molino on Sunday evening of September 11, even though their meeting with J.R. had begun the previous evening. This showed that the brethren at Gum Spring were dedicated to making the Molino work prosper. The two congregations are only about seventeen or eighteen miles apart, allowing J.R. to preach at Gum Spring in the morning service and preach at Molino in the evening service. Bradley then had to ride back to Gum Spring very early next morning to continue speaking at Gum Spring. Keep in mind that he has hardly had more than a day's break from preaching or traveling for nearly a month, and there were several weeks left in his meeting schedule.

The Molino work still survives today (2019). Most of the churches established by Bradley do still exist. It is important to instill in each generation the need to be faithful, and that is what he always did wherever he traveled and preached.

It appears that J.R. closed the Gum Spring meeting on the morning of the 16th, since he began a meeting on the evening of the same day at Minnow Branch, northwest of Pulaski, Tennessee, and southwest of Lynnville. He wrote his report on the Gum Spring meeting on September 17th. That was the day after he began the Minnow Branch meeting (*G.A.* Sept. 28, 1887, p. 610). In that report he clearly stated that the Gum Spring meeting ended on the 16th, which is the same day he had just begun the Minnow Branch meeting; therefore, a morning service at Gum Spring and a night or evening service at Minnow Branch. Not one hour of rest from one place to the other was found by him.

To add to his weariness, follow the work he did within the next month. From September 16th until September 20th he conducted a meeting at Minnow Branch. The following night, which was September 21th, he preached at Crawford's Schoolhouse and baptized one person. From there he went to Odd Fellows' Hall and baptized three people. From there he went to Robertson Fork and preached on September 23rd. One placed membership there (*G.A.* Oct. 12, 1887, p. 642). J.R. could now go home and visit Mary and take the first night of sleep in his own bed in over a month. This was September 24th.

The following morning, which was the fourth Sunday of September, J.R. traveled a few miles eastward and began a joint effort with W. H. Dixon at Gnat Branch (which would be known as Gnat Grove). This meeting continued through the following Saturday (October 1st). They closed with five baptisms and received one from the Methodists. J.R. said that not much interest was shown until about the close of the meeting. Rain caused lack of interest in the meeting until near the end on Saturday. He traveled from Gnat Branch straight to Odd Fellows' Hall and preached. On Monday (3rd) that work was organized into a proper congregation

(*G.A.* Oct. 12, 1887, p. 642). J.R. remarked about this: "I am at this place now. We expect to set our little band "in order" tonight, so that they can keep house for the Lord. This will be one of our preaching points next year (the Lord willing) and hope for much good" (*G.A.* Oct. 12, 1887, p. 642). Odd Fellows' Hall is still a viable congregation in 2019. J.R.'s field of work was expanding and getting fixed on a more permanent footing.

J.R.'s health was good at this time, and he began to feel the need for more land to use in his farming. A three-acre parcel of land came available, which adjoined his farm. He bought the land from two brothers, James H. and V.C. Wright, and the amount he paid was one hundred dollars (Lincoln County, Tennessee, Deed Book, 1887, p. 512). This was probably the second-best land deal that J.R. would make in his lifetime. This made the Bradley farm contain five and a half acres. That would be enough land upon which J.R. and Mary could survive. J.R. worked his land and still met his regular appointments.

One report concerning this field of labor is described, not by Bradley, but by T. C. Little of Fayetteville, Tennessee. He wrote:

> The work for the Master is progressing finely in most places in Lincoln County. For some time, we have been giving special attention to preaching in new and destitute fields, the old churches supporting the work in part. The result is very satisfactory. Several new churches have been built and another will be soon. Bros. Bradley and Dixon have done the principal part of the preaching this year, all the work I have been able to do has been done in this field, my sore throat has prevented me from holding any meetings this year, in fact I have spoken only once or twice a month. I am glad to say that there has been some improvement recently, and I hope to be able to resume my work next spring. I shall not attempt to speak through the winter (*G.A.* Nov. 23, 1887, p. 751).

In this correspondence, T.C. Little says that Bradley and Dixon had done nearly all the work, accomplished in Lincoln County,

Tennessee. This may explain why J.R. was on such a busy summer schedule.

J.R. had met his entire meetings scheduled by the end of October and had settled down into his regular winter routine. He would preach on weekends at his monthly obligations. He described the work at Molino and Odd Fellow's Hall as follows:

> Our brethren of Molino and vicinity are still determined, by the help of the Lord to have a house of worship. We need about two hundred dollars more money, but, I think we will have but little trouble in raising that amount. Two were added by obedience, at my last visit there. One of them, I think, intends to worship at Gum Springs. On last Lord's day and night, it was my pleasure to be with the good people at Campbell's Station, in Maury County. I have labored with these brethren and sisters in by gone days. Bro. F.C. Sowell is their preacher now. They are doing well, I think; they have a good Lord's Day school. We had two additions by letter there. Our little band at Odd Fellow's Hall, Giles County, is doing wonderfully well; they have bought the Hall and lot from the Odd Fellows very cheap and have new seats and a new stove. It makes a very neat little church. They have prayer meeting and Lord's Day school there (*G.A.* Nov. 30, 1887, p. 759).

It seems that Bradley had helped the Molino and Odd Fellows' Hall brethren get on firm enough ground, spiritually, to begin standing on their own. This may explain why J.R. would take on two new preaching points, which were in the beginning stages. With this report, J.R. reported his "end of the year" work with the churches. We know that he continued to meet his weekly appointments, however, because he was always faithful to his commitments.

Two of his last communications for 1887 were concerning weddings that he had performed. On November 30, he conducted the wedding for Dr. T. N. Jenkins of McDowell's Mill and Miss Nannie G. Holbert, of Cyruston, both of whom were from Lincoln

County. On the 31st, he performed the marriage between Bro. W. B. Dagget, of Robertson Fork, Marshall County, to Miss Nora Pigg, of Brick Church, Giles County (*G.A.* Dec. 14, 1887, p. 797). His very last note was written on Christmas Day of 1887. He married the young couple at the residence of the bride's father. Mr. J.D. Collins was the groom and the bride was Miss A.V. Collins (sometimes know as Sister Donnie). J.R. said that she was "one of our fairest and brightest young ladies, and, best of all, a good Christian" (*G.A.* Dec. 28, 1887, p. 831). Sister Collins was a member at Philadelphia. He wrote of the groom: "Mr. Collins is one of Lincoln's most civil and courteous young men" J.R. wished the couple "much happiness, success in life, and a home in heaven" (*G.A.* Dec. 28, 1887, p. 831).

Thus, was closed one of the busiest years of labor that J.R. had ever had. He loved being used for God's Kingdom and he loved watching the Gospel change the hearts of men into something pliable and useable for God's purpose. J.R. never, throughout his entire career as a minister, complained about his work schedule, nor the distances he had to travel to accomplish that work. He truly manifested the servant attitude toward God and His kingdom, and it was never more clearly shown than in 1887. The next year held promise of being just as busy.

The first big event to warrant Bradley's attention for the year of 1888 was a debate at Lynnville, Tennessee. J.R. had lived in that community and had preached for the brethren at Lynnville and Robertson Fork, which was just four of five miles east of Lynnville. Here he would meet old friends and make new acquaintances. Several members attended from Limestone County, Alabama, including one of J.H. Hundley's daughters-in-law, from Mooresville, Alabama. Also attending this debate were the three sisters responsible for the Randolph Street Church of Christ's establishment —sisters Hundley, Collins and McMullen. The debate was conducted between James A. Harding and a Mr. Nichols of the Methodist Church. It was agreed upon by both parties to print the debate. H.F. Williams said, "It does immense good to know that good folks think you do a good in the cause" (*G.A.* Feb. 15, 1888, p. 5). Apparently, the people of Lynnville thought a good work had been done.

Another report was made by J.W. Grant of Guthrie, Kentucky. He wrote concerning preachers who were in attendance at the debate:

> It was my good fortune to attend the debate recently held at Lynnville, between our James A. Harding and John H. Nichols, of Grub-Ax fame. Some points from it may prove interesting to the readers of the Advocate. The Christian preachers present whom I now call to mind were: J.R. Bradley, J. H. Morton, H. F. Williams, M. H. Northcross, Thomas G. Nance, Arthur Growden, Felix Sowell, H. J. Spivey, Kirby, Petty, Murphy, and the writer. There were probably others whose names I have forgotten. Brother Anderson, who has charge of Lynnville Academy and preaches for the congregation, was also in attendance, having dismissed his school for the occasion. There were four Methodist preachers in attendance, besides the debater, and two Cumberlands. Arthur Growden took a stenographic report of the debate, which will be published in book form after the speeches have been carefully revised by the speakers.

J.R. saw many old friends at this debate. He enjoyed a good debate, and this was a good one.

Just two days after the Lynnville debate report was printed in the Advocate, one of J.R.'s friends and helpers died. He was John Lee Fowler. J.R. wrote in his obituary the following words:

> Our dear old brother and tried friend, John Lee Fowler, of Wilson Hill congregation, Marshall county, Tenn., has left the stormy shores of time, to enter into "that rest that remains for the people of God." Bro. Fowler was born May 6, 1812, died February 17, 1888, aged 74 years, 9 months and 11 days. For many years he was an elder of Wilson Hill church. Always enjoyed the worship as much as anyone I ever saw, I think, during our services there. Many, many times has the writer

been there at his appointments and could see old brother Fowler, about the time for services, coming to church afoot. He lived some two miles away. His companion, our dear old sister still lingers with us, but is very feeble, though strong "in the faith once delivered to the saints" (*G.A.*, June 6, 1888, p. 11).

J.R. concluded that obituary with the words: "We pray the care and blessings of God upon the friends and relatives of our departed brother" (*G.A.*, June 6, 1888, p. 11).

In the very same issue of the Advocate, he reports the death of another brother. J.R. was touched deeply over this young man's death. Columbus Hartsell was only three months beyond his twenty-eighth birthday. He had been a member of the Methodist church, near Gnat Grove, in Lincoln County Tennessee. Bradley had baptized Fowler during the meeting that he and W.H. Dixon conducted the previous September at Gnat Branch. J.R. wrote that Fowler died of consumption. He was married to Miss Willie Trigg of Diana. He left behind Willie and three little children, the oldest one being a little more than four years old. J.R. was called to his bedside just a few hours before he died. Concerning his final hours J.R. wrote: "I was called to the bedside of our brother just a few hours before he departed. In his conversation with us, said that, "he was willing to go at the bidding of the Lord, but so much hated to leave Willie and the babies" (*G.A.*, June 6, 1888, p. 11).

J.R. further stated: "We pray the blessings of our Father upon our sister, and the "little babies," and that they all may be fitted to meet an immortalized husband and father, "over there" (*G.A.*, June 6, 1888, p. 11).

He explains in his next report why, maybe, he had not reported much work, thus far, for 1888. He had come down with the chills in early spring and was still suffering their effects as late as the second week in June of '88. His report is just too good to dissect and re-word. We give the following report in its entirety:

Our work for the summer, in protracted meetings, will soon commence. I greatly fear that I am not going to be able to go through the campaign. I have been having chills this spring, Cough very much, and pain in the side and under shoulder blade. It may be consumption. I had a sister to die with that dread disease. If I must go this way, who can help it? I can not; the Lord knows best. By his help I intend to preach, pray and try to save souls, as long as my strength will admit. I think we are getting along moderately well in the bounds of my work. The new house at Molino, this (Lincoln) county, is in process of erection. It will be a splendid frame building, I think. Our brethren there, and the workmen think that we can use it for protracted meeting commencing on the second Lord's Day in August. The meeting at Wilson's Hill is appointed for the fifth Lord's Day in July. These brethren expect a good meeting. They desire to co-operate with us in one of two meetings, at destitute points, this summer. The meeting at Odd Fellow's Hall, Giles county, is appointed to commence on the third Sunday in July. These people have done very well indeed. They have a splendid Lord's Day school. At our appointment there, last Lord's Day, we had one confession and baptism. Our Roberson Fork brethren have not said anything to me, as yet, about the time of their meeting, but I suppose it will in-clude the fourth Lord's Day of August or September. Dear Brethren, many of you have been with me in our meetings. You know I have nearly always led the singing. Now, let me tell you all who read these lines, that I am done singing, unless I can get so that it will not hurt me so. Our dear brother, Dr. McMullin, at Molino, and other physicians, too, have told me that I must quit. Pray that I may be able to work in my Master's vineyard, this year at least (*G.A.* June 13, 1888, p. 14).

This is just the beginning of the affliction that will plague J.R. for most of the remainder of his life. One can see this deep desire and dedication to preach and save the lost. We must sympathize with him.

A short note in the *Gospel Advocate* announced the wedding between S.P. Williams and Lizzie Hayes, which was conducted by J.R. He remarked about the newlyweds as follows:

> While Mr. Williams is not a member of Christ's body, he is a kind, civil young man, and we think a believer of the gospel. We hope that Sister Lizzie may be an instrument in the hands of God in persuading her husband to put his faith in practice (*G.A.* June 20, 1888, p. 10)

J.R. also stated in this article that Lizzie was a member of the Gnat Grove congregation. (*G.A.* June 20, 1888, p. 10). Even though he would marry non-members to members of the Church, he was always concerned that the believer would convert the non-believer. This could clearly be seen in this note from J.R.

His first meeting for the season was held at Beech Hill schoolhouse in Giles County, Tennessee. The meeting began on the 2nd and ended on the night of July 5, 1888. He wrote: "This is a very strong Methodist community, but we had a fine hearing most of the time" (*G.A.* July 18, 1888, p. 14). He said that the rain hindered the meeting twice. He could not hide his disappointment, however, when he wrote: "Never saw such interest, to be only one added" (*G.A.* July 18, 1888, p. 14). He expressed his desire to hold another meeting there in September. Even though disappointed with the outcome of this first meeting, he was no quitter. He was willing to try again "toward the last of September."

His next meeting was held at Odd Fellow's Hall, beginning on July 14 and continuing through July 23, 1888. F.F. Dearing of Bellbuckle, Tennessee, helped J.R. part of the time, during the meeting. J.R. wrote of Dearing: "He has endeared himself, very much, to the people of Odd Fellow's Hall. We hope that he may be able to visit us again in the near future soon" (*G.A.* Aug. 8, 1888, p. 2). J.R. said that fourteen were added to the church at that place during the meeting. He also stated concerning the brethren there: "We have some noble brethren and sisters, who I think will never surrender the good work at 'the Hall'" (*G.A.* Aug. 8, 1888, p. 2). Bradley expected Wm. B. McQuiddy to come and preach some in their meeting, but McQuiddy could not come.

J.R.'s next appointment was with the Wells' Hill congregation. He began preaching on Saturday night (July 28, 1888) and continued through August 5th. They had only one addition. He told of a new kind of distraction they had to overcome during part of this meeting. He wrote: "Barbecues (sic), pic-nics (sic), and Brand-dances (no doubt he meant "barn dances") hindered very much, I think. All of this was carried on at, or near the church spring during the meeting. The writer could hear music while he was preaching" (*G.A.* September 5, 1888, p. 14) These were the kinds of methods the Devil used in different communities to disrupt the preaching of the Gospel. J.R. saw his share of disrupting factors in his long life as a minister of the gospel. The "power of the gospel," however, always prevailed, and it always will. The members at Wells' Hill were special to J.R., and especially Brother McAllister. He provided a meeting place for the church, in his own shop. He was the "John D. Wade" of Well's Hill.

On August 11th, J.R. and T.L. Weatherford, of Limestone County, Alabama, began a meeting at Molino. Bradley commented on the new building at Molino: "Our brethren here are very proud of their new house. I think they deserve great credit for their earnestness. Had six additions at this place" (*G.A.* September 5, 1888, p. 14). From Molino, he went south eastward a few miles and began preaching in a grove. This was in the community called Camargo. Camargo sits on Pea Ridge, southwest of Fayetteville some seven or eight miles. This meeting began in the evening of August 19th, after Bradley closed the meeting at Molino that Sunday morning of the same day. J.R. said this community was strongly Presbyterian, but they still had a good attendance. J.R. did all the preaching in this meeting. He was feeling much better. Of his physical condition, he wrote: "I am a great deal better now than I was early in the spring. My cough is much better. My wife is not able to be up much of the time now. Our doctor says it is torpidity of the liver" (*G.A.* September 5, 1888, p. 14).

From Camargo, he went to Roberson Fork and began a meeting on August 26, 1888. He had looked for Wm. B. McQuiddy to come to his aid at Roberson Fork, but McQuiddy could not come. He said the congregation was disappointed. McQuiddy had been having health issues, just as J.R. was having. More and more these two men would come less and less to some of their appointments because of sickness. He closed his lengthy report by saying that he had six more meetings for the season. He asked the brethren to pray for him, "that he fails not," in this great conflict (*G.A.* September 5, 1888, p. 14). The meeting was a success, because six were baptized and another, who had been baptized during T.W. Brents' meeting at Lynnville, placed membership at Roberson Fork (*G.A.* Sept. 12, 1888, p. 3). Bradley wrote in his second report for September, that "Bro. W. B. McQuiddy greatly disappointed us in not being at Robertson Fork." He said that he always wanted to have a co-worker in these meetings, because he got hoarse from continued speaking. The following Sunday (September 2nd), Bro. J.H. Burrow filled the pulpit at Roberson Fork, as J.R. was beginning a meeting at Gnat Grove that night. This allowed J.R. to stay home while he preached in the meeting at Gnat Grove, because this church was within a short riding distance of his home at Reuben (McDowell's Mill). He wrote: "I am home today, for the first time in about ten days. Found my dear woman in bed. She has not been able to be up but little in four weeks. A sickly woman, who is a preacher's wife, is greatly to be pitied.... If my wife is not worse, I shall go back to the Grove to-morrow" (*G.A.* Sept. 12, 1888, p. 3).

His friend, J.H. Morton was holding the meeting at Philadelphia, which was one of J.R.'s preaching points. That resulted in twenty-eight additions (*G.A.* Sept. 26, 1888, p. 3). J.R., as well as other preachers, helped during the meeting. This meeting ran parallel to his meeting at Gnat Grove. The Gnat Grove meeting ended on the 7th, mostly because of rain. W.H. Dixon helped J.R.

three nights of the meeting. This rested J.R.'s vocal chords and throat considerably. By this time in the season he needed the rest. He left Gnat Grove and traveled directly to Gum Spring and preached four times with one baptism (*G.A.* Sept. 26, 1888, p. 2). This would have been September 9-10, 1888 (1888 calendar). Throughout the remainder of that week he, along with other preachers, aided J.H. Morton in his meeting at Philadelphia (*G.A.* Sept. 26, 1888, p. 3). The next week J.R. would spend near home, taking care of Mary and attending his farm chores. He would be able to attend some of Morton's meeting on Cane Creek, which had begun on September 16th.

J.R. started his next meeting at Beech Hill Schoolhouse in Giles County. He began it on Saturday night (September 22nd) and continued through Thursday. He had four additions at Beech Hill. He said that they were all from the Methodists. This was a new preaching point at which none of our brethren had ever preached. He had preached his first lesson there back in July. He said, "I have been preaching here at 'odd times'" (*G.A.* Oct. 10, 1888, p. 3). He further wrote that "Lord willing" he would go there and preach monthly in 1889. He closed the month out by beginning a meeting in a Baptist church building called Antioch (*G.A.* Oct. 31, 1888, p. 3). That meeting continued through the following Friday night, which was Oct. 5, 1888. There were no conversions there at Antioch.

From Antioch, J.R. traveled southward to a recently established work at Cash Point School-house. T.L. Weatherford worked jointly with Bradley in this meeting. This meeting began the first Saturday night (6th) of October and continued until the 12th. There were two added to the work at Cash Point. Weatherford left for home on the morning of October 11th, leaving J.R. to finish the meeting on his own. He then gave a very good description of the work at Cash Point Schoolhouse as follows:

Now I desire to say to our brethren and sisters of Lincoln County, that is a good mission field. I speak of Cash Point. We have about four brethren and twenty-five as good sisters as there are in Lincoln County. They want a monthly appointment from some of our preachers and are willing to do all they can. Some good men, who are not Christians, who live in the community, say they will help. 'Said without being asked." Now let the congregations of Lincoln County send to sister J.W. Gatlin, Cash Point, Lincoln County, Tenn., say five dollars each, in order that these sisters may have some good brother to teach them and their neighbors the gospel as much as once per month next year. This Cash Point is on the south side of Lincoln, in about two miles of Ala. Surely the brethren and sisters of our county will not pass by this call unheeded. I came home from this trip, having been gone eight days. Found my wife still in bed and not any better. She has been in bed for three months. I came home with the worst cold, sure the worst I ever had. Dear brethren and sisters do please consider the appeal of Cash Point (*G.A.* Oct. 31, 1888, p. 3).

One can see from this report that J.R. was concerned for the success of the church at Cash Point. He was constantly remembering and praying for the success of all the new churches; not just the ones he had started. Cash Point, however, can be added to the ever-growing list of churches that had been established by J.R. Bradley. It is also noted in this report of the deteriorating health of Mary. J.R. was also becoming ill more often than in the past.

Illness in those days could be deadlier than now simply because of the lack of medical attention or lack of medicine. One of the last acts performed by J.R. in November of 1888 was to preach the funeral of a little eight-year-old girl, named Pearlie Willeford, whose father was T.Y. Willeford. J.R. wrote: "I attended the funeral of the subject of the above sketch, and sung two of her favorite songs, "Evergreen Shore" and "Are You Ready," Made a talk to a large crowd" (*G.A.* Dec. 12, 1888, p. 14).

This must have broken J.R.'s heart for two reasons. First, he loved little children. Second, Pearlie's parents, T.Y. and M.E. Willeford, were his friends. T.Y. was one of the men converted and trained by J.R. to preach. He would preach in some meetings with J.R.

This was the last report of J.R.'s to be published in the *Advocate* for 1888. This year had turned out, despite J.R.'s frequent illness, to be the most productive year, perhaps, in J.R.'s preaching career through the decade of the 1880's. He was anxiously waiting to see what the New Year brought. He could joyfully look back over the year and praise God for the wonderful works that God had performed, using him as one of God's messengers to the lost of Giles and Lincoln Counties, and other places also. Churches had been planted and strengthened and souls had been saved.

5

SUPPORTING PREACHERS CONTROVERSY

Despite all the good J.R. had accomplished in the past year, there was only one thing lacking in J.R.'s life. He had purposefully worked with either poor churches, or new churches, which really were not established financially. This made it difficult for J.R. to survive, because they gave him hardly any money at all. He needed money to pay doctor bills, medicine, and food to eat. He needed financial help, but he did not want to be accused of "preaching for money." For this reason, he had not taught very much on giving. This had already come back to haunt him in a financial way. A little more than a year before, his old horse had died, and he had to have another one to fill his regular preaching and meeting appointments. He only had part of the amount ($25.00) to pay on the horse, leaving him with a note of $100 that he was to have paid within the next two years (*G.A.* Nov. 20, 1889, p. 747). This left J.R. with a lot of debt and no money. During the winter of 1888-89 J.R. was faced with this and it lay heavily upon his mind. He was a little depressed.

His worries were increased by his wife's deteriorating health. She was mostly housebound by that winter and had been for some time. Her care fell upon him and a few good neighbors, since both of them had no family leaving within miles of them. Their families lived several miles to the west in Lawrence County,

Tennessee, and Lauderdale County, Alabama. J.R.'s health was going down and he could not get outside very much. Some of the time he felt well enough to meet some appointments. Other times he was not well enough. This gave him more time to worry how he was going to pay for his horse. That note had at least two friends tied up also. How would he pay it back? He knew just faith by itself could not pay it. The note was coming due by the next fall and this created stress and anxiety upon a good man who was already overloaded with burdens that were affecting his preaching.

His work was at a minimum pace through the middle of May in 1889. His wife was still bedfast, and he needed to plant the garden and a few acres of corn for the continuation of life on Bradley's small farm. The first report on J.R.'s work for May of 1889 was made by H.F. Williams, who had worked on occasions with J.R. and apparently had heard J.R. preach in Pulaski in the early days of May. He called J.R.'s sermon "an excellent discourse" (*G.A.*, May 15, 1889, p. 307). Williams recorded some of Bradley's sermon as follows:

"I forgot," So many people forget. So many people so often forget so many good things for so many trifling excuses. "Oh, I forgot it.'

They forgot that forgetfulness is a ruinous habit that furnishes the soil for many sinful seed.

Moses says, 'Lest ye forget the covenant" "Beware lest thou forget the Lord." David says, 'The wicked shall be turned into hell and all the nations that forget God." "Forget not all his benefits" "I will not forget thy word."

Paul says, "Forgetting those things which are behind us and reaching forth unto those things which are before, I press (sic)." "Be not forgetful to entertain strangers," "to do good and to communicate forget not."

James says, 'If any man be a hearer of the work and not a doer, he is like a man that beholds himself in a glass for he beholds himself and goes his way and straightway forgets what manner of man he was," So let's not forget that we can forget. There are some things we must forget. There are others that should never be forgotten. Don't forget this (*G.A.*, May 15, 1889, p. 307).

The overall title to this sermon was on the "unity of God's people," but Williams was especially impressed with Bradley's part on "not being forgetful." This portion of the sermon may have been presented especially to those who promised to aid preachers and then failed to do so. Maybe they had made this promise to J.R. and had failed to keep their promise.

His next correspondence to the *Advocate* was brought forth over churches not supporting the preachers who labored with them. He began by asking the following questions:

> How can you give to foreign missions to the exclusion of home missions? Why report work done in the Indian Nation through our paper, money sent, etc., when within ten miles of, and in the same county with you, an earnest brother is preaching to large audiences of eager listeners of unconverted people, without support from any source?
>
> Why not announce, urge upon our congregation to give "one Lord's day contribution," to that brother's support?
>
> "Why that would look too little." "We want to appear Big." "Therefore, we will announce, beg, press, scold, threaten, and do nearly anything for a foreign work, because that will blow our horn."
>
> How many have asked their Sunday schools, their congregations, for one Lord's day contribution for our Pulaski mission? O yes, that looks too little does it? (*G.A.* June 5, 1889, p. 359).

You can see the anger as he penned these lines. He was concerned that preachers such as himself could no longer pay their debts, due to the lack of support that the churches in Southern Middle Tennessee withheld. You could feel his hurt as he chastises his friends at the *Advocate* for what he perceives as supporting "foreign work" to the exclusion of "home work." Perhaps J.R. was justified to be hurt over the neglect, by the churches, to support their ministers. That is why most preachers in Giles and Lincoln Counties had to farm to live. He writes further and gives us a clue to what sent him into a state of hurt and anger:

> Last Monday morning, the writer of this, was returning from an appointment, and while passing through one of our county towns, there was a pleasant faced little girl, of probably ten years of age, darted into the street before him holding out her hand, and remarked: "Mister, can't you give us just one nickel for our 'foreign missions'."
>
> Now I want it distinctly understood that I am not opposed to our Indian Mission, as such, but to the idea that foreign missions are to be sustained to the exclusion of supporting those at our doors (*G.A.* June 5, 1889, p. 359).

J.R. ended this letter with an appeal:

> In conclusion, I want to ask my brethren to just look around a little bit and see if I have over-drawn the picture on this sheet. In the south-west corner of Lincoln County, at a place call (*sic*) Cash Point, I am preaching every first Lord's Day. I get large crowds to listen to the work. They are nice looking people. Seem eager to hear. I have received $13.00 for this work, and five of that from a man of the world. Three from a school teacher who is Methodist. Ought I quit? What must I do? Trust the Lord? (*G.A.* June 5, 1889, p. 359).

J.C. McQuiddy, W.B. McQuiddy's brother, and former classmate of J.R.'s at Mars Hill, undertook to address the above letter.

It appears J.C. McQuiddy was very much on the defensive concerning what J.R. had written. But this did not stop him from also saying something good about Bradley. He stated:

> We know Bro. Bradley well, having been associated with him in school at Mars Hill College, and some protracted meetings since that time. He is a good meaning brother, but we think he is wrong in some of his views on missionary work (*G.A.* June 5, 1889, p. 359).

This is one of those 'he is, but" compliments that is really a sort of "backhanded" compliment toward J.R. It seems that many years of journalism had made McQuiddy defensive of any criticism that might come the *Advocate*'s way. He then began to give a few examples of churches that did right opposite of what J.R. described. He missed J.R.'s point, which was that he and the Southern Middle Tennessee preachers were nearly destitute, while in that very area churches were raising money for the Indian Mission work. Bradley was not against helping men like Robert Wallace Officer of Indian Territory but thought it a shame to help him and others in Indian Territory and not help the local workers also. Keep in mind that Bradley was friends with Officer; he had worked with Officer and Askew. Askew was another friend of J.R. and Officer, who had worked in Indian Territory. McQuiddy missed the point. Had he been one of those struggling preachers from Giles and Lincoln Counties, he may have seen J.R.'s letter in a different light.

McQuiddy continued his defense:

> We know one congregation that has given more by far to the "Indian mission" than all Giles county and it has not only done this, but we are satisfied it has done more to help plant the cause in Pulaski than all the churches in Giles outside of Pulaski (*G.A.* June 5, 1889, p. 359).

Pulaski was a new mission work, planted by J.R. Bradley and J.H. Morton with the help of a few others, whose names are unknown now. McQuiddy was making some very broad assumptions in his defense, with statements such as 'but we are satisfied' and "We know one congregation that has given more by far to the "Indian mission' than all Giles county ..." How did McQuiddy know this? Did he know every single church that had sent money directly to Officer? (These churches *personally* knew him)? Did McQuiddy personally know every single individual in Giles County who may have contributed? To further illustrate McQuiddy's broad assumptions, we give the following statement by him:

> Lynnville has also been making some effort, *I believe* (underlining is the writers), to have the gospel preached in destitute portions of Giles county. I call to mind that Rural Hill some five or six years ago did something in the way of having the gospel preached to the destitute of their own county. We have not heard of their doing anything in this line recently. Giles county, we are sorry to say, has as a county been behind in doing either home or foreign missionary work (*G.A.* June 5, 1889, p. 359).

One can see that McQuiddy was speaking to things which he was not sure about or things about which he had no knowledge. It is very interesting that in 2019 Giles county Tennessee has as many Churches of Christ as any county in Southern Middle Tennessee, unless Maury County would be counted as Southern Middle Tennessee. Someone must have supported the works. J.R. was concerned about the little churches not contributing to their local preacher's support. It may be that McQuiddy took J.R.'s letter as a personal attack upon him (McQuiddy).

McQuiddy further wrote about J.R. after saying that Giles County churches were in their duty toward mission work:

> Here is a good chance for Bro. Bradley to show his ability to get churches enlisted in home missionary work. When he has done this, we will give him a chance to work up an interest in foreign work, as he thinks many will contribute to it because it sounds "big," With all our announcing urging and

beseeching, we have not succeeded in getting many to contribute to the Indian mission in Giles County.

Perhaps, if Bro Bradley will try his hand on them, they might
do better. And when he gets them to giving liberally, he will
find that they will not only give liberally to Pulaski and other
points in said county, but they will give liberally to the Indian
Mission. They will be ready to go and preach the gospel to
every creature. We are not saying the brethren of Giles county
are naturally less liberal than others, but we are sure their
preachers have not pressed this matter of giving on them as
they should. Teach the churches, Bro. B. that they "who
preach the gospel, shall live of the gospel," "the laborer is worthy of his hire," and that "the Lord loveth a cheerful giver,"
and further "that it is more blessed to give than to receive."
Let us see that they teach these scriptures. The church that
knows the truth and then will not support the preacher is not
worthy the name, church. But don't let any preacher imagine
that the reason he is poorly supported is because it is given to
the Indian mission, for the very churches that are supporting
him so poorly are doing nothing for missions. The churches
that give liberally to missions are liberal in the support of the
gospel at home (*G.A.*, June 5, 1889, p. 359).

McQuiddy was so defensive in his rebuttal of J.R.'s letter that he
could not see the immediate need of Bradley. J.R. needed help at
that time, and not months later. McQuiddy almost had the philos-
ophy of "You made your own bed now lie in it." He offered no
help for J.R. and the preachers in Giles and Lincoln counties.
McQuiddy had gone to Nashville after Mars Hill, and he had never
gone through the poverty that J.R., W.H. Dixon, J.H. Morton and
others had experienced. It was easy for him to point the finger of
blame at J.R. and his fellow-workers. He never understood that
the mindset of J.R. and his friends was not to appear that they
were only preaching for money. Therefore J.R. always wanted to
work with "new preaching points" or "poor churches,"

Maybe J.C. McQuiddy's observations were correct, but he displayed a total lack of compassion toward J.R., his friends, and Giles County in general. McQuiddy lacked the compassion demonstrated by his own brother, William B. McQuiddy, who showed his several times. It is a wonder that J.R. ever communicated with the *Advocate* again, but he was bigger than that. He could take criticism quietly most of the time. If he ever responded to McQuiddy's comments, they were never printed in the *Advocate*. As a matter of fact, J.R. never again asked for help directly through the Advocate. If his needs were ever again made known, someone else would do it from the kindness of their heart.

Despite J.R.'s need for financial help, he kept riding on a horse that was not fully paid for and preaching in destitute points. His next report was concerning his work at Antioch (a Baptist building) and at the Bradshaw Schoolhouse. These were new points for him and he spent half of his time for 1889 in preaching for points such as this (*G.A.* July 3, 1889, p. 430). The other half of his time he spent preaching for established works, such as Gum Spring, which had been mentioned in this report. He did, however, write about the lack of churches' liberality again. He wrote:

> Am getting nothing, or but little, in the way of remuneration
> for it. Brethren of the churches say, "go ahead Bro. B. that is a
> good work, the Lord will hold up your hands." Maybe the Lord
> will, but I don't believe they think there is any obligation rest-
> ing upon them (*G.A.* July 3, 1889, p. 430).

His financial woes were piling up and no doubt he must have questioned himself, as to whether he should continue preaching and trying to care for his sick wife or should he go into secular work. The answer was clear. He had a fire in his soul, a passion for lost souls, and he would preach until he starved. He would never take his hands from the Lord's plow.

J.R. continued to plow in the Lord's fields and to gather in the harvest. He reports a joint effort with T.Y. Willeford at a schoolhouse in Giles County, about six miles north of Pulaski. He continued in his report that the meeting had begun on "last Lord's Day" (July 28) and ended on Thursday night (Aug. 1). They had six additions (*G.A.* Aug. 14, 1889, p. 526).

With this report J.R. sent a rather strange article to the Advocate and it was published in the second issue of August that year. It was seemingly written to explain why he did not write more than he did. He wrote:

> In passing about I often meet with brethren and friends who ask me the above question (The Article's title was "Why don't you Write?"). I concluded this morning to state a few of the "whys," It is a good plan to only speak when you have something to say, and I dare say the same rule is equally as good for writing. Perhaps it is more applicable, in as much as one is recorded permanently in words that can be seen and read by all, while the other is recorded in the minds of only a few and may never recall it. Hence, he who writes, writes perhaps for generations yet unborn, and the influence may increase, if not for good, to the destruction of future generations. Hence the scribbler should write with these thoughts before him, and there would be less "slashin: and' "blazin" in the things that are written (*G.A.* Aug. 14, 1889, p. 517).

He went on to say that the writer who "would write often and in words that burn, had better embrace something else besides the plow handles" (*G.A.* Aug. 14, 1889, p. 517). Here J.R. was referring to Cincinnatticus, the mythological figure that drank so much that he had to support himself on the plow handles as he plowed. It seems that this article by J.R. was a double-edged sword. It would partly show that J.R. had learned his lesson about writing. Remember that his bout with Walling during 1884 got rather ugly, on Walling's part. His last article was attacked by J.C. McQuiddy, who took it personally. No wonder J.R. had slacked from writing in any paper. The second edge of that sword may have been for the benefit of J.C. McQuiddy, concerning the way he tried to tear J.R. to shreds. Maybe J.R. decided to just refrain from giving any more opportunities to anyone to get harsh with him over something he had written. The solution, to him, was not to write anymore. He intended this article to be his *swan song* to the career of writing.

He further wrote:

> Again, I have been taught that he who speaks only for confusion and strife had better keep silent. And I am doubly sure that this idea is more needful to the scribe who would write of the Kingdom of God, its laws and ordinances, and hence, it suits me to be a listener—a reader—rather than a writer. Again, I have heard it said it was easier to be a judge than a lawyer in a case in court—and I do not see why it should not apply to judging and criticizing the things written than to write the things, and my experience teaches me that we have more judges—critics—than writers. I do not see why I should not class myself with the former rather than the scribes (*G.A.* Aug. 14, 1889, p. 517).

He further pressures writers who would promote themselves, rather than the cause of God's Kingdom. He continued:

> Stand up ye scribes, ye mighty men of the pen, ye writers. We judge your writing good as they coincide with our opinions, the nearer and the better you write our opinions, the grander and more sublime your writings, and we applaud you in these grand efforts to express our opinions upon the many things which you write. But if you write things in opposition to our opinions you become an old fogy or a crank, and deserve to be either given up to the tender mercies of us judges, or placed in the asylum of dilapidated fanatical writers and fed upon all the evil mixtures of our opinions that the unlimited resources of conception can hatch up, until you are made to down the hinges of your minds and the sinews of your arms and fingers, so as to compel your pen to write our thoughts and opinions, instead of your convictions of God's word. Then will we be

the judges and you writers become as one mighty giant in the land to overturn all opposition to our own opinions whether emanating from God, Satan, or man (*G.A.* Aug. 14, 1889, p. 517).

J.R.'s bitterness, as to the way some writers were treated, came out in this stinging charge toward writers who had set themselves up as authorities, and yet their authority was from their own opinions or the opinions of readers, whom they were trying to please, rather than relying upon the authority of God's word. He wrote:

...many noble writers that were once moved by the authority of God alone, are weakening day after day, giving up the demands of God's word or adding our opinions by a continual silence on a "thus saith the Lord," or worse still, a complete submission to all of our "opinions," While recognizing these opinions as driving out the authority of our God and substituting man's instead, tearing down the walls of God's house, and rebuilding with temporal mortar, driving union and harmony out of the Lord's Kingdom, and bringing schisms, strife and alienation (*G.A.* Aug. 14, 1889, p. 517).

He was always concerned with peace and harmony in the church. He wanted the "unity" preserved, but not at the cost of throwing aside God's word.

He concluded his article by pointing out the reason some wrote in the above manner. He asked:

"And for what?" That a single soul may be happier and holier? That God, our Father and his Son, our Savior, might be more exalted, or that the law of the spirit might rule and reign in the hearts and lives of all God's children? No, No. But simply that our opinions may be sole ruler in spiritual as temporal things. Scribes, how have you written? How do you intend to write? How are you classed by us judges? Are you a fogy, and crank, or do you belong to us judges? You may be ashamed to write your confession, but we know, and we have already passed judgment upon some of you, while upon others there is but a few more articles needed to put you upon the food of reconstruction, or final judgment of condemnation awarded to those who "speak as the Bible speaks, and are silent where it is silent" (*G.A.* August 14, 1889, p. 517).

J.R. was concerned that many who wrote were either afraid to write the truth, in fear of being ridiculed, or they had sacrificed God's word for man's desires, to be pleasers of men rather than of God. J.R. could never be accused of doing that. He was from southern Lawrence County, Tennessee and his people spoke their mind, based upon their convictions, not what others thought they should have said. This article was printed without comment.

J.R.'s next meeting was at Gum Springs, Lincoln County, Tennessee. The meeting began on Saturday, August 24th and ended on August 30th. W.H. Dixon and M.H Northcross aided him in this meeting. W.H. Dixon wrote of this meeting: "Bros. Bradley and Northcross were with me, none added. Congregation helped much. Old place, our attendance was small owing to a busy time in work on a new railroad" (*G.A.*, Sept. 11, 1889, p. 579). J.R. did not report since Dixon made a report on the meeting. J.R. never cared who gave a report on meetings in which he co-labored, if God got the glory.

J.R. began a meeting at Antioch, a Missionary Baptist Church Building on September 1, 1889. The meeting lasted five days. He had one to confess Christ and three more were to make confessions at the creek, but heavy, steady rains prevented this from happening. He had to leave to begin another meeting before baptizing anyone. He wrote: "This, I think, was the wettest week I have ever seen since I began preaching. I think good can be accomplished at this place" (*G.A.* Sept. 25, 1889, p. 641). He began preaching on Saturday night before the second Lord's Day of September at New Union, on Egnew Creek in Giles County,

Tennessee. The meeting continued for eight days and nights, from the 7th until the 14th (*G.A.* Sept. 25, 1889, p. 641). He had seven baptisms and seven restored at this place. He wrote: "Hope and pray that these brethren may keep house for the Lord" (*G.A.* Sept. 25, 1889, p. 641) This indicates the church at this place was not yet organized.

From Egnew's Creek he traveled to Greenwood. He preached two sermons on September 15th. He described the audience as being "large" (*G.A.* Sept. 25, 1889, p. 641). He promised to return and hold a meeting for them on the third Lord's Day in October. From Greenwood he traveled to help Bros. Morton and Dixon in a meeting at Cane Creek on September16th. J.H. Morton had begun the meeting the day before, which was the third Sunday of September. Bradley and Dixon would share in the preaching at Cane Creek. You may remember that Cane Creek was in Marshall County, Tennessee. This month had been busier than any September since J.R. began preaching. Maybe this was a sign of things to come. He had written this letter to the *Advocate* on the night of September 16. He had just returned home from Cane Creek for the night. It was good that he could be back in his own neighborhood and so close to home.

His next meeting was back at Gnat Grove, with W.H. Dixon. It began on September 29th and continued for eight days. He had preached at this point many times in the last year or two. He preached ten sermons and baptized three persons. From Gnat Grove, J.R. traveled to his childhood home at Antioch, in Lawrence County, Tennessee. He wrote:

> Second Lord's day in this month [October 13, 1889] I delivered two discourses to a large crowd of my old friends and relations at Antioch, Lawrence County, Tenn. Continued through the week at this place, Iron City, Hamburg, and Cold Creek. Two confessions and baptisms. Then to Greenwood preached seven times, one from the Baptists (*G.A.* Nov. 6, 1889, p. 707).

J.R. was always filled with joy whenever he could visit his old homeplace (sic) and spend time with his old friends and family. It may be noted here that Antioch, Wolf Creek School, Iron City and Hamburg all lay in the Shoal Creek Valley, except for Hamburg, which was only about two miles west of St. Joseph, Tennessee, and about the same distance north of Wolf Creek. The Greenwood mentioned in this report was on Weakley Creek which ran on the Giles—Lawrence county line, just north of Bodenham. This was on J.R.'s way home back to McDowell's Mill in Lincoln County.

The next time J.R.'s name appears in the Advocate was not of his choosing. He would have preferred that it not appear as it did: attached to an appeal made on his behalf. After McQuiddy's last words about J.R. and his Giles—Lincoln County friends, he would have preferred starvation and bankruptcy than to have made another appeal for help. This appeal, however, was made by Sister Molly DeFord of the Gum Spring congregation, Lincoln County. J.R. did not know that the appeal was being made. It reads as follows:

It is with some feeling of reluctance that I ask permission to make the following appeal through the columns of the Advocate and were it not for the worthiness of the person for whom this appeal is made, I would refrain from doing so. The person to whom I refer is Bro. J.R. Bradley, of McDowell's Mill. Bro. Bradley is an earnest and efficient worker for the cause of Christ, and has, for many years, labored at various places in Maury, Marshall, Lincoln, and Giles counties. From some of these places he has received good pay, from others but little. His work this year has been mostly in destitute places, what remuneration he has had, coming from brethren of other churches. Sister Bradley has been confined with illness for the most part, since August of last year, and this, of course, increases their needs. Two years ago, he purchased a horse, and having but $25 at the time, he borrowed the remainder ($100) from a brother, giving his note for the same, and another brother going security. It is now time that note should be paid off, and Bro. Bradley has not the money to do it. Will not those congregations for whom he has worked so faithfully, and with whom he is now working, put their shoulders to the wheel and raise the desired amount? This is a shame! Is not "the laborer worthy of his hire?" Is not "the workman worthy of his meat?" (*G.A.* Nov. 20, 1889, p. 747)

The dear sister had taken this matter upon her own shoulders to try to help J.R. and his predicament, but her motives may be impugned somewhat, as we shall later see.

She wrote a disclaimer to show that Bradley had nothing to do with the letter. They did not get together and plan for this letter to be written. She wrote it on her volition.

She wrote:

> Bro. Bradley would much rather that his name were (sic) not publicly noted, but this seems to be the best way of getting it before the midst of the people; and bear in mind, this is only asked of those for whom he has been, and is now laboring. I am a member of the church at Gum Spring, Lincoln County, where he has been preaching for three years, and know my statements to be correct; that he is not only sadly in need of this help, but well worthy of it. Bro. Bradley's address is McDowell's Mills, Lincoln County, Tenn. (*G.A.* Nov. 20, 1889, p. 747).

J.C. McQuiddy felt compelled to write a trailer to this letter of appeal by Mollie DeFord. He wrote as follows:

> I know Bro. Bradley well, have labored with him in meetings in the past and know him as a worthy and efficient preacher. If he was not such, the congregations for which he labored, would be excusable in not supporting him in his work, but as it is, there is no excuse to be made for them (*G.A.* Nov. 20, 1889, p. 747).

He began his comments as though he was sympathetic with J.R., but you will see his mood change through the rest of his comments to thrashing sister DeFord and her home congregation. He wrote that it was "a burning shame and lasting reproach that these congregations would allow a worthy preacher to be reduced to such penury" (*G.A.* Nov. 20, 1889, p. 747).

J.C. continued by saying:

> It is strange that Gum Spring church where Bro. Bradley has labored for three years would have such an appeal as this made. A church? and yet will not raise $100 to relieve a worthy preacher of debt, when doubtless their lack of liberality helped very largely to reduce him to such poverty. Know Bro. Bradley's condition, the continued sickness of his wife and as our sister says that he was "not only sadly in need of help; but well worthy of it," it is passingly (sic) strange that this church could see no shorter and better way to help him than by sending this appeal to us (*G.A.*, Nov. 20, 1889, p. 747).

> McQuiddy has jumped to conclusions that probably were not true. He insinuates that the Gum Spring congregation got sister DeFord to send that appeal, when she indicates that she sent it on her own out of honest concern for Bradley and his needs. He also does not know the circumstance of the people at Gum Spring. Maybe if they had the money they would have already helped J.R. Furthermore, McQuiddy hinted that all the congregations were a part of the appeal, that, maybe, they all knew the appeal was being made, when he wrote: "It is still a great reproach that all or anyone of them is willing for this appeal to be made public, thereby exposing their stinginess and lack of religion" (*G.A.*, Nov. 20, 1889, p. 747).

That sounded like he believed that more than one church knew that Sister DeFord was writing the appeal. McQuiddy had a lot to learn before he would become a "level headed" writer. This kind of treatment was no doubt what had caused J.R. to refrain from writing. Every time an honest appeal was made by an honest soul, it was turned on them by McQuiddy. Why didn't Lipscomb, or Sewell or Srygley answer this or at least offer their comments? At this point in his career, J. C. McQuiddy was more like a "bull in a china shop. "

He did offer one bit of consolation for J.R., when he wrote:

> No doubt, if Bro. Bradley had said to these brethren unless you pay me so much, I will not preach for your church, many would have cried out, "preaching for money!" Well how much worse to preach for money than to live for money? Neither is right and the man who does it will see his mistake when it is too late. I am glad to say that our preachers as a rule are the most earnest, liberal and sacrificing men we have (*G.A.*, Nov. 20, 1889, p. 747).

McQuiddy did at least end on a more positive note than he seemed to be headed for in the middle of his comments.

Oddly enough, J.R.'s next meeting was held at McQuiddy's schoolhouse in Marshall County, the home place to J.C. McQuiddy and his brother William B. J.R. began the meeting on the fourth Lord's Day (27th) of October. J.R. and a Brother Love did the preaching, even though Wm. B. McQuiddy was there. J.R. preached through the following Friday (Nov.1st). Love stayed behind and preached "a few more sermons." J.R. wrote:

> Don't know the result. Three confessed and were baptized before I left. I think this is a good missionary point. Five dollars received from my old yoke fellow and brother, W. B. McQuiddy, of Normandy, Tenn. To help pay off the $100 note. Thank God for such a friend. (*G.A.*, Dec. 4, 1889, p. 771).

We wonder how much J.C. sent to J.R. to help him pay his $100 note. If he ever gave any, it was never noted in the pages of the *Advocate*.

McQuiddy wrote another article concerning J.R. in the second issue of the Advocate for December of 1889. It was titled: "More About Supporting the Preacher." This was after J.R. had personally visited the office of McQuiddy. He wrote:

A few weeks ago, I had an article in regard to the support of Bro. Bradley by the churches for which he labors and has labored in Giles and Lincoln counties. Since that time Bro. B. has been to the office and has given me full facts in regard to his labors and support. He wishes it to be distinctly understood that he is not appealing to the brethren generally for help in order to pay what he owes on his horse, but simply asks the churches for which he has labored, to pay him what they justly owe him. "They that preach the gospel shall live of the gospel." "The laborer is worthy of his hire." ... Some of the churches for which Bro. B has labored promised him that they would do the best they could in supporting him." "The best they could" or did do was to pay him fifteen or sixteen dollars during the year for the support of the gospel! I hear many of the members quoting frequently, "The Lord loveth the cheerful giver," and "It is more blessed to give than to receive"! Other churches of hundreds of members promised to give him sixty or seventy-five dollars for his years' preaching, but he closed out the year with the marvelous sum of $17.00. Of course, they imagine "this is the best they could do," and that when they were done with the aches and pains of this life, "They would hear the welcome plaudit," well done thou good and faithful servant, enter thou into the joy of the Lord" (*G.A.* Dec. 11, 1889, p. 787).

Thus far McQuiddy seems as though he is sympathizing with J.R.'s needs. He continues:

It is a little amusing, but more saddening to hear the members of such churches quoting, "Ye cannot serve God and mammon." They know well how to lecture the preacher who dresses neatly and occasionally wears a high hat. [This was certainly not J.R.'s style. Probably a clean white shirt and old woolen pants. These are the writer's comments]. He is too worldly minded and thinks too much about dress. Their Bibles say, "Be not conformed to this world, but be ye transformed," etc. "Set your affections on things above.: The same loving merciful Father says: "Thou hypocrite, first cast out the beam out of thine own eye, and then shalt thou see clearly to cast out the mote out of thy brother's eye" (*G.A.* Dec. 11, 1889, p. 787).

At this point McQuiddy sounded as if he favored J.R.'s plea, but he ended by making the following statement:

> I cannot close without saying that Bro. Bradley is largely responsible for this state of things. He acknowledges he has taught them very little on their duty to give. This is a mistake. Many preachers are afraid somebody will say "Preaching for money." I always teach that only the man, as a rule, will make such charge who loves money so well that he never drops over a nickel into the contribution basket. Teach "the whole counsel of God," and leave the results with him (*G.A.* Dec. 11, 1889, p. 787).

McQuiddy seems almost as though he has a vendetta against J.R. for some reason. It is as though he could do or say nothing that would meet with J.C. McQuiddy's approval. Then again one never knows how to read McQuiddy. In this same issue of the Advocate he reported: "J.R. Bradley spent some time with us last week and preached for the South Nashville church on last Lord's day. We were sorry to learn from him that his wife was not better" (*G.A.* Dec.11, 1889, p. 794).

It was good of McQuiddy to step down from the pulpit on that Sunday and let J.R. preach. This was probably the first and only time that J.R. would ever have an opportunity to speak to a "big" church.

J.R. wrote, concerning his trip to Nashville and his preaching for the south Nashville congregation, in the following words":

Was much pleased with my visit to Nashville last week. Formed some new acquaintances of brethren at the office of Gospel Advocate Pub. Co. It seems that we ought to double our energy in work for our literature, seeing that our brethren of the Advocate are working so hard to give us something good. Preached for South Nashville congregation on Sunday and Sunday night. [J.R. wrote this letter on December 10, which is a Tuesday. This would have made him preach on December 1st, because he said his trip was "last week"]. Oh, what a booming good Sunday-School these good brethren have! Fine audience out both day and night. Seemed to appreciate my poor efforts at preaching the old Jerusalem gospel. These good brethren and sisters remembered me kindly in contributing $20 to help me and my sick woman along: $5 to pay traveling expenses, and $15 to help pay off the $100 note spoken of by sister DeFord. May God bless and prosper these good workers in his kingdom. Also, one dollar and forty-five cents from Pulaski brethren for the same purpose. One dollar from an unknown friend, through Bro. Sugg, of Gum Spring (*G.A.* Dec. 18, 1889, p. 803).

We do not know what took J.R. to Nashville and the office of the Advocate. It could be that he had some business there, which he never mentioned. And one also wonders if McQuiddy may have engineered the whole trip to show J.R. that he did understand his situation. After all, it was McQuiddy's congregation that helped J.R. so much. Only the heavenly "Recorder" knows the real reason for the trip and the way things turned out for J.R.

It seems that J.R. was reporting two weddings that he had conducted earlier in the year. Why he was just then reporting them, we do not know. It may be that he had overlooked these items, or it may be that they had been at the Advocate's office for a while and they were just now being published. He had conducted one wedding for R.M. DeFord and Eliza Halbert on November 21st at Gum Spring. Both were members there at that place. On November 26th, he married Jack Clark and Pamela Mayfield, both were of the Bradshaw Community, Giles County, Tennessee (*G.A.* Dec. 11, 1889, p. 794).

In the same issue of the Advocate, J.R. wrote a commendation for the *Christian Hymns*, which was a new song book produced by Gospel Advocate Publishing Company. He wrote:

> I think Christian Hymns, of Gospel Advocate Publishing Company to be the best thing yet gotten up for our congregations, and Sunday –schools. Every congregation should get the note edition and get enough to scatter around over the church, so all the congregation can sing (*G.A.* Dec. 11, 1889, p. 794).

A few observations would be in order at this point concerning J.R.'s commendation.

First: J.R. was an accomplished singer and recognized by others to be so. He loved this new song book. Even though McQuiddy played a large part in the publication, J.R. would still recommend it. He held no grudges toward J.C. McQuiddy. Bradley still considered him to be a good friend. Second: because of his persuading churches to buy the "note edition," inferred that the churches, for the most part, did not use the notes in worship. This is a transitional period of the church song books; from books with the words only to books that have musical notes. Third: This inferred that the churches were not in the habit of buying enough books to supply the entire congregations so that everyone could sing. This gave a typical picture as to how the churches worshipped God in singing. The modern-day reader realizes that we have conveniences to make worship so much easier for us today. We should not take these improvements for granted. J.R. was living during a marvelous time of change from primitive to modern. He saw his entire world transition from one age to another.

His last report for 1889 was a short one. As he was now getting ill and his wife still bedfast, he could only do monthly appointments as health would permit. He reported no baptisms, but only who had sent money to help him pay off the outstanding note.

The report was dated December 13, 1889, from McDowell's Mills, Tennessee.

The Lynnville church sent him $2.95, which was "one Lord's day contribution for their church." It was "to be paid on the $100 note." He concluded by saying "Many thanks dear brethren and sisters" (*G.A.* Dec. 25, 1889, p. 826).

No doubt, this year had been the worst year in J.R.'s life. Maybe the next year would be better. He needed a turn-a-round in his life, so he could do the work he loved to do—the labor in the Lord's kingdom. This may have been the turning point in J.R.'s life. From now to the end of his life, he would not report near as much work as he had during the decade of the 1880's. One reason his productivity would decline is that he would be sicklier, and his wife's health would not improve. Bradley is just one example of many men such as him, who worked in Middle Tennessee and North Alabama. Their lives would reveal the same type of gladness and sadness that J.R.'s life reveals to us today. His life would continue for over three more decades, still filled with the same joys and heartaches he would endure. He would never give in to the hindrances in his life. He would overcome them one by one and grow stronger in faith in the process.

The year 1890 began with the brethren still sending money to help J.R. pay for his horse. *Gospel Advocate* published that he had only received about half of the amount needed to pay for the horse (*G.A.* Jan. 22, 1890, p. 58). In February someone who wished to remain anonymous sent $5.00 to help pay off the note on the horse (*Gospel Advocate* Mar. 5, 1890 p. 147). His new horse was being used for the work of evangelizing. He demonstrated this by writing of his appointments for that year as follows:

"My preaching points for this year are, 1st Lord's Day at Verona, 2nd Lynchburg, 3rd Green Wood, and 4th at Molina and Stoney Point, alternately with Bro. W.H. Dixon. Have just returned from Lynchburg. This was my first visit" (*Gospel Advocate* March 19, 1890, p. 179).

These appointments at Lynchburg and Green Wood (now spelled Greenwood) had developed into life long friendships. J.R. would come back even the last few years of his life and preach in meetings, and especially at their homecomings. He wrote of the Lynchburg congregation after his first visit: "I am much pleased with these good people. "They mean business," Also, their Sunday school is a success. May God bless us in the good work" (*G.A.*, March 19, 1890, p. 179).

He had written this letter from McDowell's Mill on March 10, 1890. The work of a minister is not always joy and fun. Sometimes there are sad occasions, also. The following excerpt demonstrates this very clearly. Bradley wrote of John Corpier's death:

Confessed Christ and was baptized by Brother J.H. Morton in August 1888. His only regret was that he did not enter into the vineyard of the Lord at an earlier date. He died April 14, 1890, of cancer. Was 68 years, 1 month, and 18 days old. Bro. Corpier was a fine man of great firmness, his hope for heaven, was no doubt, founded upon the Bible. The writer spoke to a large crowd of his friends and neighbors from Rev.XX:6. Then his remains were laid carefully away in "Bee Spring" grave yard... (*G.A.*, July 2, 1890 p. 428).

The local papers bore accounts of many funerals conducted by him.

The last half of July 1890 was filled by meetings at Green Wood and Stoney Point. His letter of August 8, 1890 read as follows:

Preached a week for Green Wood Brethren embracing third Lord's day in July. Had good attendance all the time, but no good done, I fear. A Bro. Kelley from Lawrence County was with us in the meeting and did some good preaching. He is young but does well. Including fourth Lord's day in July, I preached about a week for Stoney Point brethren. Had two confessions and baptisms up to Thursday night (*G.A.*, Aug. 13, 1890, p. 531).

Green Wood was formerly known as the Weakly Creek congregation and was established by Wade Barrett in November of 1846. That makes this the oldest of J.R.'s preaching points.

He began a meeting at Green Hill School house in Franklin County, Tennessee. The church at Lynchburg had established this effort as a missionary effort. Now that Lynchburg is one of Bradley's regular preaching appointments, he was holding the meeting. He wrote of the meeting:

> Began at Green Hill on the last Lord's day night. Could only preach at five o'clock in the evening or at night, on account of school. This is a new place for our brethren. Great many separate Baptists here, and also many Methodists. We had a fine hearing. Grew better to the close. Had one confession and baptism. Promised to hold another meeting there beginning second Lord's day night in September (*G.A.*, Aug. 27, 1890, p. 546).

Two weeks after the Green Hill meeting, he began a meeting at New Union and preached for seven days. He baptized six persons and had one restoration. The following day (fifth Sunday) after meeting closed at New Union, he began a meeting at Sumac near his home. He had only preached for two nights when he wrote this report to *Gospel Advocate*, dated September 1, 1890 (*G.A.*, Sept. 10, 1890, p. 578). Another report was sent by him on September 5:

> Had three confessions and baptisms at Sumac, Giles county. A fine hearing all the time. Began the fifth Lord's day in August and closed the Friday following. One good Methodist said, "he

would be better pleased if Bradley would preach remission of sins before baptism" (*G.A.*, Sept.17, 1890, p. 594).

The third Sunday of August finds Bradley preaching at McQuiddy's School House near Farmington, Tennessee. One may recall that in the 1880's William B. McQuiddy was preaching and traveling with Bradley. This same Wm. B. McQuiddy grew up at Farmington, and the school was named after his family. The connection between J.R. and William B. McQuiddy lasted throughout their lives. T.J. Burrow wrote of this meeting at McQuiddy's school house in a letter dated August 25, 1890. It read as follows:

> Bro. J.R. Bradley held meetings at McQuiddy's schoolhouse near this place beginning the third Lord's Day in this month. Preached ten discourses upon such themes as "The Word," "Grace," "Forgiveness," "Christian Union," etc. There were good audiences and good attention, but no additions. Bro. B "outdid" himself preaching and we hope some good will result from this meeting yet. But for the fact that the people about here are wedded to the "isms," such preaching as Bro B does would accomplish much good. And he is doing a noble work in portions of Lincoln, Franklin, Moore, Giles, and Marshall counties, for less that "half for the round trip" (*G.A.*, Sept. 10, 1890, p. 579).

To highlight the people being "wedded to the 'isms', is illustrated in the fact that Wm. B. and J.C. McQuiddy's mother never left the Baptist church even though three of her sons were preachers in the church of Christ. The church was finally established at Farmington and still meets today (2019). J.R. would make other trips and preach at this place.

He returned to Green Hill, as promised, and held a meeting, which began on the second Sunday of September 1890. He preached twice before writing his report to the *Advocate* and reported seven confessions and baptisms. He continued through Friday of that week. He left there and went to Long Branch in

Lawrence County, Tennessee to preach in another meeting (*G.A.* Sept. 24, 1890, p. 611).

Another report was sent to the *Advocate* about the meeting at Green Hill. This report was written by J.T. Silvertooth and was dated September 18, 1890. It read as follows:

> Elder J.R. Bradley, of McDowell's Mills, Lincoln County, has just closed a series of sermons, delivered at Green Hill Academy, this place, with good results. Through the kindness of the congregation of Lynchburg, for which church he preaches, his appointments were extended to this place. He has filled two appointments at this place and as a result of his labors fourteen additions have been made to the church of Christ, eleven conversions, two from the Baptist church, and one restored member. We will meet at a private house and organized on next Lords Day and prepare for more work in the future. (*G.A.*, Oct. 1, 1890, p. 626).

Thus, another congregation added to the list of churches established by J.R. Bradley.

In September, Bradley had secured the right to hold a gospel meeting in the Methodist Meeting house in Booneville, which was a few miles from his home, in the eastern part of Lincoln County. He wrote of that meeting:

> Began preaching at Booneville the fourth Lord's day night and continued till Friday night, and closed with two confessions and baptisms. We were rained out one night. New Herman and Stoney Point brethren sustained this meeting. Our Methodist friends allow us to use their house. I think much good can be done at this place (*G.A.*, Oct. 15, 1890, p. 659).

Before the year's end, Bradley had established the Booneville congregation. This congregation is still a strong rural congregation today.

In the first part of October, he held a meeting at Marsh Academy near Lynchburg. This effort resulted in two baptisms and one restoration. Opposition from the denominations was so strong that he sounded discouraged concerning this effort. He wrote: "We have some noble brethren and sister in range of this place, but I fear but little good will ever be done here on account of opposition "(*G.A.*, Oct. 22, 1890, p. 675). Bradley ended the meeting on Wednesday night, which is an unusual time to end, as most meetings continued until Friday or Saturday night. It seems that he had a special reason for this unusual end. He reported that F.D. Srygley was holding a meeting at Bradley's home congregation, which at the time was Lynchburg. He wrote in the *Advocate* as follows:

> Bro. Srygley is with us here this week. Don't know how long the meeting will continue. Large audiences. Only three sermons have been preached. If the people continue to come as they have been doing, and the preaching continues to be good as it has been, the meeting will doubtless be a success (*G.A.*, Oct. 22, 1890, p. 675).

A week later Bradley reported that large crowds were attending the Lynchburg meeting, "with fine prospects for a good meeting" (*G.A.*, Oct. 22, 1890, p. 685).

The months of November and December of 1890 were relatively uneventful. He preached for his circuit of preaching points and even from house to house. Except for an occasional wedding or funeral, he spent that winter in study and preaching. The last week of November was spent in preaching funerals. He preached Mary Worsham's funeral on November 25th, and two days later he preached Charlie Hughey's funeral. He had baptized Mary Worsham on July 22, 1888 in a brush arbor meeting at Beech Hill. On December 17, 1890 the *Advocate* gave J.R.'s final report for 1890. It read as follows:

I have held fourteen meetings of a weeks' duration, since the third Lord's day in July, with forty-three additions. This is by far, the smallest number, during protracted seasons, since I left school in '79. Don't know why. I have pleased myself in preaching better than any year before. Had good order at all places, and large crowds. Three took membership at Center Point fourth Lord's day in November, that are not included in the forty-three. Pray for me and mine (*G.A.*, Dec.17, 1890, p. 815).

Sometime during the winter of 1890-1891, J.R. became ill and was unable to do very much preaching until the summer of 1891. Lipscomb underscores this fact when he wrote the following about Bradley:

Bro. Bradley has been afflicted with "La grippe." He did not fill his appointment at Mulberry on this account. This is the first appointment he has missed for two years. He has also been suffering from hemorrhages. He hopes to be well soon and finds much comfort in the letters of Bros. Elam and Kidwell. He says: "We think we are doing tolerably well in the bounds of my work. The Sunday-school at Stoney (sic) Point has taken on new life. Molino has let her's die out, but we hope new life will be diffused into it before long. I think the singing there, will be an important factor along this line. Lynchburg Sunday-school is all right. Church not doing what she ought, I fear. Odd-Fellows Hall doing well, for a small, persecuted, and young congregation. Mulberry brethren and sisters are determined to succeed. Brethren please pray for us" (*G.A.*, March 18, 1891, p. 170).

A reunion was being planned by former Mars Hill students at this time. J.R. really had wanted to go to the reunion, but his illness had impeded his work so much that year, that he was in a strait as what to do. He wrote:

I want to be at the Mars Hill reunion very much. It is at a time when nearly all the brethren in my field of labor want their meetings. I don't want to say that I will go, and I know that I shall be hurt if I don't get to go (*G.A.*, March 18, 1891, p. 170).

Apparently, he never got to go. His name was never mentioned in anyone's list of those who attended, and Bradley never mentions having gone.

His illness lasted longer than Bradley first thought, and the effect was greater than he had expected. This was evident in a letter, written by him, dated August 20, 1891. It read as follows:

The reason I have not reported work done for the Master, is, that I have done but little. Been waiting to see if I could get something to report. And even now, though am (sic) writing this, I am ashamed to see it alongside of the reports of my brothers whose work has been so abundantly blessed. Bro. Dixon and I were at Stoney Point, Lincoln County, embracing third Lord's day in July, remained there till Thursday night following with only one addition. I began fourth Lord's day at Molino, and continued till Saturday night following with four additions, three of these were confessions and baptisms, the other one restored. We should not have closed this meeting as soon as we did, but I was under promise to the Lynchburg brethren to begin a meeting on Farris Creek. Went on there early Lord's day morning, only to be disappointed. Just closed at Green Hill, Franklin county, a meeting embracing the second Lord's day in this month with no additions. Very fine audiences every night. Preached in daytime under a large elm tree near Bro. J.A Silvertooth's house. Nine-tenths of the people in that county are strongly opposed to the church of Christ. May God help the cause in that country (*G.A.*, Sept. 2, 1891, p. 556).

From the above writing, one can sense a degree of depression in Bradley's tone. He was still living at McDowell's Mill at the close of 1891.

His next letter was more upbeat. He began with, "We have just closed a glorious meeting with the New Hermon brethren near Flat Creek, Bedford County" (*G.A.*, Sept. 23, 1891, p. 601). The meeting began the first Sunday in September and went for twelve days. The meeting closed with fifteen baptisms and four restorations. He wrote of the meeting:

> We had some rain and some old Baptist association to contend against, but still we had a fine hearing all the time. These brethren and sisters are greatly revived...They were not only kind to me while visiting them in their families and at their homes but remembered me in a substantial way when I went to leave. May God abundantly bless them (*G.A.*, Sept. 23, 1891, p. 601).

He was to return for another meeting on the 5th Sunday in November. He began a meeting at Molino on the fourth Sunday of September. This meeting lasted four days and nights. Four baptisms resulted. That was the exact same number he had had earlier in the year at this place. He said that these were the first responses the church at this place had seen in two years. They had not been meeting regularly and promised that from that time forward they would meet on a regular basis (*G.A.*, October 5, 1891, p. 649).

He began a meeting at Mulberry, a little village between Lynchburg and Fayetteville. This meeting began on October 4, 1891. Apparently, Bradley did not like the results. He never reported it to *Gospel Advocate*.

In November of that year, Lipscomb reported of the preachers of Middle Tennessee. He wrote as follows:

> Such preachers as Bros. Floyd, Bryant, Bradley, Hoover, Dearing, Morton, Ridley, Dixon, Land, and a host of others are doing a very excellent work in advancing the Kingdom of Jesus Christ in a quiet way. It is not the preacher who makes the

greatest show that is doing the most valiant service every time, for "empty wagons rattle the loudest" (*G.A.*, Nov. 26, 1891, p. 749).

From Murfreesboro southward to the Alabama-Tennessee line, the above-mentioned men were the shining stars of the south Middle Tennessee "Restoration Movement."

The year 1892 began with a change of address for J.R. Bradley to McBurg, Lincoln County, Tennessee. He had established a church at that place. He labored with the brethren and farmed to support his wife and himself. Farming and preaching are what he did best. His first communication to the *Advocate* was a very sad report of a young girl's death by fire. It read as follows:

> Early on the morning of the 16th of February last, little Iva, daughter of Bro. J.F. and sister (sic) Lulia Davis ... being near the fire with her back to it, her dress caught on fire, and began to flame frightfully, at which little Iva became alarmed, and broke out doors, running around the house. Her sister (Mrs. Smith) ran after her, and caught her, but Iva pulled loose, and kept running until nearly all her clothes burned off. A colored man not far off heard the screams and ran to her and helped to extinguish the remaining clothing that had not burned off. Poor creature! She was so badly burned that she died the 17th, in her 13th year. She told her mother just a few days before the sad accident, that she was reading the Bible, "by another year mother," she said, "I will be prepared to join the church." Bro. and sister Davis are members of Stoney Point congregation, Lincoln county. Hard indeed to give up such a sweet, promising little child, but God knows best (*G.A.*, March 31, 1892, p. 204).

The move to McBurg was not a happy move. That year was filled with more sad notes than happy ones. Bradley seemed to be despondent from his prolonged illness. He did not send regular reports to the *Advocate*, as had been his custom in the past. There were, however, some good things to report.

Some of this good news began to be seen the middle of July, that year. In his first report in nearly five months Bradley gives a synopsis of his summer's labor. He also explains:

> I have neglected to report my meetings so long that I have almost forgotten results of some of them. Began at Antioch, Lincoln County, the fourth Lord's day in July, and closed Thursday night following with one confession and baptism, and one took membership. The next meeting began at Greenwood, 5th Lord's day in July and continued eleven days. Bro. R.F. Carter of Lynnville, Tenn., assisted me in this meeting for six days. He left to meet another engagement. Up to that time seven had obeyed. The five remaining days we had eight confessions and baptisms. I think the church greatly revived. Second Lord's day in August I began at Molino, Lincoln County, Tenn.; continued five days with four confessions (*G.A.*, Sept.1, 1892, p. 556).

While at McBurg, he and J.B. Trigg, of Diana, Giles County, Tennessee, held a meeting at Oddfellow's Hall, also in Giles County. They began on the third Sunday of August and continued for twelve days and nights. This resulted in seventeen baptisms, two restorations, and twelve placed membership – thirty-one responses in all (*G.A.*, Sept.1, 1892 p. 556; Sept. 15, 1892, p. 584).

By the middle of September, having been at McBurg for less than a year, he had moved to Booneville. He had strengthened the work at McBurg and had preached there in several meetings. He had conducted several weddings and funerals. One such funeral was reported in the *Advocate* of September 8, 1892 on page 576. He preached the funerals of friends. He had baptized Marmaduke Clifton and his wife Sarah in 1880. They died just hours apart, it seems. They were laid to rest near their home. This would be J.R.'s last communication from McBurg to the *Advocate*. He would be concentrating on the work in the north central part of Lincoln, Moore and southern Bedford Counties.

6

NORTH CENTRAL LINCOLN COUNTY

Within two weeks J.R. and Mary moved to Booneville, northwest of Lynchburg, and bought a house situated on an acre of land adjoining the Booneville Methodist Church property. His morning began on Friday, September 23rd, unlike his usual days, but filled with anxious excitement. He had moved among old friends and acquaintances and before the day's end, he would sign the deed to his new house (Lincoln County, Tennessee, *Deed Book*. 1892. pp. 270-271). He had established the church there in Booneville in 1890. He announced his change of address from McBurg to Booneville in the *Advocate* (*G.A.*, Oct. 20, 1892, p. 664). Before moving to Booneville, Bradley had held one meeting at Philadelphia, between Lewisburg and Columbia. We learned this through a letter written by J. B. Trigg, of Diana. He said that Bradley started the meeting by himself on the second Sunday of September 1892, and that he (Trigg) came to help a day later, and that there were two baptisms and one restoration. Trigg wrote: "The brethren at Philadelphia have been lukewarm for some time, but they say they are going to do better" (*G.A.*, Sept. 29, 1892, p. 620). From this report we now know that Bradley did not report all of his work, therefore we only get little glimpses into his life and work.

His health was not very good after so many months of hard labor to sustain his wife and himself. From his report on September 29, 1892, until January 10, 1893, he had only baptized four persons. He also reported that his wife had been sick with pneumonia for two weeks, and that he had been caring for her. There were no children in J.R.'s household; therefore, all care for his wife was upon him. This explains why he said: "I have not been here long – have been a little confused" (*G.A.*, Jan. 19, 1893, p. 40).

After a few weeks Bradley was able to begin his regular preaching visits. One such visit was at New Hermon, just four or five miles north of Booneville. He would visit them the first Sunday of each month. He wrote in the *Advocate*: "The first Lord's Day in each month we are with these dear people of God. They have a very interesting Sunday school. Well attended. The spiritual interest seems to be growing at this point" (*G.A.*, March 23, 1893, p. 189).

The following week J.R. sent another report to the *Advocate* concerning the work at Molina and Booneville. This letter was rather lengthy, as compared to his other reports. He told of A.B. Lipscomb preaching for the Molino congregation on the night of March 20th. He wrote of Brother W.H. Dixon's nephew, Earl Dixon, being baptized. He also spoke of the work at Taft and Elkwood as having a good future (*G.A.*, March 30, 1893, p. 193). He further wrote in this letter:

> I visited Booneville, Tennessee, and preached last Sunday and Sunday night. We have several brethren and sisters in Christ there. They have no house of worship in Booneville, but a splendid school house. A few years they met regularly upon the Lord's day, but for some cause have quit. Our home was with these dear people several years ago. And we learned to love them very much (*G.A.*, March 30, 1893, p. 193).

He reported one week later (March 30th) that two had been added to the congregation at Molino. He wrote that he hoped for a "fruitfull year at Molino during 1893" (*G.A.*, April 6, 1893, p. 220). He also reported his attendance at a funeral of an eight-year-old child at New Hermon (*G.A.*, April 27, 1893, p. 268). Most of Bradley's circuit was now improving. The circuit now was Booneville, Taft, Elkwood, and New Hermon. Taft and Elkwood were about three miles apart, Taft being in Tennessee and Elkwood in Alabama. The first three congregations had been started by Bradley; only New Hermon was the exception. It had been established by Henry Dean in 1830. Bradley did seem to favor the brethren at New Hermon because they showed endurance and steadfastness. This was opposite of the Booneville brethren, who were only a few miles down south of New Hermon. Bradley had started the Booneville work when he had lived there a few years before. Upon his return to this community he had found them in a state of complacency and unfaithfulness. He did, however, set those things that were lacking, straight.

Now that his field of labor was turning around for the better, he began to make plans to establish a new congregation in 1893. J.C. Martin had issued a challenge to every preacher who read the *Advocate* to commit to establish one new congregation in 1893. J.R. Bradley took the challenge and submitted his name to Martin's list of the *Advocate*. He wrote the following to Martin:

> For fifteen years I have tried not to be like the father, whose little boy-when asked if his father was a religious man, answered "Yes-sir-ee, but he is not working at it now," But to establish a new congregation, means more probably than some of us think. But if the congregations already established, could but hear, and be impressed with your whisper to them, as co-workers in this business of establishing new ones, oh how much lighter the job! I with a bow, join your band (*G.A.*, May 4, 1893, p. 281).

One can easily see that Bradley planned a goal and he would reach it as we shall see later.

To reach that goal, he would go into poor communities and work. He, being raised in a poor community and on a farm, never forgot his humble roots as is shown in the following report. He wrote:

> Please say through the *Advocate* to my brethren, especially of Tennessee, that I would like to correspond with those who desire meetings during July, August, and September. I have the 4th Lord's Day of these months on which I can begin meetings to continue two weeks if necessary. I prefer to correspond with poor congregations (*G.A.*, May 4th, 1893, p. 280).

From this it can be understood that his desire was to help poor and maybe struggling churches. Who among 21st Century preachers would advertise as Bradley did?

By the third week in June of 1893, J.R. Bradley had received some requests from some of the poor congregations to come and hold meetings. The church at Molino had secured a promise from him to hold a meeting beginning on the 4th Lord's Day of August 1893 (*G.A.*, June 22, 1893, p. 392). He had received a request from his old home congregation at Iron City, Tennessee, to come and hold a meeting for them. He stated his intention to preach about a week at Iron City. He also listed other protracted meeting appointments as follows: "Chestnut Ridge, first Sunday night of August: Stoney Point, third Sunday in August: Molino, fourth Sunday in August; New Hermon, First Sunday in September" (*G.A.*, June 22, 1893, p. 392).

Concerning New Hermon, this was one of his regular preaching points; however, they desired him to hold an extended (protracted) meeting for them. He also tells of the new meeting house they were building at New Hermon. He wrote: "New Hermon is to have a new house of worship soon. We gave the old house and six hundred dollars for the new one. It is 48X30 feet.

We are occupying the schoolhouse while the new house is being built" (*G.A.* June 22, 1893, p. 392). In that same letter Bradley reported he still had about time enough to hold three more meetings if anyone was interested. He also reported one addition to the church at Chestnut Ridge on the second Sunday in June 1893.

On July 23rd Bradley began a meeting at Stoney Point, which continued through August 1st, a total of 10 days. They had 3 baptisms at Stoney Point. Two came from the Baptists, one of these being Allen Rozier. Rozier was a Separatist Baptist preacher, but for two years he had been leaning toward the New Testament Church. Bradley said, "His faith and preaching for about two years have caused quite a commotion in the Baptist Zion," He also preached three sermons in the earlier part of the meeting (*G.A.*, Aug. 10, 1893).

Bradley reported his next meeting three weeks later in the *Advocate*. The meeting was a ten-day meeting that ran through August 16 at Chestnut Ridge. There were four additions to the church there. Bradley reported that Allen Rozier and a brother Gammill had helped him in this meeting. (*G.A.*, Aug. 31, 1893, p. 556). Two weeks later he reported on his meeting at Molino. His letter read as follows:

Our meeting at Molino closed last night, having continued six days and nights. Eleven sermons-six by Brother W. H. Dixon, and five by the writer. Eleven confessions and baptisms, one from the Baptists, one restored, and three took membership. Two of those baptized were from the Cumberland Presbyterians. One lady came from the United Presbyterians, who had formerly been a member of the church of Christ but being young and somewhat untaught went over to the "U.P. church" to be with her husband, but she attended our meeting and concluded that she could not live happily in the church of her husband (*G.A.*, Sept. 14, 1893, p. 595).

He further stated that he would begin a meeting at New Hermon the next day (September 3rd). His work was very pressing during the fall of 1893. As usual he would work himself too hard and would get ill during the winter. This would be his pattern until his death. Until illness would overtake him he would continue working very hard and would continue to do a very good job of preaching the gospel, as was demonstrated at his New Hermon meeting.

He reported the following week concerning the New Hermon meeting. The meeting lasted five days and nights with eleven baptized, one restored, and two placed membership. That was fourteen additions in five days. In 2009 there were only eight people still worshipping at New Hermon; about half of what Bradley's meeting added in five days in September 1893. There is a lesson in this for all churches to keep lively and not grow complacent in the work of the Lord. Bradley also reported the following about the New Hermon effort: "Brother A.H. Rozar, lately from the Baptists delivered two sermons during the meeting with good results. Brother Gammill of Chestnut Ridge preached one sermon satisfactorily" (*G.A.*, Sept. 21, 1893, p. 601).

The reason these two other men preached during Bradley's meeting was that he was probably getting very tired. He had been holding meetings almost constantly since the middle of July. These meetings consisted not only of evening sermons, but sometimes there would be two preached during daytime. That would take a toll on a man's health after a couple of months of constant preaching without a break. This was not solely Bradley's style, but the way everyone held meetings at that time. This style continued into the twentieth century. Thus, it would be a welcome relief to have someone else, such as Rozar and Gammill, to preach a few sermons for him. Bradley also seems to be giving these men some training to work with him, since brother Gammill was just a member at Chestnut Ridge and had not preached very much at all, and

A.H. Rozar had just recently converted from preaching for the Baptists. These men would need some patient grooming, and that seems to be what J.R. Bradley was doing in the meeting at New Hermon.

The meeting at New Hermon had closed on September 8, 1893, and it was a week before J.R. began a meeting at Awalt. This break from constant preaching gave him a week of badly needed rest. He began at Awalt, in Franklin County Tennessee, on September 15th and concluded on the 21st with four baptisms and one who placed membership. Bradley had begun sowing the seeds of the kingdom in the Awalt community two years earlier. His first meeting there had been a success. He had baptized fourteen souls. He organized the Awalt congregation of twenty-five members. The brethren said that they would build a house of worship. From Awalt, he went to Estill Springs, near Dechard, Tennessee. He began preaching on the fourth Sunday of September and preached six days and nights. Apparently, he had no visible results in this meeting, but he did say that he had a "Good hearing all the time" (*G.A.*, Oct. 12, 1893, p. 652). The Estill Springs' work was still being organized during Bradley's work in that area. He promised to hold a tent meeting for them the next June. Bradley had written that report on October 3rd, and it was printed 9 days later by the *Advocate*.

By the end of October, J.R. reported to the *Advocate* of his establishing a church in Bedford County Tennessee (*G.A.*, Nov. 9, 1893). No more details were given at that time. In another report he wrote:

> Since my last report I have baptized two at Chestnut Ridge, at my regular appointments. I begin a meeting at Watson's Chapel the fourth Lord's day in October, but closed on Tuesday night following, on account of my failing health. I don't think I ever made a start for a meeting and had to close on account of failing health before. I think much good would have been accomplished if I could have remained for eight or ten

days. This church is near Tullahoma in Franklin county. My cause for stopping the meeting was hemorrhages. I think of the lungs. I thought I had gotten much better, till last night, when I had another hemorrhage, and am still spitting up a little blood this morning. 1 hope my brethren off some distance from home will excuse me from filling my regular engagements with them during the coldest part of the winter. I hereby ask you to do this. May be that if I will expose myself to the severe cold, I will be able to be with you some next spring and summer. 1 shall try to fill my appointments that are nearby. (*G.A.*, November 23, 1893, p. 744)

He further wrote of weddings he performed during November:

Three marriages since my last report. Brother G.M.D. Creason to sister Dora Alexander, Brother Joseph Lane to sister Maud Waggoner, and Mr. D W. Ashby to Miss Willie Harris. May God's blessings overshadow them all! (*G.A.*, November 23, 1893, p. 744)

He also mentioned a debate in which he was a participant:

There is a debate between Brother William Erwin, of County Line, and of the 'Separatist Baptists" Church, and the writer, announced to begin at New Hermon. Mr. Erwin affirms that he and his brethren teach the doctrine taught by Christ and the apostles—I deny. I affirm the same for myself and brethren —he denies. I may not be able to do the speaking on account of the trouble mentioned above. Dear brethren, pray for me, that the Lord may bless me in my trouble. If any of you feel willing to help us a little, so, that we may get through the winter, it would be appreciated very much indeed. I speak or the brethren in my work, and who appreciate my efforts in the good work. We have received very little these hard times, J.R. Bradley (*G.A.*, November 23, 1893, p. 744).

His illness would plague him throughout the winter. This seemed to be his pattern for the remainder of his life. He would not correspond with the *Advocate* until March of 1894. He did, however, perform a few weddings while confined mostly to his house. One such wedding is recorded in an old family Bible. It was between E.L. Parks and Ella Ermine Foster on February 4, 1894 at Booneville in the home of Bradley ("Family Bible" of E.L. Parks). Even currently he was still unable to preach.

His first correspondence to the *Gospel Advocate* for 1894 announced the marriage, on Feb. 24, between Oliver Anderson and Fannie Weddington, of the Sylvan Mills congregation. (*G.A.*, March 14, 1895, p. 168). His second was announcing three additions at Sylvan Mills (*G.A.*, March 14, 1895, p. 176). His third correspondence was a series of questions that he had concerning articles written by a brother Oakley. He had written an article in which he had seemingly separated Abraham's faith from his works. Bradley asked the following three questions: "(1). which law is "by deeds of which no flesh shall be justified" (Rom. 3:20, 28)? (2) "When was the scripture fulfilled which saith, Abraham believed God, and it was imputed unto him for righteousness, and he was called the friend of God? (See Gen. 15:6; Rom. 4:3; Jas. 2:23) (3) When was Abraham converted?" (*G.A.*, March 29, 1894, p. 199) From this correspondence, J.R. had a very keen mind and knew how to use it. Keep in mind that this letter was written while he was still ill. Concerning this illness, he wrote:

> I wish to say to the brethren that I have greatly improved my health from what I was last winter. My physician, Dr. W.C. Griswell, of Bellville, advised the free use of cod-liver oil, hypophosphite, and egg, during the winter and early spring, and now I am heavier than ever before in my life. I weigh 154 pounds. I am sure that I feel as well as I ever did (*G.A.*, June 14, 1894, p. 376).

He further added that he was willing to do some meetings during the months of August, September, and October. This would be in addition to his regular circuit appointments. He stated: "I would prefer new places or congregations that are to be built up" (*G.A.*, June 14, 1894, p. 376). You may recall that in the May 4th *Gospel Advocate* of 1893, he had expressed a similar thought about working with the poorer churches.

Apparently, while Bradley was sick, the church at New Hermon nearly split. He wrote:

> I am happy to say that our trouble at New Hermon has been satisfactorily settled. Those dear brethren and their families have come back into the service and work of the church, and everything seems all right and everybody happy. Thank God! There was a large crowd there at our regular appointment last Lord's Day, and the brethren and their families who have been absent from the services so long were in their places and feeling good (*G.A.*, June 14, 1894, p. 371).

One can only speculate as to what the problem might have been. We are tempted to wonder if building a new building might have brought on some of the problem. Remember that Bradley had announced in the *Advocate* of June 22, 1893 that New Hermon was in the process of building a new house of worship. The congregation had been meeting in that older building for over sixty years and no doubt some tradition had developed among the members. It was in this building that Joshua K. Speer, Thacker Griffin, Tolbert Fanning, and other pioneer greats had proclaimed the Gospel of Christ to the masses. It is understandable that human nature may have kicked into play. Whatever happened, Bradley helped put it back the way it was supposed to be. He helped bring peace back to New Hermon.

The next several weeks, J.R. would continue to work and heal the wounds at New Hermon. By the middle of July, he began to fill meeting appointments. His first to be reported in the *Advocate* for the late summer was a meeting at Watson's Chapel in Franklin County, Tennessee. The meeting began on the fourth Sunday in July and continued until the fifth Sunday. The meeting ended with four baptisms. J.R. developed a very bad chest congestion and had to get his friend, and son in the gospel, to do most of the preaching. The congestion was probably connected to the bout of "La Grippe," which was very much like pneumonia. He would be plagued by this type illness the rest of his life.

J.R. wrote the following, concerning the meeting and then another one to follow:

> I hope much good is accomplished. Brother Rozar did some splendid preaching. I desire to announce an arbor meeting beginning on the third Sunday night in September, near Buckeye Baptist church, in this county (Bedford) (*G.A.*, Aug. 9, 1894, p. 503).

He would report the results at Buckeye in a letter that he wrote to the *Advocate*, dated September 25th, from Booneville (*G.A.*, Oct. 4, 1894, p 630).

His next correspondence was dated September 7 and was written from home at Booneville. It read as follows:

> Our meeting at Chestnut Ridge began Saturday before second Sunday in August and continued nine days and nights with two confessions and baptisms, and three restored. We began at Molino third Lords day in August and continued seven days and nights with three confessions and baptisms. We began first Lord's Day in this month (September) at New Hermon. Eighteen additions to date. Brother Dixon is with us. Very large audiences and good interest. May close Sunday night (*G.A.*, Sept. 20, 1894, p. 599).

It may be noted here that J.R. said the meeting at Chestnut Ridge began on the Saturday before second Sunday of August and ended nine days later. That would mean that he would have had to preach on the third Sunday to preach nine days and nights at Chestnut Ridge. You will also notice that he said "We began at Molino third Lord's day in August..." Perhaps J.R. preached at Chestnut Ridge Sunday morning and then rode on horseback 18-20 miles and began the meeting at Molino on Sunday night. If this was the case, you can understand how J.R. had a difficult time overcoming illness. It was also possible that W.H. Dixon, who assisted J.R. in this meeting, preached on Sunday for J.R. Keep in mind that transportation was either buggies, wagons, horses, mules, or walking. None were very fast. Much time was spent by J.R. and his preaching companions traveling to and from meetings, such as were just described in J.R.'s letter.

In J.R.'s former report he had stated that their meeting at New Hermon was in progress and that it probably would close on the second Sunday of September. At the time of his writing of that report, he reported eighteen additions. The results had been so good that the meeting did not close until the following Monday. The meeting concluded with a total of twenty-three additions at New Hermon (*G.A.*, Oct. 4, 1894, p. 630). Apparently, things had gotten back to normal at New Hermon, because he further stated three more persons took membership there. We cannot imagine that the meeting results would have been the same with grave problems still occurring at New Hermon.

J.R. also reports the results at Buckeye as follows:

> I preached a week in Buckeye Baptist church, beginning the third Sunday night (September). Brother W.B. Freeman, who lives there, with a few other brethren, built an arbor for us, but the Baptist brethren kindly tendered us the use of their large and commodious house. I think the meeting will do good. I am at Stoney Point now. Began last Sunday (fourth Sunday). Good Crowds (*G.A.*, Oct. 4, 1894, p. 630).

By way of observation, we can see that J.R. preached the truth firmly, yet with love and concern. This was very much like his old teacher, T.B. Larimore. The Baptists respected Bradley enough to allow him the use of their building, even after an arbor had been built. This was not the first time that a denominational group would open their house to J.R. This tells us that he preached the truth without being offensive to others. Keep in mind that he converted many Baptists, Methodists, and Presbyterians.

In November he reported on the total results of the meeting at Stoney Point. His letter reads:

> Our meeting at Stoney Point began the forth Lord's day in September, and closed Tuesday night after the fifth, with six confessions and baptisms and one restored. Brothers Dixon and Rozar helped us in the meeting. There were two confessions last lord's day at Brother Rozar's appointment. Our little congregation there is growing both in numbers and grace. I hope (*G.A.*, Nov. 1, 1894, p. 694).

This was the last report by Bradley to be published in 1894; however, another report written on the same day (October 24th) concerning his labor for October through December was sent to the *Advocate* by a sister Ellis of Sylvan Mills, Tennessee. She wrote as follows:

> I desire to report a meeting held at this place mainly by our Brother J.R. Bradley, of Booneville, Lincoln county, Tenn. It had been announced for some time that our meeting would begin the second Lord's day in October, and that Brother Bradley would be here. He came up on Saturday. Though there was no announcement for preaching for Saturday night, it was circulated in the factory, that he would preach that night, and so we had a respectable hearing and two additions that night (a Baptist preacher and his wife). On Lord's day our crowd began to increase. We have had preaching only of nights (except Lord's days) for eleven days, and during the time, there have been fifteen confessions and baptisms, three from the

Baptists, four from the Methodists, and eight restored. Brother W. H. Dixon came up and delivered two splendid sermons, and did other valuable service. Brother Dixon is to be with us again on Monday night after the second Lord's day of next month [November], and Brother Bradley will come back the fifth Lord's day in December (*G.A.*, Nov.1, 1894, p. 694).

This report gave the summation of J.R.'s work for the last quarter of 1894. The old year was on its way out and another long winter lay ahead for J.R. and Mary.

7

ILLNESS HINDERS WORK

The year 1895 was not a good year for J.R. He had some illness early in the year. He did, however, get to plant a small crop to sustain Mary and him through the next winter. His first report was sent on February 26th and was very short. It reveals a new preaching point in his list of appointments. It reads as follows: "There have been three additions to the congregation at Sylvan Mills since the last report" (*G.A.*, March 14, 1895, p. 176). This was a new congregation near J.R.'s home and was in Bedford County, Tennessee. Due to the brevity of the report, one can see that J.R. was not feeling very well at the writing of his report. He had worked himself too hard during his protracted meetings of '94. He also included in this report a notice of a wedding he had performed, two days earlier, at Sylvan Mills between Oliver Anderson and Fannie Weddington, Both were members at that place (*G.A.*, March 14, 1895, p. 168). After his short report of February 26th, his voice fell silent in the pages of the *Advocate*, as far as reports on his work, until November of that year. This was not typical of J.R. He would usually send in reports on individual meetings, weddings, and funerals, and he would have especially reported a debate that took place in his own home community. F.B. Srygley debated a Baptist preacher at Booneville, which was

J.R.'s home and he never mentions it (*G.A.*, July15, 1895, p. 456). This shows that something was ailing him. From his silence, we gather his physical state and maybe even depression hindered his correspondence. Even though he sent no reports to the *Advocate* on any work, he did write an article challenging his Baptist friends to answer some questions he had posed. (*G.A.*, March 28, 1895, p. 206).

On or about July 30th of that year, he took very ill with indigestion. He sadly wrote as follows:

> In the first place, I must say that I have done less work than ever before, since I have been trying to preach. About July 30th I took an indigestion trouble which caused me to give up three meetings entirely. I would come home, and after a few days rest and taking medicine would get better. Then I would go off to the next meeting, get worse, and must go home again. I kept on this way till frost began, then I began to improve. Now I can eat most anything and not suffer from it. I have held four meetings since I began improving, and in all I have had seventeen additions. I am now beginning to feel almost well. I had promised to hold three meetings in Indiana — the appointments all made and was to be the third Lord's day in October, but was fearful on account of my stomach trouble, and wrote them I would not go. I greatly desired to make the trip (*G.A.*, Nov. 28, 1895, p. 765).

From his above information, his illness sounds like he may have been suffering from the very painful problem of a bad gall bladder.

In the foregoing excerpts from Bradley's letter he mentioned three meetings that he had to cancel in Indiana. It is tantalizing to ask questions about his Indiana plans. Where in Indiana was he planning to preach? Who arranged these meetings for him? Who did he know in Indiana? After all, he was just an old "Tennessee Plowboy" from Iron City, Tennessee. Maybe some possible answers may be suggested in another excerpt from Bradley's letter.

On the meeting at Chestnut Ridge, Moore Co., Tennessee he wrote:

> Brother G.C. Waggoner, of Lynn, Indiana held our meeting at Chestnut Ridge. He began the third Lord's Day in August and continued about ten days —had twenty-four additions. I was to have been with him through the meeting but had to go home on account of indigestion. I only preached twice. Brother George did some as fine preaching as I ever heard, though (*G.A.*, Nov. 28, 1895, p. 765).

This may be an indication as to where in Indiana J.R. was to hold his meetings. It may also explain who J.R. knew in Indiana. How he knew Waggoner is still a mystery.

J.R. continued to tell of hopes dashed because of his illness. He wrote:

> I was to have been with Brother Granville Lipscomb at Molino but did not get to go at all on account of my trouble. He had a fine meeting there. All were pleased with the preaching and results. He had nine additions. He then went over the river just four miles to Old Gum Springs (another of J.R.'s preaching points), preached a few days, and had a good meeting - about twenty additions, I think (*G.A.*, Nov. 28, 1895, p. 765).

You can just see how J.R.'s absence from these meetings ate at him. First, he loved being able to preach. Secondly, he loved to hear good preaching. Due to his illness he could do neither. Earlier in J.R.'s letter, he had mentioned that he had held four meetings after he began to feel better. He told of those four meetings:

> The places where the four meetings were held were: Sylvan Mills, Corder's Cross Roads (both in Tennessee), Reunion, Ala, and Well's Hill, Tenn. We had twelve additions at Stoney Point. Brother A.H. Rozar did most of the preaching. I only

spoke twice. He and I were to have both worked together in that meeting, but on account of my sickness he did all but two sermons (*G.A.*, Nov. 28, 1895, p. 765).

From this letter we can see that J.R. was frustrated with his condition. He really wanted to preach at all his appointments but was hindered by his illness. His two reports give an insight into the depression that must have afflicted him because he could not preach. This mental pressure seems to have been reflected by his omission of dates of meetings, how long they lasted, and who were some of the people attending those meetings. He omitted many details that normally would have been found in his reports.

Another sign of his depression was reflected in his complete omission in his reports for all of 1895 of the debate conducted between F.B. Srygley and Dr. M.W. Blaloch (a Baptist). The debate was held in Lynchburg, just less than six miles from J.R.'s home. It began on March 19th and continued through March 22nd. Two days were given to each disputant's proposition (*G.A.* April 11, 1895, p. 230). The debate was reported by J.D. Floyd, who lived farther up the valley from Lynchburg than J.R. What is most surprising about this failure to discuss or report the Lynchburg debate is that F.B. Srygley was an old Mars Hill classmate and a very dear friend. If J.R. even attended the debate, nothing was mentioned about it. It could have been that J.R. was sick at this time, or even Mary, who had been bedridden for more than two years. Setting all speculation aside, it is still unusual that J.R. never mentioned it in his November report. This was truly J.R.'s worst year since he left Mars Hill. He could only hope for a better year in '96. It appears J.R. and Mary did have a better winter and spring. J.R. was getting stronger by the day. He would be able to plant another small crop for necessities. He preached at his appointments whenever he was well enough and that was improving more. He did an occasional wedding and some funerals. He sometimes, during his illness, gave appointments to other preachers as is seen in a report given by R.C. White:

Unionville, Sept. 2. On the third Lord's day in August I preached at Sylvan Mills on my way to Powell's Creek School-house (Shake Rag as better known), where I began a meeting that afternoon... Brother J.R. Bradley advised me to go to that place, and I will never regret it, because I think seed was sown in good and honest hearts. I hope to return there and reap the fruits of the good seed sown. (*G.A.*, Sept. 12,1895, p. 588).

This is the first year in his preaching career that he had to give appointments away because of illness. 1895 had truly been J.R.'s worst year for his labors.

8

ALABAMA IS CALLING

J.R.'s first report for 1896 was about a funeral of a dear friend. The report read as follows:

> On the 12th of April, Sister Martha Jane Duncan of Chestnut Ridge congregation, passed over the cold river of death, and as we trust, "into Abraham's bosom." Just as were gathering at her church for worship her spirit was being gathered safely home. The writer preached over her remains on Monday, April 13, from John 11:24, to a large crowd of her friends (*G.A.*, June 11, 1896, p. 379).

He admonished her two daughters and two sons to "get about the preparations that they have to make to meet dear mother in 'the sweet land of rest'" (*G.A.*, June 11, 1896, p. 379).

His first meeting for the year of 1896 was at Reunion, Limestone County, Alabama. This had been old Brother J.H. Dunn's congregation. The meeting began on the fourth Sunday of July and continued through the first Sunday morning of August. He began at Big Creek on the first Sunday night. J.R. wrote of these meetings as follows:

There was a good attendance and marked attention through-out the meeting [at Reunion]. I certainly think that the church is greatly strengthened spiritually by the meeting. There were twenty-one additions from all sources – twelve by confessions and baptisms, four took membership who had obeyed at other meetings, three from the Methodists, and one from the "Ste-phenites" (whatever that means) (*G.A.*, Aug. 20, 1896, pp. 540-541).

At Reunion J.R. had probably preached to several who had been baptized by John Henry Dunn (J.H.) or had been encouraged by him. Reunion had been one of the key centers of the church in Limestone Co., Alabama for several years.

From Reunion he went immediately to Big Creek, in the same county. He wrote:

On the first Sunday night, after preaching twice (that same day) at Reunion, I began at Big Creek (same county) in Brother Morton's place. I preached seven sermons and had eleven confessions and baptisms. Brother Hardy had one on Sunday, making twelve baptisms. Three were restored, mak-ing fifteen added at this place. I think that the brethren aim to get Brother George Waggoner, of Indiana, to continue this week. I had to come home, and I will begin at Chestnut Ridge tomorrow (*G.A.*, Aug. 20, 1896, pp. 540-541).

It seems that J.R. was just "filling in" for brother Morton (J.H.). Maybe Brother Morton was sick or tied up in another meeting and could not get free. It does seem, however, that J.R. was conven-ient to the location and was glad to take Brother Morton's place. All turned out well. His new Indiana friend, George Waggoner, would take over the meeting when he (J.R.) went home.

And go home he did, because he was to begin a meeting at Chestnut Ridge in Lincoln County, Tennessee, the next day (Au-gust 8, 1896). This meeting was begun on Saturday before the second Sunday and continued through the third Sunday night. Two were baptized and one took membership. Apparently J.R. was getting very tired this early in the season because he allowed J.B. Trigg to do most of the preaching. J.R. left the meeting at Chestnut Ridge at some point during this meeting to begin a meeting at Maplewood in Giles County, Tennessee, on the Saturday night before the third Lord's Day in August. This meeting closed on the fourth Sunday night. J.R. related a very sad story of this congregation as follows:

> Maplewood is a new house, about five miles north of Shoals Bluff. The building of the new house came about in this way: They had torn down the old log house, and had a nice frame building nearing completion, when it was discovered that one of two of the brethren had a paper going around, getting all they could to sign, for putting an organ in the new house when completed. So the brethren who are desirous to have the worship conducted in the apostolic manner, after doing all in their power to include them to desist from the "organ-nation," went to the site above named, and now they have a nice new building fully complete, and so deeded that the worship (and the preacher too) must be after the divine model (*G.A.*, Sept. 24, 1896, p. 621).

Maplewood was formed by Shoals Bluff brethren who refused to worship with instruments of music. They also took precautions so a problem, such as the above mentioned, could never divide them again. One can only imagine how J.R.'s heart must have been pained upon receiving this news. He continued in his letter:

> O how I did hate to find things thus! Two of the finest meetings of my life were at old Shoals Bluff. Brother W.J. Hudspeth and the writer held them a meeting seventeen years ago, embracing two Sundays with forty-seven additions. Nine years ago, I went there and continued over the Second Sunday, with

145

thirty-three additions. There was no organ in that work. I do pray that these brethren may see the error of their course and agree that the house may be finished without "binding a yoke" upon those faithful brethren which they nor their fathers were able to bear (*G.A.*, Sept. 24, 1896, p. 621).

It seems from J.R.'s letter that the Shoals Bluff building was still not completed, and perhaps would not be, unless the promoters of the organ ceased. We do not know what caused these few brethren to show their hand, but we do know that O.P. Speegle and his followers were doing some probing into the churches in this region of Alabama and Tennessee. The two men who had been so influential upon Shoals Bluff had been dead for nearly twenty years. That would be J.H. Dunn, who died in 1877, and M.M. Nance, who started Shoals Bluff, and who had died in 1879. Their influence had passed with the passing of many of the original members, who remembered Dunn and Nance. They were slowly losing the biblical emphasis that so many of the older members had known. All of this made a sad scene for J.R. when he had arrived in the Shoals Creek Valley. He reported only two baptisms and eight had taken membership at Maplewood (*G.A.*, Sept. 24, 1896, p. 621).

From Maplewood he went to Union Grove, Limestone County, Alabama. We do not know exactly what J.R. did the week following Maplewood, because his meeting at Union Grove began seven days afterwards. We do not know if he traveled home for a few days or if, perhaps, he visited with old friends. Brother T.L. Weatherford did live in the area and he and J.R. had been friends since their Mars Hill days. At Union Grove he reports four baptisms and one united from the Methodists (*G.A.*, Sept. 24, 1896, p. 621). The meeting ran from August 30th through September 4th (first Friday).

Bradley continues his letters:

> We began on the first Sunday [6th] in this month, at an arbor
> near Bethel, Limestone County, Ala., and closed on the second
> Sunday, with seven additions – four from the Baptists, two
> from the Methodists, and two reclaimed. This was the work of
> the Bethel brethren. Brother T.L. Weatherford, of O'Neal,
> Ala., was to have been with me at Maplewood, but was too un-
> well to be there. He came to the other two meetings, and
> though feeble, did a grand work and part in the services. He is
> improving rapidly and has not lost a particle of his zeal. His
> pathos is about the same as when we were in school at Mars'
> Hill, nineteen years ago (*G.A.*, Sept. 24, 1896, p. 621).

Bradley loved Brother Weatherford and held him in high esteem.
He could sympathize with him in his illness, since Bradley was no
stranger to the discomforts of pain and illness. He concluded his
report by giving his next appointments:

> My next meetings are: Richmond, third Sunday in September;
> Sylvan Mills, fourth Sunday in September; Noblitt's Chapel,
> first Sunday in October; Paint Rock, [Jackson County] Ala.,
> beginning on the 14th of October at night. I shall spend two
> weeks with most of them (*G.A.*, Sept. 24, 1896, p. 621).

While J.R. was away for these meetings, the four-year-old
daughter of his friend, and "son in the gospel," A. H. Rozer, died.
This was reported to the *Advocate* by one of Bradley's friends,
Robert Creson (*G.A.*, Sept. 24, 1896, p. 621). This was sad news
for J.R. to have received while on the road. When he received the
news he also reported on Little Ethel's death. You can read the
sympathy toward the family in every line he wrote. He wrote:
"The grand father and grand mother, living nearby, seemed to
suffer the affliction as keenly as the parents..." (*G.A.*, Oct. 1, 1896,
p. 636).

In the *Gospel Advocate* for October 8th, some unnamed source reported on Bradley's meetings at Richmond and Sylvan Mills as follows: "Brother J.R. Bradley has recently held meetings at Richmond and Sylvan Mills, in Bedford County. There were a number of additions at each place about four at the former and two at the latter named place" (*G.A.*, Oct. 8, 1896, p. 648).

It could have been that J.R. was very busy and had someone else to send the reports, or he may have sent the reports to the *Advocate*, himself, and one of the editors could have summarized the report. The former suggestion is more plausible, since J.R. sent a report himself, one day after the report appeared in the *Advocate*. His report was dated October 9, 1896. The report stated:

> At Richmond, during a meeting which began on the third Sunday in September, one was baptized, and one restored. At Sylvan Mills, where I began on the fourth Sunday in September, I baptized one, and received one from the Baptists. I am now at Noblitt's Chapel, where I began on the first Sunday in October. To date there have been thirteen baptized, one received from the Baptists, and four restored. I have time to preach four more sermons here. I begin the night of the 14th at Paint Rock, Ala. Brother J.L. Holland assisted us at Richmond. He did some very fine preaching. Love to all. Praise the Lord! J.R. Bradley (*G.A.*, Oct. 22, 1896, p. 684).

You may have noticed some inconsistencies between J.R.'s report and the one made earlier by someone else concerning the same two meetings. The earlier report seemed to have been made by someone who did not have all the facts. J.R.'s reporting was always accurate, even to a fault. He would sometimes report so much that one might say, "I did not need that much information." He also gave the vicinity for the location of Noblit's Chapel. Up until now, no one, at least in the pages of *Gospel Advocate*, had given the location of Noblit's Chapel. J.R. let us know that it was near Minor Hill.

Noblit's Chapel was organized about 1870. The church building was built on the land donated by Thomas H. Noblit. Thomas was an elder in the congregation. The building was situated on the banks of Puncheon Creek. Noblit's Chapel would eventually become the Puncheon Church of Christ ("National Register of Historic Places Continuation Sheet," Section Number 8, page 24, June 11, 2008). A note attached said that Puncheon was still meeting in the old log building (2008). That would be the same building they meet in presently (2019), with a remodeled look. J.R. probably spent time in visits with the Noblit family and maybe lodged there with the Noblit family when he held meetings at Noblit's Chapel.

J.R.'s report was not the only report made on the meeting at Noblit's Chapel. Brother R.C. Abernathy sent a full report on Bradley's meeting. We include the letter in its entirety because it contains a very good insight into Bradley's preaching. Abernathy wrote:

Brother J.R. Bradley, of Booneville, Lincoln County, commenced our protracted effort the first Lords' Day in October [4th], and continued eight days, with unabated interest till the close. The day he closed was a rainy one; never the less, the house was well filled, and splendid attention was had. There were six additions at the last sermon. I think I understand why he had such good attention: Brother Bradley is clear and forcible speaker and delivers his sermons with zeal and earnestness that few surpass; and, again, the spirit that he manifests is love, gentleness, and kindness. This disposition will arrest the attention of the most vicious when rightly wielded. Brother Bradley has a wonderful tact of gaining the attention of his hearers; and when gained, he tells the sweet story of the cross in such loving-kindness that he wins the hearts of many who hear him. Brother, if your congregation is cold and lifeless, get him; he will infuse new life. If you are a lively, working congregation, get him; he will teach you how to love and do more for the Master. Ours was a grand meeting. The church was much edified, the community thoroughly taught, and seed were sown that we are confident will bring fruit in the near future. We had thirty additions – eighteen baptisms, two from the Baptists, two from the Methodists, and eight took membership. We engaged Brother Bradley to hold our meeting in September 1897, beginning Monday night after the first Lord's Day.

R.C. Abernathy. (*G.A.*, Oct. 29, 1896, p. 701).

Abernathy's prediction came true, concerning Bradley's sown seed bringing forth "fruit in the near future." He reported to the *Advocate* on November 8th that "A Baptist preacher and his wife united with us at Noblit's Chapel the fourth Lords' day in October. He is a man of culture and refinement" (*G.A.*, Nov. 19, 1896, p. 748). Bradley made many lasting friendships in Sugar Creek Valley and Noblit's Chapel. From this appointment, he traveled home to rest for a few days. For some reason he began his meeting at Paint Rock, Alabama, two days late. It may have been he needed more medical attention than usual. He did finally leave home on the fifteenth and headed for Alabama.

He began the meeting at Paint Rock, two days late, as has already been noted. The meeting began on October 16th, which was a Friday. The meeting continued through Monday night, October 26th. He described the people of Paint Rock Valley as follows:

The people of this little town are kind and hospitable, and very much desire the "kingdom of heaven" to prosper, except possibly a few who very much detest the idea of "campbellism." There is an invitation for me to take this field for the next year. There are some four or five congregations that seem to be very anxious to have a good, sound, and earnest man locate among them. I hardly think that my present condition will allow me to accept the invitation. We baptized two. One came over from the Baptists and one from the Methodists, and one was restored, making five in all (*G.A.* Nov. 19, 1896, p. 748).

Paint Rock was the farthest east that J.R. had been up to his point. It would not be his last time in this area of Alabama.

His next appointment was just down the road from Paint Rock. He would preach seven sermons at Whitakers Chapel, located seven or eight miles from Paint Rock. He baptized four and received two from the Baptists, making six. Bradley wrote: "I am told that they are as fine people as can be found in that country" (*G.A.* Nov. 19, 1896, p. 748). The meeting began on October 27th and ended on the 31st. He preached three sermons. He described the people at Kennamer Cove as "very fine people." Bradley concluded the report by saying:

> I was gone on this trip one month and six days, and held three meetings, resulting in forty-one additions from all sources. During thirteen weeks in protracted meetings I have added one hundred and four to the "one body." "Praise God, from whom all blessings flow" (*G.A.*, Nov. 19, 1896, p. 748).

This turned out to be a good year in J.R.'s work, even though he had a rough beginning to the year. This goes to show that only God gives the increase, and he can do it even when the messenger has ill health. Think of the work accomplished by the Apostle Paul, the man with "a thorn in the flesh." J.R.'s thorn was his recurring illness, but God still used him in 1896.

Whatever lay ahead in the coming year, J.R. took courage from his experiences during the past two years. He also learned that God's work would prosper, with or without J.R. This is a lesson that we all need to learn today. We should never think that we are so valuable that the work would fail without us. We are not suggesting that Bradley ever did feel that important. He was too humble by nature for such feelings. He did, however, hurt when things went undone while he was incapacitated by sickness. That was the sign of a great Christian worker.

The New Year (1897) was ushered in with some old baggage from previous years and the church would have to deal with it. Some of these old problems were not only lingering, but also growing. The question concerning "Sunday School" was becoming a big problem. As early as 1880, G.W. Elley had connected the work of "Sunday School" to the missionary societies (*G.A.*, 1880, p. 356). The original idea had been introduced through the societies. The brethren in the south had found another way to have Sunday Schools without a Society. The original concept involved the sending of a superintendent (teacher) from the missionary society into a community and set up a school without the local elders being involved. Total control was retained by the society, and not the local church. The *Gospel Advocate* fought this arrangement, because it was not biblical. The local church was responsible for such schools and not a missionary society. J.R. was against any kind of organization that took away the control of Bible studies from the oversight of the elders. The elders are the ones charged by God's Word to "feed the flock" (Acts 20:28) and not some organization outside the local congregation, such as a missionary society.

The idea of "Sunday School" was not a bad idea. The church did need to be fed spiritual food; in other words, they needed to study the Bible. Sunday school was a way for the church to be fed. Many churches in the south began to organize their own schools under their own elders. As is always the case, some brethren objected to even a locally organized Sunday school. They could not distinguish between a society Sunday school and a congregationally sponsored school; thus, the anti-Sunday school movement began. So many issues were put forth by the anti-Sunday school brethren that the *Advocate* published many articles on the subject. You may ask, "How does this tie into J.R. Bradley's life?" It very much ties into the field in which he labored. J.R. had made references, in a good way, to Sunday schools before, such as the one in South Nashville, where J.C. McQuiddy was the minister (*G.A.*, Dec. 18, 1889, p. 803). He mentioned the Sunday schools in other places, yet always in good light, if organized by the leaders of the local congregations. He could not see why some brethren were so adamant against them, if they were only an extension of the Sunday services.

He decided it was time for him to have his say on the subject. Sometime during the winter months of 1896 or 1897, he wrote on the subject. His article began by saying:

> Please allow me to say a few words through the *Gospel Advocate*. Has not too much already been said in the *Gospel Advocate* on the Sunday school? Have not positions been taken and not sustained? I know of one large congregation, some of the best members of which have almost quit reading and studying the Bible in the classes, claiming it favors a society too much for them. The negro said that his board tree was so straight him lean a little to one side?" Are not some of our "divines" getting so straight on this Sunday school question that they are leaning a little to one side? Now, then, I just want to say that I never expected to get that straight. Nearly every congregation I have preached for in side of at least six months is troubled and their work hindered by some of the brethren being almost crazed over this thing (*G.A.*, Feb. 11, 1897, p. 91).

One can sense J.R.'s frustration over these issues. It was difficult enough to work among the denominational groups, and now his brethren were creating more difficulties. The "Sunday School" issue should have never arisen. Brethren should have been smart enough to distinguish between a Sunday school operated by a society and one conducted by a local congregation. J.R. knew that if brethren would just study their Bibles more, these problems could be laid to rest.

He felt that the churches were paralyzed by these wranglings. He knew that the main issue for the church was evangelism and not "fussing and fighting" over issues. J.R. was becoming more like his old Mars Hill teacher, T.B. Larimore, towards issues. Larimore would not allow himself to be drawn into taking sides over issues. He just wanted to preach the "Gospel of Christ," He believed that was the key to Christianity, not quarreling over issues. J.R. wrote further in his letter about the silliness of some well-meaning folks concerning the Sunday school question. He stated:

> Why, they will say: "See what Brother So-and-so said in the Advocate about Sunday school being societies." "No sir" I am going to quit the Sunday school." The elders will go on in their zeal and great desire to work for the Lord, and appoint or place over the Sunday school, or those disposed to "learn of Him," a superintendent, a teacher for class No. 1, a teacher for class, No. 2, and so on: all the time the leaders supervising or overlooking the whole thing. Now, then, for someone to "pop up" and shriek out "too much like a society (sic)!" Where and how does it favor a society brother? "O, well, Brother So-and-so said so in the Advocate." Brethren, this life is very short. Let us, O do let us hush up so much quarrelling and go at the work of getting ready for the judgment. Societies have not scared me as yet so badly that I feel like discouraging in the least, the Sunday school. They have always been under the care of the elders where I have been trying to labor (*G.A.*, Feb. 11, 1897, p. 91).

He went on to recommend the Gospel Advocate Sunday School literature. He said, "I think it is as good as the best." He explained the children's literature and why it was so effective: "Those little lithograph cards are not as inducement to the children, because they are so pretty; but they help to impress the thought of the lessons upon their blank minds" (*G.A.*, Feb. 11, 1897, p. 91).

There are many of us still around that remember those little lithograph cards in our classes at church. J.R. said enough to tip his hand a little to one side, the right side. J.R. had hardly ever written lengthy correspondence to the *Advocate*, unless he had serious concerns. This letter was one of those lengthy correspondences that revealed J.R.'s concerns.

His next correspondence was a very short one, but very sad. One of his dear friends from the County Line congregation in Moore County, Tennessee, the Gentry Family, was saddened by the death of Mary C. Gentry. She left behind four children, three sons and one daughter. Bradley said that all four were Christians. Mary's husband had died a few years before. J.R. was always saddened by the death of a friend, and especially close friends. He was touched by the children's loss of their mother. He wrote: "May God bless them in their sad bereavement" (*G.A.*, April 1, 1897, p. 199).

J.R.'s next report, written almost six weeks after his report on Mary Gentry's death, was published in the *Advocate*. He reported on his preaching appointment at Chestnut Ridge on June 13, which was the second Sunday of the month. He reported two confessions and baptisms at Chestnut Ridge. J.R. explained that one of the subjects had come forward during a lesson by T.C. Little some two or three weeks before. The Saturday night before J.R.'s appointments, W.M. Gammill of Utica, Miss. did the baptizing. J.R. said that Gammill "preached a fine sermon on last Saturday for us at the same place" (*G.A.*, June 24, 1897, p. 397).

J.R.'s next meeting was in Limestone County, Alabama. His next two meetings were held in that county. His first meeting was on Big Creek, on the north side of the creek at "Shanghai" Schoolhouse. The second meeting was on the south side of Big Creek at the Pleasant Point Schoolhouse. Bradley thought that the brethren in both communities should build a house of worship for themselves. He wrote:

> There are several brethren and sisters accessible to both of these schoolhouses. I think they ought to build a house of worship. The schools hinder the meetings at these schoolhouses, and the meetings hinder the schools. Brother T.L. Weatherford was with us just one day. He had a meeting of his own at another place (*G.A.* Aug. 26, 1897, p. 541).

When J.R. said the brethren should "build a house of worship" he obviously meant one house for the brethren of both communities to use, in other words, a joint effort. He did say that there were several "brethren and sisters" close to both locations. J.R. was a practical man and he knew that the church would do much better in a building of their own, under their control. J.R. had developed a great respect and love for the Limestone County brethren and loved preaching in that county. He had already preached at other locations around the Athens area.

From Limestone County, he just went northward a few miles to Giles County, Tennessee, to the Maplewood Community. Here he found some of the Shoals Bluff brethren meeting. You may recall that the Shoals Bluff congregation had stopped building on their house of worship over two families trying to get the organ installed in the new house. So, most of the new congregation of Maplewood was formed just four or five miles north of Shoals Bluff brethren. This pained J.R. very much. He recalled: "Two of the best meetings of my life were held at Shoals Bluff" (*G.A.* Aug. 26, 1897, p. 541). The Maplewood congregation was full of zeal at this time and had invited many people to their meeting. Bradley described the meeting in the following way:

> Our meeting here (Maplewood) began yesterday [August 8, which was second Sunday]. A very large crowd was present

not over half of the people could be seated. These are part of the old Shoal Bluff congregation of brethren and sisters. We all remember their split over the organ. The house of that organ faction is still standing unfinished. The ones who contended for the organ do not attend at the new church at all. I am so sorry of such a state of things...we are having an old-fashioned basket meeting-two sermons and dinner every day. We are hoping for a good meeting here (*G.A.*, Aug. 26, 1897, p. 541).

J.R. had to mail this report from Minor Hill, Tennessee, as there was no post office nearer to Maplewood. From here J.R. would join T.L. Weatherford for a meeting at Union Grove, Limestone County, Alabama.

On August 27, 1897, J.R. sent a report to the *Advocate* jointly with T.L. Weatherford concerning the meeting at Maplewood and Union Grove. The report was a rather lengthy one; probably bearing thoughts from each preacher yet written in J.R.'s peculiar style. The report stated:

Our meeting at Maplewood, which began the second Sunday [8th] in this month, closed the third Sunday, with seven additions from all sources. We had dinner on the grounds every day for eight days, and two sermons every day. This was indeed, a meeting which we both [J.R. and T.L. Weatherford] enjoyed very much. These brethren are for the "old paths" in everything. Because of an organ proposition at the Shoal Bluff church (five miles below), some two or three years ago, this house was built [Maplewood]. One Monday after the Maplewood meeting closed we began at Shoal Bluff, being invited and earnestly solicited to do so by all members except four, these being the two brethren and their wives who favored the organ proposition. The older one of these and his lady attending the meeting all the time, or nearly so. The other brother was out only one time toward the close, though his lady came several times. A new organization was affected toward the close of the meeting, though (the four mentioned) did not enter into the new body. It is hoped that they will do so at an early day. The meeting closed on Monday following with nine baptisms. We left these brethren and sisters very much encouraged. They had a new "church book" on which they placed their names, agreeing to take the New Testament as their rule of faith and worship. We surely think the trouble is settled, and that the new house will be completed at an early day. They have not been meeting for two years. Work on the new house was suspended two years ago. It has been damaged some by the weather but will be a splendid house when finished (*G.A.*, Sept. 9, 1897, p. 573).

J.R. must have been overjoyed to make this report. The brethren at Shoals Bluff would always have a special place in his heart. An unusual schedule developed for J.R. at the Shoals Bluff meeting. It closed two days into the meeting at Union Grove in Limestone County, Alabama. Since the Shoals Bluff meeting was an impromptu meeting, it would have to work within the boundaries of his scheduled meetings. Since the meeting at Union Grove was conducted during the daytime only, it may be assumed that the Shoals Bluff meeting was at night only. Union Grove was not too distant from Shoals Bluff. This would explain the overlapping of the two meetings.

The Union Grove meeting began on the fourth Sunday of August and continued through the fifth Sunday. Bradley and Weatherford reported nine confessions and baptisms at Union Grove, and one restoration. They wrote:

This also was a meeting where all the preaching was done in the daytime, with dinner on the ground. Such work, we believe, is better for both preachers and audience. On this trip, forty-two from all sources have been added to the congregations. Our work together in this field has been very pleasant to us and we hope, profitable to the cause (*G.A.*, Sept. 9, 1897, p. 573).

J.R.'s reference to "this trip" refers to the work that began at Maplewood and ended at Union Grove. Weatherford and J.R. had worked together in other meetings in Alabama and South Tennessee, but never as long, at one time, as was this tour. It would have been interesting to hear these two old soldiers of the cross reminisce about their days at Mars Hill and how their hopes and dreams did or did not materialize. J.R. announced in the foregoing report that he would begin a meeting at Noblit's Chapel, Giles County, Tennessee, on the first Sunday [5th] of September. He also wrote that from Noblit's Chapel, he would travel to Paint Rock, Alabama, and hold a meeting.

The meeting at Noblit's Chapel was determined by Robert Abernathy to have been a success. He wrote the following:

> Brother J.R. Bradley, of Booneville, Lincoln County, Tennessee has just closed a nine-day meeting with us at Noblitt's Chapel, and a grand meeting it was – not in a large number of accessions, but in seed sowing and an honest and faithful effort to present the truth as it is in Jesus. We had seven additions – two from the Baptists, two from the Methodists, and three from the world – all baptized. Brother Bradley delivered sixteen sermons and Brother Thomas Weatherford one (*G.A.*, Sept. 23, 1897, p. 605).

J.R. had made lasting friends at Noblit's Chapel, such as Abernathy. The church at that place always appreciated the efforts of Bradley and let him know it. Weatherford may have visited the one time during this meeting, which may explain why he only preached the one sermon. It was customary, at that time, to allow visiting preachers to preach some during the meetings.

Abernathy had been observing how the churches treated men like Bradley and Weatherford in a financial way. He was disappointed as is seen in his conclusion. He wrote thus:

Why is it brethren, that men like Brothers Bradley and Weatherford go at their own charges? Two-thirds of their preaching is in destitute places, with no remuneration whatever. Is this right? My brother, in your confession you said, "I believe that Jesus Christ is the Son of God." Are you acting out this faith? Where is your fruit? Jesus says to the preacher to go and he will be with him. Does this not mean through his church, through his disciples? Yes, you say. Then are you carrying out this promise for the Master, when you fail to contribute of your means for the preachers' sustenance (*G.A.*, Sept. 23, 1897, p. 605).

Abernathy pointed to a plan whereby six congregations could contribute $300.00 toward the support of one preacher in the South end of Giles County. He ended his letter by saying: "My brother, there is more in the Christian warfare than just enlisting" (*G.A.*, Sept. 23, 1897, p. 605). J.R. would never give up on destitute fields nor would his friend 'Uncle Tom' Weatherford, as he was affectionately called by the people of Limestone County, Alabama. We do not know if the plea by Abernathy did J.R. any good. By the end of the year J.R. would be changing areas of the country in which to labor.

Another letter was written to the *Advocate* on behalf of Bradley. We do not know who wrote the letter. Their name was not published, but we do believe that the author of the letter was from Alabama. The letter began as follows:

Brother J.R. Bradley has been doing some good work in Alabama. The churches where he has labored should seriously ask themselves the question: Have we done our duty in supporting him in the work? It is as much the duty of the church to support the faithful preacher in his work as it is for the preacher to go and preach the gospel of Christ. The churches need this fruit to abound to their account. The preacher who is constantly with us, who 'has borne the burden and heat of the day." should not be forced to go away empty-handed, while the "big evangelist" comes along and for one week's work reaps the harvest of shekels. This is not treating home talent fairly and is a very effective way of driving them from the field (*G.A.* Nov. 25, 1897, p. 744).

We do not know if J.R. had been talking among friends about his consideration to move to another region of work, but it is highly possible. Friends do confide in other friends when there are trials before them. We do know that support to preach had been a problem for J.R. for several years. Friends such as Abernathy of Noblit's Chapel and even Weatherford of Limestone County, Alabama would be concerned if J.R. was to move away. Maybe J.R. had mentioned that he was considering a move to Jackson County, Alabama. This would explain the letter from Abernathy in September and, now the present letter under consideration. The letter may have been written by Weatherford to get help for his old friend, J.R. Bradley.

The writer of this letter continues to point to the failing of the churches to support the evangelists in the field of labor. He wrote: "It will be fearful for them (churches who fail to support preachers) in the Day of Judgment" (*G.A.* Nov. 25, 1897, p. 744). That was a serious charge against some laded congregations toward their duty of aiding the evangelists who labored for and with them. He continued: "The Christ is constantly placing opportunities at our doors. Will we improve them as they come and go? By so doing we may be entertaining angels unawares" (*G.A.* Nov. 25, 1897, p. 744). Despite the pleas to secure help for J.R. he was forced to move to Jackson County, Alabama, to support Mary and himself.

Midway into December the *Gospel Advocate* published the following letter from J.R.:

After this week please send my paper to Gurley Alabama. Please announce in the Advocate that our address is changed from Booneville, Tenn., to that place. Wife and I both dislike having to leave Tennessee. We are Tennesseans by birth. Please say to our brethren, sisters and friends in our native old state: "God be with you till we meet again," Four congregations in Alabama —Kennamer Cove, Whitaker's Chapel, Paint Rock, and Garth-have invited us to their field of labor. There is no society or clique of men moving us in this work, but just simply an agreement, these earnest workers and myself agreeing together to cultivate that field. Please let us have the prayers of our old Tennessee brethren and sisters. Since we have lived at Booneville we have worked, more or less, with the following congregations: County Line, New Hermon, Stoney Point, Chestnut Ridge, McBurg, Molino, and Richmond. A part of the time I have had such mission points as Watson's Chapel, Sylvan Mills, Green Hill, Light's Schoolhouse, and Coffee's Creek. I am sorry that my work in this field has not resulted in more good than it has, but it seems that we all did what we could under the circumstances; anyway, it is a thing of the past, and we must meet the record of it in the judgment day. For five long years we have been forming acquaintances here at Booneville. We are much pained at the thought of separating from them. They have treated us kindly. Booneville is a pleasant little town in which to live. We are not going away from choice but feeling a sense of our duty to God and ourselves. We are having to sacrifice little things that cost us money in order to make the change. The move is about fifty-five miles. May God bless us all.

J.R. Bradley (*G.A.* Dec. 16, 1897, p. 797).

You can almost see tears pouring down the face of a broken-hearted man as he pens this final letter from Booneville. No doubt that finances played a large part in this move, but J.R. always liked a challenge. This new field would be a challenge. He would have to acquaint himself with people of a different temperament than he was accustomed to seeing back in Tennessee.

This year, without a doubt, would go down as one of the saddest years for J.R. At least the ending of 1897 would be so. He had to completely uproot himself and his beloved Mary and move among strangers, for the most part. He was leaving behind old friends that he may never see upon this earth again. Works with which he had labored would constantly be in the back of his mind, always wondering about their conditions. He would now have to make new acquaintances to integrate into the life of his new community.

J.R., as was typical of him, was looking ahead to all of the opportunities that he would have in preaching the Gospel. After all, he did say he was making the move to Alabama because he felt it was his duty to God.

We know hardly anything about J.R.'s work in 1898. His name only graces the pages of the *Gospel Advocate* two times. J.R. never sent a single report to the *Advocate*. We do not know the reason for this lack of reporting. Was he depressed from moving to Paint Rock Valley, from Tennessee? Was Mary much worse from depression or sickness, or both? Did he not think his success was worth reporting? There are so many questions we could ask about this unusual behavior on J.R.'s part, but we do not know the answers. We do know that he continued to work some in the field. We know that J.R., if well enough, would always keep his appointments.

There were two appointments of J.R.'s that were recorded in 1898. One was at Maysville, Madison County, Alabama and was reported by J. L. Hucks, the preacher at that place. His report states:

Our meeting of two-weeks' duration is ever. Brothers J.R. Bradley and J. S. Kelly assisted the writer in the preaching. The immediate result was twenty-nine additions to the one body—

twenty-five by baptism, three restored, and one from the Baptists. Taking all things into consideration. this was the best meeting ever held in this community. Brothers Bradley and Kelly are sound gospel preachers and know how to preach it plainly and simply. (*G.A.*, Sept. 8,1898, p. 576).

The second report was sent to the *Advocate* by R. N. Moody of Albertville, Alabama. It reads as follows: "Brother J.R. Bradley begins a meeting at Blessing's Schoolhouse, in Marshall County the forth Lord's Day in this month" (*G.A.* Sept. 8, 1898, p. 579). That was the sum of the report. We do not know of the success of the meeting nor do we know if J.R. held the meeting. If he was well enough, we know that he would have kept this appointment at Blessing's Schoolhouse.

Blessing's Schoolhouse is no longer there, but it is recorded as having been one of the historical sites in Marshall Count, Alabama. Blessing, the community of today (2019) is located about three miles southwest of Kilpatrick, in Marshall County. There is a congregation of the Lord's church still meeting there. It is possible that J.R. had a hand in organizing a church there, along with R.N. Moody, who was the established minister in Marshall County.

For all the facts and speculations from the above paragraphs, we can conclude that 1898 was not even close to being one of J.R.'s best years in the field. He must have been doing good whenever able, because John E. Dunn wrote in the following year about Paint Rock Valley: "This has been a neglected field, but now Brother J.R. Bradley is doing a good work here" (*G.A.* Sept. 21, 1899, p. 605). Thus, we know that J.R. was doing what he could do, and with some degree of success.

One such example of him trying to do good wherever he might be is drawn from an article that he wrote and had published in the *Firm Foundation*, a brotherhood paper published in Austin, Texas and edited, at that time, by Austin McGary. The article appeared under the heading: "A Review Reviewed." Even though the article was published in June of 1899, it related to a discussion that had occurred sometime in the latter months of 1898. J.R. describes the setting for the discussion as follows:

> In *The Sabbath Advocate* of January 17, of this year [1899], (a paper edited at Stanberry, Mo., in the interest of the ancient Sabbath day) appears "a review" over the signature of E.W. Williams of Rains, Ala., [now Rainsville in 2019]. This "review" proposes to be an answer to some remarks by the writer of this, upon the ancient Sabbath day. Said conversation took place at the house of Brother John A. Miller of Lot, Ala. Mr. Williams and myself were the principal ones in the conversation. He was, it seemed then, always pitching in to somebody with his Sabbath talk (*F.F.*, June 6, 1899, p. 355).

From that place in the article, J.R. began to present the body of his article as a written debate. Williams began his review as follows:

> "J.R. Bradley affirms that the covenant of Heb. 8:13, which is called old, and is ready to vanish away, is the covenant that contains the Sabbath day." He then says these words verbatim; "There was no Covenant made by the writer of Heb. 8:13 nor of him" (*F.F.*, June 6, 1899, p. 355).

J.R. responds:

> E.W. Williams, what do you mean by that sentence? Did I contend that "the writer of Hebrews" ever made a covenant? Unless you are a bigger gump than I then thought you were, you know I never intimated such a thing. Then tell us please, what you mean by "nor of him" in the sentence. What noun is the antecedent of the pronoun "him" in the sentence? I do wonder if there is a man in the state of Alabama that can parse that sentence. I'll just "fess up" that I cannot.

Williams continues:

> "J.R. Bradley what stirred you up against the ten command-
> ments? Was it the verse I asked you to read in 1John 5:3?"

J.R. answers:

> No, I was not stirred up against anything in that conversation
> by what you said. I do believe your looks and crooks upon that
> occasion ought to have stirred up something, but you failed
> wholly to do anything in that way. I believe and preach every-
> thing in 1John 5:3: "For this is the love of God that we keep
> his commandments, and his commandments are not griev-
> ous." Where to be found on earth, is the body of people that
> dwell more upon keeping the commandments than the body
> with which I stand identified? Let Mr. Williams show that the
> command to keep the Sabbath is in "the ministration of the
> spirit," "the new and living way," "the new covenant," "the
> New Testament," or "will" and we will "whoop up" the Sab-
> bath with all our power. But we know that even the great and
> learned Dr. E.W. Williams cannot find the command to keep
> the Sabbath day in the will of Christ. But we do find plenty of
> commandments in the New Testament, and therefore we be-
> lieve and teach that the people should keep the
> commandments of God.

Mr. Williams spoke of a "no law theory."

J.R. responded by saying:

> It was all gammon and deserves no notice by me. But here are
> some stunners for Mr. Williams: "Wherefore then serveth the
> law? It was added because of transgressions, till the seed
> should come." Gal. 3:19. To what was the law added? Why, to
> the law of circumcision, an account of which is given in
> Gen.17. If it was added to the Abrahamic covenant, it surely

became a part of that to which it was added, and then when the thing added to, was done away; surely the thing added was done away also. Now Mr. Williams, you have tied yourself into a knot.

Williams said:

If the ten-commandment law was done away, or vanished away, there would be no law to condemn anyone, "for by the law is the knowledge of sin." Rom. 3:20.

Williams further claimed that the law of the 20th verse was not done away.

J.R. responded:

...Paul says, (right there in that 20th verse) "Therefore by the deeds of the law there shall no flesh be justified, for by the law is the knowledge of sin." By what law is the knowledge of sin? It surely is the same law by which no flesh can be justified. We are then to keep that law by which no flesh can be justified. Mr. Williams this is your logic.

In the very next verse (21) your logic is clearly condemned. Paul says: "But now the righteousness of God without the law is manifested." Let Dr. Williams rise and explain how the righteousness of God is manifested without the very law which he contends is still binding. Mr. Williams had you noticed in Gal 3:19 that the apostle says, that "the law was added till the seed should come?" What seed is this? Remember that Paul asked the question, "Wherefore then serveth the law?" and then in the 23rd and 25th verses: "Wherefore the law was a schoolmaster to bring us to Christ, that we might be justified by faith. But that after faith had come (faith here means the law of Christ) we are no longer under a schoolmaster." The only conclusion from these passages is, that Christ is that seed that should come, and that the law of this whole chapter, schooled and prepared them for Christ, and that the school-master—the law—was no longer binding since Christ had come.

E.W. Williams says of this law:

If the ten-commandment law was done away, or vanished away, there would be no law to condemn anyone, "for by the law is the knowledge of sin." Rom. 3:20.

J.R. again responds to that thought:

We have these same thoughts in Col. 2:14-15-16-17: "Blotting out the hand-writing of ordinances that was contrary to us, and took it out of the way, nailing it to the cross." Mr. Williams are you prepared to say that this "hand-writing of ordinances" does not contain the Sabbath day? Be careful old fellow! Take the next verse (15th) "And having spoiled principalities and powers he made a show of them openly, triumphing over them in it."

Now, for the 16th verse, which knocks Mr. Williams "off the Christmas tree:" "Let no man therefore judge you in meat, or drink, or in respect to a holy day, or of the new moon, or of the Sabbath" (days). Remembering that "days" here is a sup-plied word and not in the original at all. So, you see Dr. Williams that the "hand-writing of ordinances," which Paul says was "blotted out," does contain the Sabbath.

The 17th says the "meat," the "drink," the "holy day," the "new moon," and the "Sabbath" "are a shadow of things to come, but the body is of Christ." Do we need the shadow, Mr. Williams, after the substance has come? Why hold on to the shadow—Sabbath—after Christ, the substance has come?

Hold on Doctor, I am not done piling it on you yet. Just open your mouth and take your medicine like a man. 2Cor. 3:6-7-8-9-10-11, "Who has also made us able ministers of the New Testament not of the letter but of the spirit, for the letter killeth, but the spirit giveth life." Dr. Williams, what is this called the "letter" here? Do you say this "letter" does not contain the Sabbath? Hush! be still, I hear wild geese. No, Doctor Williams, it was you I heard.

Now for the 7th verse: "But if the ministration of death, written and engraven in in stones was glorious, so that the children of Israel could not steadfastly behold the face of Moses, for the glory of his countenance, which glory was to be done away." Now then, what is the ministration of death, Doctor? It was written or engraven on stones. Mr. Williams, was anything, by the finger of God, ever written on stones, in the shape of a law, but the Ten Commandments? Now sir, if you cannot show a law in the Bible, other than the Ten Commandments, written in stones, you are badly left on the commandment law. I say, without fear from Dr. on earth, that God has never written, or engraven any law in stones, but the Ten Commandments.

Your uncle Joe Smith, Dr. claimed a law written on gold, but God had nothing to do with that matter you know.

Paul says that written in stones "is the ministration of death." (7th verse) Do you say it is the ministration of life? Take the 8th: "How shall not the ministration of the spirit be rather glorious?" What is the ministration of the spirit? Why it is the gospel, or law of Christ, which is rather or more glorious than the law written on stones, --the Ten Commandments. 9th verse: "For if the ministration of condemnation be glory, much more doth the ministration of righteousness exceeds in glory." Do you claim the ministration of condemnation for your law, Dr.? I don't want it, and I dislike knowing of any of my old friends, like you, taking it as their rule of action. Dr. be persuaded to take in its stead the ministration of righteousness. 10th verse: "For even that which was made glorious had no glory in this respect by reason of the glory that excelleth." Yes, the glory of the "law of liberty" by far excels in point of glory, that which was written in stones—the Ten Commandments—the fourth of which is "Remember the Sabbath day to keep it holy."

169

The 11th and the last verse that I expect to notice now: "For if that which is done away was glorious, much more that which remaineth is glorious." Now, friend Williams, I shall soon tell you goodbye, but hold a little while. What does the apostle mean in this verse by "that which is done away?" Please instruct us just a little bit before you go. Does he mean anything but that which was written on stones? If you cannot show some law, besides the Ten Commandments that "was written on stones;" "Is done away," is the name of your theory, given by Paul 2 Cor. 3:11.

Dr. E.W. Williams, dear old soldier friend, goodbye till we meet again (*F.F.*, June 6, 1899, pp. 356-357).

With the closing of this article, J.R. ended the longest article he ever had published. It is interesting that the article was published in the *Firm Foundation* and not the *Gospel Advocate*.

J.R.'s first report of 1899 was a short one and more about John E. Dunn's labors in that field than about his own. He writes:

Brother J.E. Dunn of Murfreesboro, Tenn., is in this field. He has just closed His third week in meetings. We have baptized eleven persons, and two have united from the denominations – thirteen in all. Brother Dunn will remain here in my field till about October 15. I think he is the man for us in these untaught churches and uninterested places (*G.A.*, Oct. 4, 1899, p. 634).

One can see that J.R. was not his usual self, when writing this report. He usually would write "eleven by confession and baptism," instead of "baptized eleven," He also usually wrote "received thus and thus from the Baptists or Methodists" instead of "two have united from denominations." In other words, his usual "flowery" words were not in this report. This may reflect his emotional status at this time. Maybe that depression was taking its toll upon Bradley at this time. A mystery soon develops over when J.R.'s moved back to Tennessee.

9

RETURNING TO TENNESSEE?

Even though J.R. seemed to have been battling illness or depression he had improved enough, by October, to hold a meeting at Smithland, Tennessee. Smithland was in Lincoln County, Tennessee, about five miles east of Fayetteville. The meeting began on the fourth Sunday of the month. A report was sent in by some church members at Smithland. It read as follows:

> Beginning on the fourth Lord's day in last October, Brother J.R. Bradley, of Gurley, Ala., held a meeting for us here, which was continued for eight days and nights and resulted in two persons being baptized. He also gave us practice in music for a week beginning on Monday night after the third Sunday in November (*G.A.*, Jan. 25, 1900, p. 61).

The letter was signed by seven members of the Church at Smithland. This report hints of J.R. having already moved back to Tennessee, since he went back so soon after he had held the meeting at Smithland to teach the singing school. Gurley, Alabama, was a long way from Smithland and Bradley could not afford to travel much. Remember he was a very poor man in worldly goods and would likely not have money to do this kind of travel. In December it was announced that: "Brother J.R. Bradley, of Gurley,

Ala., is a duly authorized agent of the Gospel Advocate Publishing Company, and we will appreciate any favors shown him as such" (*G.A.*, December 14, 1899, p. 606). This shows that J.R. wanted to get more involved with the *Advocate* in his field of labor. It also indicates that he still lived at Gurley. This just adds to the mystery surrounding where J.R. lived at that time.

To further confuse the question concerning his moving back to Tennessee, a report was sent concerning a meeting at Unionville, near Shelbyville, Tennessee. The report was as follows:

> Brother J.R. Bradley, of Gurley, Ala., held us an eight-day meeting which began on the first Lord's day of this month [August 1900] and closed on the second Lord's day night, resulting in six confessions and baptisms. We had good attendance at night and everybody seemed to enjoy Brother Bradley's preaching. He delivered many instructive lessons, and he shuns not to declare the whole truth written in God's revealed word. May he live long upon this earth to declare God's holy and righteous will, is my prayer. To God be all the praise (*G.A.*, August 23, 1900, p. 541).

By this reference to Bradley as being from Gurley, Alabama, makes it appear to the reader that he still lived in Alabama. It could have been that he had just recently moved back to his old home area. Nothing is ever said concerning his change of location back to Tennessee, either in the *Advocate* or any other existing sources.

We know that J.R. had moved back to Lincoln County by May of 1900, because a deed is recorded in Fayetteville which shows that J.R. purchased land near Fayetteville, Tennessee, dated May 4, 1900 (Lincoln County, Tennessee, 1900, Deed Book, p. 284). J.R. promised twelve hundred and fifty dollars for the property. He paid a down payment of three hundred and fifty dollars and promised three payments of three hundred dollars each year, until paid in full. The above information just increases the mystery surrounding J.R.'s northeast Alabama experience.

The second time that we hear from J.R, through the *Advocate,* was in a letter sent by W.H. Dixon. He reported on a meeting at Molino, southwest of Fayetteville, Tennessee. Dixon and Bradley worked in the meeting together. He wrote: "Brother J.R. Bradley and I are having a good meeting here (Molino, Tenn.). We have given out meetings until August 26, 1900" (*G.A.*, Aug.30, 1900, p. 560). Somehow, he had returned to Tennessee from Jackson County, Alabama in his work. Most of his meetings were now in Tennessee, and he had moved back to Lincoln County, near Fayetteville, Tennessee. We have no knowledge as to when or why J.R. had returned to Tennessee. We do know that J.R. and Mary both were sick more often, for the last few years. By the end of the year he was teaching a Sunday school class at the church in Fayetteville.

1901 began with some hope that J.R.'s health was improved enough to do a full schedule of work. In February he had a question to arise from a Sunday school class concerning the time of the Lord's Supper and "foot washing," He wrote to David Lipscomb at the *Gospel Advocate* about these issues. His letter stated:

Brother Lipscomb: I promised two of our sisters in Christ that I write you a few words regarding the Sunday school lesson for February 10, 1901, "Jesus Washes the Disciples' Feet." These ladies, as well as myself seem not to be able to harmonize a part of the "Explanatory Notes," in the *Advanced Quarterly*, with the scriptures. The language is this: "This could not have been the supper of our last lesson in Simon's house; that was six days before the Passover; at Bethany." The reference given as proof of this is John 12:1. We fail to find the proof either in John 12:1 or anywhere else in the Bible that the supper of the previous lesson, in Simon's house, was six days before the Passover. John 12:1,2 seems to teach that the Savior "came to Bethany" six days before the feast and "there they made him a supper." But does not Mark14:1-3 teach us that this same supper was served only two days before the feast? Surely the supper or "sitting at meat," in Simon's house is the same supper referred to in John 12:2, because the woman – Mary – is spoken of in both places as coming and anointing the Savior. Therefore, we conclude that our Savior only came to Bethany six days before the Passover and had been there four days before the supper was made for him (*G.A.*, March 7, 1901, p. 158).

Lipscomb explained that he had previously held the exact same view that Bradley had described, but later concluded differently. He gives a lengthy explanation as to why he no longer held that view. Apparently, J.R. was satisfied with Lipscomb's explanation because he never responds in the *Advocate*.

J.R. was satisfied, but other brethren were not. A brother in Wilmington, Kansas, by the name of Jack Turner, wrote to Lipscomb concerning the answer that he gave to J.R. He wrote: "I do not think you answered the main argument in John13:29" (*G.A.*, April 25, 1901, p. 265). He could not see that Jesus washed the disciples' feet at the same feast. Lipscomb wrote in response to Turner:

> "I have no hope of settling the times of the suppers. This has been a question of doubt and discussion for at least fifteen hundred years and I presume it will be till we lay aside the fleshly hindrances; yet some things are well agreed upon" (*G.A.*, April 25, 1901, p. 265).

Lipscomb, like so many other great men in leadership roles, hated to be wrong or to be challenged on one of his views. He continues to try to prove his point, even after admitting that he had "no hope of settling" the matter.

J.R. wrote a lengthy article for the *Gospel Advocate* under the heading of "God No Respecter of Persons." He developed the lesson with the following four points:

1. God has proven he is "no respecter of persons" (Gen. 12:3; 18:18; 22:18).

2. God has proven he is "no respecter of persons" in the fulfillment of that promise in the gift of his Son (Luke 2:10, 31; John 3:16-17).

3. God has proven in the death of his Son, our Savior, that he is "no respecter of persons" (2 Cor. 5:14-15; 1 Tim. 2:5-6; 1 John2:2).

4. God has proven in the proclamation of the gospel that he is "no respecter of persons" (Mark 16:15; Matt. 28:19; Luke 24:47).'

He concluded by reviewing the above four points. He summed everything up in the following statement:

> My brethren in Christ, remember that neither the promise of a Savior to all, his gift to all, his death for all, nor the gospel being preached to all is in and of itself sufficient to commend us to God: but on our part we must fear him and work righteousness, or do righteous works, in order to be "accepted with him." We must "labor to enter into that rest." May God help us so to do (*G.A.,* April 25, 1901, p. 271).

This was constructed like a sermon. It may have been one that J.R. had preached or taught in some congregation.

His summer was filled with some farming to survive. He and Mary always had a garden large enough to carry them through the year. He would always have a corn patch to grow food for their animals and chickens. He had been hindered from doing these things at times in the past, due to illness. This year was different. He was up to the task, and since he was a farm boy, he farmed as his health permitted. His late summer preaching appointments rapidly approached. He was booked for the rest of the meeting season. He was definitely back home in Tennessee.

10

Money Problems

His first appointment was at Molino, a congregation that he had helped to organize a few years past. A Sister Minerva A Hays reported the meeting to the *Advocate*. The report read:

> Our protracted meeting at this place began on the third Lord's day (sic) in August and closed at the water on Wednesday morning after the fourth Lord's day. Brother J.R. Bradley, of Fayetteville, and Brother Charley L Talley, of Howell, did the preaching, and it was of a very high order. Both of these brethren have been preaching for us occasionally for several years, and they shun not to declare (sic) all of the council of God. As a result of our meeting, fourteen precious souls were added to the church of Christ – thirteen by confession and baptism, one restored, two from the Presbyterians, and one from the Methodists. The church was greatly encouraged. Pray for us that we may keep up the interest at this place (*G.A.*, Sept. 19, 1901, p. 604).

A month later, Charles L. Talley put a footnote to the report of the meeting at Molino. He wrote: "On August 17, I was with the body of worshippers at Molino, being assisted by Brother J.R. Bradley, where we worked until August 28. Fourteen persons

were added. Thirteen by primary obedience and one restored"
(*G.A.*, Oct. 24, 1901, p. 685). Talley was one of those preachers
from the Fayetteville – Lynchburg area that had been encouraged
by J.D. Floyd, T.C. Little and J.R. Bradley to preach. He became a
very popular preacher throughout the southern states.

It is noticeably clear that J.R. did not write either of these reports on the Molino meeting. As a matter of fact, he never
reported on one single meeting for the entire year of 1901. Had
he lost interest in reporting on his work? Did he not feel that his
work was worth reporting anymore? We do not know the answers to these questions; but we do know that he was involved in
meeting work for the latter part of the year. It could have been,
also, that J.R. did not feel well enough to write reports on his
work. He also failed to report the death of a dear friend of his
from the Campbell's Station, who died on October 22, 1901 (*G.A.*,
Jan. 23, 1902, p. 58). He would finally send that obituary in January of 1902. This was not characteristic of J.R. to delay an
obituary for so long. He had been three months late in reporting
his friend's death. Something was amiss in his activities currently.
We also know that that age-old struggle to have money for sur-
vival was working very hard on J.R. This will come to light in the
next year as we discuss the year of 1902. J.R., at some point in
time after T.B. Larimore had held a meeting in Fayetteville, had
bought a farm (*G.A.*, Jan. 23, 1902, p. 58). His constant illnesses
had hindered him from making regular payments on it. This increased the need for more money. With pressure from not having
enough money, he became ill very often. His worries were mostly
for Mary, and not himself. He worried about what would happen
to Mary if he were dead or incapacitated. The next year would
begin with new challenges for Bradley. At least 1901 saw him
move back from Alabama, to his old arena of labor, near Fayetteville, Tennessee. Apparently, the Alabama move had turned out
very badly for J.R. and Mary. He never mentions anything about
his move back to Tennessee. He was just glad to own a small farm

near Fayetteville again, even with the extra debt he incurred. He did not mind the challenge.

Our first word for the New Year from J.R. was the delayed obituary (mentioned in the previous year) in the *Gospel Advocate* about one of his friends at Campbell Station, Maury County, Tennessee. William Hobbs, who had served as an elder at that place, had died on October 22, 1901. Hobbs had served as the song leader at Campbell Station for many years. J.R. wrote that Hobbs "delighted especially in the songs" (*G.A.* Jan. 23, 1902, p. 58). Hobbs' love for church music would have made him J.R.'s friend immediately. Remember Bradley loved music and was even a music teacher.

To add to J.R.'s burden of losing a good friend, he was still very much plagued financially. The *Advocate* published the following statement under the heading of "Miscellany:"

> Elsewhere in this issue we publish a letter from Brother J.R. Bradley to Brother Larimore. Brother Bradley thinks he can meet the first note if he can raise two hundred dollars. Brother Bradley is well and favorably known and it is almost certain that some will be glad to help him in his present need (*G.A.*, Jan. 30, 1902, p. 69).

Remember that J.R. was strongly rebuked the last time he, or even friends, appealed to the *Advocate* on behalf of his financial needs.

It seemed that Bradley never intended to make an appeal in the *Advocate*, ever again. Remember the last appeal was made by a sister Molly De Ford of the Gum Springs congregation, Lincoln County, Tennessee, on behalf of J.R.'s needs (*G.A.*, Nov. 20, 1889, p. 747). J.C. McQuiddy rebuked the Gum Spring congregation for making such an appeal and rebuked J.R. for not doing better teaching to the churches on the subject of giving. That was enough for J.R. No more would he even slightly hint that he had financial needs. This printed request was totally at Larimore's request. McQuiddy could not re-act the same toward Larimore as he did toward Bradley and Gum Spring. Larimore made it clear that Bradley never intended for the letter to make it to the *Advocate*. Larimore wrote:

> Brother McQuiddy: The postman has just handed me the letter from Brother Bradley herewith, enclosed. With this note I send five dollars for Brother Bradley. I write him, telling him this: I also tell him that I request you not to consider his letter confidential, but to use it as you deem best for him, all of which you will please do. Moreover, I suggest to him to go humbly and hopefully to brethren and friends privately, tell them his troubles and beg them for help (*G.A.*, Jan 30, 1902, p. 80).

McQuiddy complied without one negative word. J.R.'s letter to Larimore is given in full as follows:

> Brother Larimore: Will you please allow me to loosen to you my greatest trouble just now? My trouble is not of a spiritual nature - no, not that; I assure you that I love the Lord just as dearly as I ever did. I love his "spiritual body," I know, and am just as anxious as at anytime in the history of my life to work for its interests.
>
> Brother Larimore, you know something of my past life; you know here my work for the Master has been – among the poorest; you know that I was well along in years when I entered school. I am not fifty-five years old. I can, and do, now think of nice country churches that have been built up under my efforts – Greenwood, Giles County, Tenn.; Molino, Lincoln County, Tenn. I was preaching at New Hermon and Richmond, both in Bedford County, Tenn., when each built a new house of worship. Well, I will not itemize any further. I think of the schoolhouses, brush arbors, private houses, etc., where I have held meetings and had many additions, to which (or whom) others have been added from time to time, and

from these interests, new houses have been built, and now some brethren who are worshiping there have plenty of money and I have to suffer.

Brother Larimore, please bear with me a little longer. I love you dearly, though I have probably never been able (sic) to prove it to you as I ought, and which I think I would have done under more favorable circumstances. You are my "father in the gospel." It is perfectly natural (is it not?) for children in the times of distresses to go to their father and mother, those whom they love. Well, you remember that I bought the little farm, just three and one-half miles from town, while you were here in our meeting. I paid a hundred- and fifty-dollars cash [the deed shows that J.R. paid three hundred and fifty dollars] (all the money that I had) and gave three notes for three hundred dollars each, making twelve hundred and fifty dollars in all. Now the first note is due (interest and all being three hundred and eighteen dollars), and I am fearful, indeed I can see no other chance except to sell the place.

Dear brother, knowing you have such a wide field, and that your influence means so much over our brethren, will you please allow me to ask you, not withstanding you have so many calls of charity and so much to think of and so many friends to remember, to think a little while for me? How many brethren of fine means – stocks in banks, money they will never be able to use – I can think of! O! If I were just in touch with them! Dear Brother Larimore, can you think of a way in Keeping with your feelings and the word of the Lord to reach their hearts and purses for me? I can raise only one hundred and twenty-five dollars and live. My crop last year was millet seed. It was a bad year for such crop. I made only one hundred and twenty-six bushels for my part. I have been waiting for a good price. I think that I will get one dollar per bushel for the seed. My little place is fine and rich: it suits me exactly, if I could only pay for it.

I have agreed to preach monthly this year at Cornersville and Molino. I may have some other appointments; I do not know as yet.

Dear brother, I do not want to bother you; the Lord knows that; but as I have more confidence in you than in any other living man, I thought of coming to you with this trouble.

Give Sister Larimore and all the children our best regards. My wife joins me in love to you all.

Please let this be confidential.

J.R. Bradley, Fayetteville, Tenn.

(*G.A.*, Jan. 30, 1902, p. 80).

From the way Larimore decided to have McQuiddy print the letter, even though Bradley had requested it to remain confidential, just accents the gravity of J.R.'s situation. It would bring a positive reaction from the brethren, just as Larimore thought it would. Maybe that would help him save his farm. Keep in mind that J.R. had to grow much of what he and Mary ate and needed tenable land, badly, for such effort. Thus, this explains why he was so worried over losing the farm.

His concerns over the possibility of losing his farm did not keep Bradley from being concerned about spiritual matters. In February he wrote to David Lipscomb and asked two questions about scripture interpretation. They were about Matthew 28: 19-20 and John 15: 1-17. His first question was about the sense in which the command: "Teaching them to observe all things what so ever I have commanded you (Matthew 28:20)?" On this question J.R. seemed to have the same understanding as Lipscomb did. On his second question about the "vine and the branches" (John 15), J.R. had a little different understanding than the explanation given by Lipscomb. David Lipscomb explained that the branches in this passage as being the apostles and those later members (including us) became smaller branches, yet attached to the vine from which comes life, through the apostle. J.R., in his questions, was a little surprised at hearing a preacher say the exact thing, in a sermon, as Lipscomb had written. J.R.'s comment was: "I recently heard a good man, a preacher, say in a sermon that these "branches" were apostles. He said he reached that conclusion from verse 16. Is he right (*G.A.*, Feb. 13, 1902, p. 99)?" In most cases J.R. seemed to reach the same conclusions, in his own studies, as did Lipscomb. It was a rare occasion for them to differ. He was always ready to hear others with their conclusions about scripture, but never believed them until he could find the answers in God's word. He loved the church and the brethren.

In March he reported the death of one of those brethren, whom he loved. It is even highly possible that Bradley baptized this brother, since he was a member of the Stoney Point congregation, which J.R. had started. The brother was John F. Davis. J.R. wrote of Davis as follows:

> Brother Davis was an elder in Stoney Point congregation; and as a Christian, and leader, and a man his life was correct. For several years he had been Keeper of a toll gate near Fayette-ville, and the duties of this position required so much of his time that he was unable to be with the brethren in their meetings and services as he desired. He was a man of firmness and decision and was always ready to give a reason for his hope in Christ (*G.A.*, March 6, 1902, p. 157).

It seems that J.R. never believed in giving flowery obituaries, just straight to the point accounts of the person's life. That was the scotch-Irish blood in him.

On March 13, Lipscomb reported:

> Brother J.R. Bradley, of Fayetteville, Tenn., joins our army of workers this week; he cheers us with a large club [this was what the *Advocate* called a large subscribers list to the *Advocate*], which is very greatly appreciated. He writes; "I think that I shall soon send about twelve more manes" (*G.A.*, March 13, 1902, p. 165).

You may recall that J.R. had agreed to get subscribers for the *Gospel Advocate* while he was living at Gurley, Alabama. He loved the editors at the *Advocate*, and especially Lipscomb, and what the paper represented.

In August J.R. wrote to Brother E.A. Elam of the *Advocate,* commending him for challenging R.H. Boll's views. Boll believed that if a man listened to any other man for advice, rather than asking God directly, he was like the missionary society people. Elam had written exposing such view. J.R. wrote of his encounter with such person:

> Please allow me to express my appreciation of your recent articles in the *Gospel Advocate* on "Trusting God for a Support," I certainly think they are timely and scriptural. A young brother sneeringly said to me at 'Yes, you trust through the brethren; I always place a man with the societies when he claims that.' This was as much as to say he did not trust God through anyone, while even he was fed and sheltered in a good brother's house. Certainly, God must send these blessings to preachers through individuals. I certainly think your 'faith-and-work' argument has completely overturned Brother Boll's theory. Some of these brethren talk as though none of us, except themselves, trust the Lord. My dear brother, continue as you have begun (*G.A.*, August 21, 1902, p. 533)."

Bradley had learned to love and respect E.A. Elam while a student at Mars Hill College and he would cherish this friendship for the remainder of his life.

During the same time Bradley wrote to Elam, he was engaged in a series of Gospel meetings near Fayetteville. On the third Sunday of August, he and Charles L. Talley began a ten-day meeting at Molino. They added twenty-nine "by confession and baptism: three from the Baptist; two from the Methodists; four restored to fellowship, and one was 'received by letter'." M.A. Hayes, who sent this report to the *Advocate* wrote: "There was much interest manifested from the first, and the large audiences attested the fact that these brethren were well adapted to this place and people" (*G.A.* Sept. 25, 1902, p. 620). Hayes continued:

> Brother Bradley recently held an arbor meeting at Rowell, which resulted in four confessions and baptisms. A movement was started in this meeting to build a new house of worship at Rowell. The brethren there have about enough money to build and will soon begin the work (*G.A.* Sept. 25, 1902, p. 620).

This was the kind of thing J.R. had complained about to Larimore in his letter, that brethren could find money to build church buildings, but never could find a way to help him when he was in need. You will also note that this new building was planned just a few months after Bradley's needs were brought before the brethren. Nothing was even hinted that the brethren contributed in any way to J.R.'s needs. The building at Rowell was begun soon after this letter was written by Brother Hayes.

Another letter was penned by a young sister, Effie Bryan, of Argyle, Lincoln Co., Tennessee, just days after Hayes wrote his. It reported of a meeting conducted by J.R. at that place. She wrote the following:

> Brother J.R. Bradley, of Fayetteville, began a meeting at the Bonner Schoolhouse, near this place on the first Lord's Day in this month [September] and closed on last Monday night, with five additions to the army of the faithful. This is a strong Methodist community. Large crowds attended the services and seemed to be most interested. We have known Brother Bradley for years and have heard him preach many sermons, and we think he did as fine preaching here as he ever did anywhere. He endeared himself to the people. I am a young Christian girl, having been baptized by Brother Bradley this year, and feel that I need the prayers and encouragement of all God's people (*G.A.*, Sept. 25, 1902, p. 620).

Oh! That our young people all had this dedication.

We learn from an article that appeared in *Gospel Advocate* of October 22, 1903, that J.R. had held a meeting at Iron City, Tennessee, sometime in September of 1902. The exact date of the meeting was not given; but since the congregation at Iron City held their fall meetings in September, and that J.R.'s prior meetings took up the first two weeks of September, he could have preached no earlier than September 21. The congregation had moved northward from the Wade farm to the town of Iron City. This was because the new railroad from Nashville to Florence, Alabama, now ran between the old Wade Cemetery and the church building. The passing trains, which ran frequently, passed and disturbed their meetings in the old building at Antioch. The meeting of 1902 was just one of many that J.R. had preached for his home congregation and would still hold more in the future.

For years Antioch had met just about a hundred yards north of the Wade Cemetery. It was here that many of J.R.'s friends were buried, including his dear friend John D. Wade. Upon his return to his old home congregation he had visited the old cemetery and found it neglected and overgrown. That was more than J.R. could bear. He was a very sentimental person and thought it showed disrespect to the dead. He encouraged the church in that place to help him clean it and get rid of the overgrowth. A friend of J.R.'s, and a member at Iron City, G.W. Sweaney wrote:

> A little more than a year ago, while Brother J.R. Bradley of Fayetteville, Tenn., was preaching for us, he asked those who were interested to meet on a certain day at the old Wade Cemetery, near this place, for the purpose of cutting away the briers, etc., from the cemetery. At the appointed time a large crowd assembled and began the work, and by noon it had been completed. The crowd repaired to a nearby spring, where a beautiful dinner was served by the good women of the community. After dinner, Brother Kimbrel (sic) read a lesson

from the scriptures and commented on it, and Brother Bradley gave a short, but pointed discourse in reference to our knowing each other in heaven (*G.A.*, October 22, 1903, p. 687).

This article could be a study in our Southern culture. It gives us a clue about the origin of our "Decoration Day" at our cemeteries. J.R. may have been the originator, as his actions related to this subject are the earliest to be documented that this writer has found.

Typically, after preaching at Antioch, he would go and preach at Wolf Creek, which was situated on the eastern side if Shoal Creek (in Lawrence County, Tennessee) and about two miles away. He usually preached at multiple points in that area, when he came, as his home in Lincoln county, Tennessee was over 70 miles away. His health, at this period in his life, would also encourage him to bundle these long-distance trips together. The following notice confirms that he preached at Wolf creek. It read:

> Bro. J. R Bradley of Tennessee has been so afflicted that he has missed holding a number of meetings during the summer. His meeting at Wolf Creek, Tenn., resulted in seven additions to the one body. (F.F., January 6, 1903., p. 7)

This note confirms J.R.'s "off and on" trouble with constant health issues. 1902 was a bitter-sweet year for Him.

11

A BATTLE FOR THE LORD FROM BED

With the beginning of the New Year, J.R. was in his usual routine. He was home with Mary nearly all the time during that winter. He had some preaching appointments when his health permitted. He would worship with the brethren in Fayetteville otherwise. On Sunday evening of January 25, 1903, the Primitive Baptists, who met within sight of J.R.'s house, were having a service. J.R. attended and heard Archie Brown, the local Primitive Baptist preacher speak. He was trying to explain why man had no part in his salvation and that God would save whomever he chose to save. This caused J.R. to write Brown a letter, requesting some answers. He ended his letter by saying:

> I kindly ask you to answer me when you have convenient time. I have some other Bible examples but will wait till some other time and see whether you feel disposed to pass a few articles with me. May I ask you to preserve this? I shall want it, whether you give it any attention or not. What hurt can it possibly do for us to write a few letters of this kind in a nice brotherly way?
>
> No, Brother Brown, I am not yet prepared to receive your sermon as true.

Yours for truth,
J.R. Bradley.

(J.R. Bradley: Can The Sinner Do Anything To Be Saved: Nashville; McQuiddy Printing Company, 1903, p. 4).

Brown responded to J.R. on February 11, 1903, from Fort Branch, Indiana, with the usual misapplication of scripture in defense of the Calvinistic doctrine. Brown did say that he would be home, back in Fayetteville, in a few days and "...if you wish to make any reply, write me there" (Bradley's Tract, p. 5). So, the written debate was on for the rest of the entire year. It was conducted with dignity and respect, both on J.R.'s part and that of Brown, also. The next correspondence came from J.R. on February 16th. J.R. showed that even though Brown had denied that his sermon taught the same as the Westminster Confession of Faith, which was a creed used by Calvinistic preachers, Brown had said exactly what the creed said. J.R. quoted Brown and the Confession, so Brown could not deny the statements he said. He only denied that he meant the same thing as the confession meant. Brown's response came on February 26th, and began thus: "Elder J.R. Bradley, Dear Brother: Your letter of February 16 was received and noted. No; I do not yet think there is harmony between the creed and my sermon as to the ability of the sinner to be saved" (Bradley's Tract, p. 7).

Brown's letter was several pages in length and ended by saying:

Now, Brother Bradley, I am done. I have something else to do. I am perfectly willing for you to believe that the dead can work to get life if you want to; but you will have to let me believe that Christ gives life to the dead before they ever can render acceptable service to him.

Your brother, Archie Brown (Bradley's Tract, pp. 10-11).

In this letter, Brown was trying to end the exchanges. He seemed convinced that his efforts could not change anything with him and J.R. J.R., however, thought the correspondence should continue.

In his next letter to Brown, dated March 23rd, he began by saying:

> Your letter February 26 and the postal card of the 11th instant have been received.
>
> You say that you are done and that you have other things to do. You also state that you are perfectly willing for me to believe as I do and that I must allow you to believe that Christ gives the dead sinner life before he can render acceptable service to him. You also state that you want me "to believe just what the Savior said," I am not willing for anyone to be in the wrong; I desire to make an honest effort to help all to see the light. I know that I want you to feel and act that way toward me. I wish to write one more letter, which I am sure –at least I feel that way—you will grant. I am sure, Brother Brown that I want to understand your position. Please answer me just one time. Of course, you want me to believe it right.
>
> It might turn out that the Lord has given me the life, as you say he must do. If so, then I am a proper subject; but if it should turn out that I am still destitute of the life, of course you will have committed no sin. I mope, in making an honest effort to teach me (Bradley's Tract, p. 11).

J.R. wrote a very lengthy letter to Brown and ended by saying:

> Now Brother Brown, do you not think that I need quite a lot of teaching? I hope you will not stop here after getting me so much interested and anxious about these things. I tell you upon honor, that I do not intend this as child's play or to perplex you: I do what light.
>
> Yours to be saved. J.R. Bradley (Bradley's Tract, p. 16).

Brown responded with a letter dated May 20, 1903. In this response he proceeds further to convince J.R. of the soundness of the Primitive Baptist doctrine. J.R. just drew him further into the discussion, insuring that Brown would not break off the correspondence.

This was very evident in J.R.'s next letter. He wrote the answer to Brown on June 30th. He pointed out many misapplications of scripture that had occurred in Brown's last correspondence. J.R., like Brown, could write lengthy letters, as this one was nearly nine printed pages in the tract. The entire letter was devoted to the wrongful application of God's word. Brown finally responded with another lengthy letter written on September 20, 1903. Brown was, at that time on another preaching trip to Fort Branch, Indiana (Bradley's Tract, p. 32). He was still trying to defend the way he used and quoted scripture. His letter was not near the length of J.R.'s previous response.

By the time J.R. had received this last correspondence from Brown, he was already becoming very ill. He was getting a terrible bladder infection; thus, his next letter was much shorter than his letter of June 30th. J.R. was not even well enough until December 30, 1903, to respond to Brown's letter of September 20th. J.R. had heard Brown, prior to these correspondences, preach on the subject of "The Rich Young Man," J.R. tried to get Brown to discuss his views on this. Brown would not discuss the subject. He wrote in his final correspondence, saying:

> I do not care to discuss the subject; but I will say that if men are to get eternal life by doing, they must do; they must keep the whole law, or the law will be against them to love their neighbor as themselves is what they cannot do (Bradley's Tract, p. 41).

J.R. wrote this note in the tract at the end of Brown's letter:

> [Brother Brown returned my letter with the above remarks written on the back. He did not sign his name. I suppose, because he did not have space on the back of my letter to do so, as he filled all the space and was crowded for room to say what he did say.] I send these letters forth, hoping and praying that they will be carefully read and that eternal good may result. Faithfully Yours, J.R. Bradley (Bradley's Tract, Page 41)].

Even though Brown's answer and J.R.'s final comments were written in early January of 1904, they actually ended the entire series of letters from 1903.

That year had been a miserable year for J.R. and Mary because both had been sickly. By the end of '03, he had developed an acute bladder infection and became confined to his house. By the middle of October, he was unable to attend or conduct the funeral of a dear friend of him and Mary. Carrah Bradford had been baptized by J.R. in August of 1892, at the tender age of fourteen years. She was a very good singer. J.R. said: "She sung so sweetly! Why may she not continue to sing a sweet song-the song of redemption-in the happy state above" (*G.A.*, Nov. 26, 1903, p. 762). She had died at the age of twenty-five and left behind a husband and three small children. J.R. always had a soft spot for good singing, and since Carrah was a good singer, J.R. was even more attached to her friendship. J.R.'s good friend T.C. Little of Fayetteville preached the funeral in J.R.'s place. It must have pained J.R. very much to not even be well enough to at least attend Sister Bradford's funeral. This was just one of several disappointments for J.R. in 1903. He hoped for a better year to follow.

The year of 1904 began with JR. confined to bed. He wrote: "I have been confined to my home for a long time, so that I have not been able to work; but during most of the time my head has been as clear as it ever was ... I ask you all to pray for my recovery. My trouble is cystitis" (*G.A.*, Jan. 21, 1904, p. 46). Cystitis is a urinary infection of the bladder. It can be caused in adults from taking a lot of medicine over an extended period. It can also be caused in males who have prostate problems. Either of these could have caused J.R.'s problem. His problem was so severe that the doctor put him in bed for an extended period.

During his stay at home, J.R. read the *Gospel Advocate* very thoroughly and encouraged the brethren, who were not subscribers, to subscribe to it (*G.A.*, Jan.21, 1904, p. 46). He also became a thorough writer while in his condition. His first appearance in the *Advocate* for 1904 was in an article he had written under the heading of "Who Then Can Be Saved." The article was a column and a half long in the *Advocate*. It was written to encourage brethren to support the Nashville Bible School. J.R., having had the privilege of studying in a school such as that at Mars Hill, knew the value of training men to preach. He begged the brethren to share their financial blessings with such enterprises as the Nashville Bible School. He wrote:

> The Nashville Bible School is not Brother Lipscomb's school, Brother Sewell's school, Brother McQuiddy's school, or anybody else's school in particular; it belongs to the cause of Christ, if I understand anything about it. You know, brethren and sisters, that it is the only school in this section that is sound in its faculty and curriculum. Brother Lipscomb is the president of the school; you all know about his soundness. Many who know me and have heard me preach remember, no doubt, that I have often remarked that "had it not been for Brother Lipscomb's soundness, his positions, and the stand that he has taken, in the *Advocate*, against societies, organs, and innovations of every kind, the congregations of disciples would have embraced all the things long ago, and, of course, would have been ruined." Now then let us help him and those associated with him in this school to prepare others who, after Brother Lipscomb has gone to his reward, will take up the

good work where he has left off, and "contend for the faith" as he has done for so long (*G.A.*, Jan. 21, 1904, p. 46).

J.R. trusted Lipscomb's judgment of the scriptures as much as he did that of T.B. Larimore. J.C. McQuiddy felt compelled to place a footnote after J.R.'s letter on J.R.'s behalf. It read as follows:

> Brother Bradley is a worthy brother. He should be remembered in a substantial way by the brethren, especially by those to whom he has preached the gospel. His affliction renders it necessary for him to cease preaching. Who will be the first to send him a liberal contribution to help him meet the expenses that must be met. "Let him that is taught in the word communicate unto him that teacheth in all good things. As we have therefore opportunity let us do good unto all men especially unto them who are of the household of faith" (Gal. 6:6-10) (*G.A.*, Jan. 21, 1904, p. 46).

It seems that McQuiddy finally saw the sincerity of J.R. and sympathized with him in his poverty. This evoked the favorable comment by McQuiddy to encourage brethren "to aid him in his present distress."

It seems that while Bradley was confined to his home he was also reading from brotherhood publications other than the *Gospel Advocate*. He cites an article by L.C. Chisholm in the *Firm Foundation*. He even clips the article and sends it to E.G. Sewell at the *Advocate*. He was trying to encourage Sewell to answer L.C. Chisholm's criticism, in the *Firm Foundation*, of Sewell's article in the *Advocate*. The article related to the meaning of the gospel and wrongfully cited something attributed to Sewell that he never did say. Bradley could not stand to see his friends assaulted editorially, or any other way. That was the Scotch-Irish coming out again. Sewell acknowledged that he read the article that Bradley referred to and concluded that since so many criticisms had been built upon what he never said, and as Sewell said..." never even thought of saying" (*G.A.*, Feb. 25, 1904, p. 121) J.R. also mentioned in his letter the "rebaptism idea" as being held by some people in J.R.'s locality. This idea was strongly advocated by Austin McGary, who founded the *Firm Foundation* in Texas, to debate David Lipscomb and the *Gospel Advocate* upon the subject. McGary contended that a person upon baptism, had to believe that baptism was for remission of sin, or he was not scripturally baptized. David Lipscomb and the *Advocate* taught that if a person was baptized to obey the command of God, that was sufficient for scriptural baptism, whether or not the person who was being baptized understood everything about "baptism for remission of sins," J.R. was dealing with this battle in his own neighborhood. Even with this extended illness, and his being confined to his home, it did not keep him from being concerned with what was happening among God's people, and especially in his neighborhood.

His next communication was in the form of another article entitled: "Who Then Can Be Saved?" It continued the theme that he had developed in his former article, only this time, instead of his naming specific people or organizations to help, he simply called the brethren to stand up to their responsibility of keeping all of God's commandments-not just some of them (*G.A.*, Mar.3, 1904, p. 131). The brethren still were not giving as they should. This was a real sore spot with J.R. since he suffered greatly while serving others, and yet they were unconcerned for him and other gospel preachers and their economic plights.

He placed a paragraph at the end of his article, to let the brethren know of his progress, or the lack of progress, as was the case with J.R. because he knew the brethren were concerned of his physical health. The note read:

> To my brethren and sisters in Christ, I would say, in regard to my physical condition; I am not as well as I was two weeks

ago. At that time my strength was better, my color had returned, and I had gained some flesh; but for two weeks past it
seems that I have, from some cause, been growing worse. I
have been sick for five months, have been almost entirely shut
in, and have suffered intense pain most of the time. I pray that
I may suffer it all out in this life and have none "in the world
to come." My dear wife has a heavy burden to bear. Please let
us have an interest in your prayers. I shall try, as long as I am
able, to let you hear from me through the *Gospel Advocate*
(*G.A.* March 3, 1904, p. 131).

Even though J.R. was a "shut-in" for all practical purposes, he kept
a clear head and was still keen in his thinking.

While a shut in, news did not come to the Bradleys very quickly.
Sometime in early March he learned of the death of an old friend
of his in the Cornersville congregation. Bradley wrote an obituary
for him and it was published the second week of March in the
Gospel Advocate. His friend's name was R.N. Thornberry. J.R. had
baptized him back in 1882 during a meeting at Cornersville. It
must have pained him to not be able to have been with the Thornberry family in their hour of distress. He always had a tender
heart toward such losses (*G.A.* March 10, 1904, p. 154).

The following week, J.R. writes and thanks two sisters for sending him and Mary some money. One sister was from Guthrie,
Kentucky and one from Murfreesboro, Tennessee. He also
thanked some others who had sent aid earlier. His words had a
tone of sadness and were as follows:

> I cannot answer all these letters in separate letters. I am sitting
> up in bed writing this letter. I have been very feeble for two
> weeks or more. My wife and I have had la grippe for about ten
> days. My other trouble was, of course, made worse. I must say
> to the brethren that I do not expect to get well (*G.A.* March
> 31, 1904, p. 205).

By J.R. being bedridden, his grief was multiplied. He could not work or preach, and his livelihood was totally dependent upon what the brethren would give him. He was never comfortable in this kind of situation.

His fear of not ever being able to preach again had plagued him greatly. His concern for what might happen to Mary if he should die lay heavily upon his mind. Then that ugly financial problem, ever looming, was staring him in the face like a hungry beast. On April 23rd S.W. Fleming and his wife Sallie filed claim for the rest of the money on J.R.'s farm (*Deed Book HH*, p. 284, Lincoln County Courthouse, Fayetteville, Tennessee).

12

SICKNESS AND DEBT

J.R. had seen bad times many times before; but this time was probably the worst. The demand for the rest of the money on J.R.'s farm evoked the plan spelled out in the following letter to the *Advocate*, as follows:

> We are in debt on our little home. One note for two hundred dollars was due on December 25; the interest on the whole debt, about forty-five dollars, was also due at that time. Now brethren and sisters, we have done without winter clothing, that we might be the more able to pay some on that note. The good brother who holds the note said: "Just pay me the interest, Brother Bradley; that is all I want now." We have paid, in all, seven hundred and nineteen dollars in money on the place. If I had remained well, I believe I could have paid it all. Our drug bill has been enormous. I took ten bottles of a very highly recommended remedy, which cost one dollar per bottle. We will have more bacon, lard, and corn than we need. About May 15 we will sell all that we do not need to pay the proceeds on our debt. We have not received enough from the brethren to pay even the forty-five dollars interest and our coal and drug bills. If I should die soon, I fear that my poor wife would be turned out of our home. I am fifty-seven years old, and, of

course cannot withstand this sickness as I could if I was younger. I have been preaching since 1878 and have been closely engaged nearly all the time. My work has been entirely among the poorer class of people. I do not expect to preach another discourse. The brethren at Fayetteville have made several liberal donations to us. Brethren pray for us; and write me a consoling letter, even if you cannot send any other gift, may the Lord help you to successfully live the Christian life and meet me on the other shore (*G.A.* March 31, 1904, p. 205).

When J.R. wrote this letter, he was very despondent and had given up on ever getting better. As a matter of fact, he believed that he was going to die very soon. However down J.R. must have felt, he never doubted his salvation, in the least. His faith in his eternal destiny was firm.

He was never worried over his eminent death, but he was concerned for Mary after he was gone. In the same way Jesus was concerned for his mother Mary's welfare when he faced death, J.R. was concerned for his wife Mary's welfare when he believed that death was eminent. J.R. loved Mary until the day he died. Mary was the same toward J.R. This is a good example for modern couples to follow, especially in a day when divorce is out of control. Through all the trials and tribulations, they endured their love for God and each other was a shining beacon in a dark world. This kind of example drew young couples to J.R. to conduct their weddings. On April 10th, a young neighborhood couple, Mary Fannie Lane and Benjamin Carol Partain, who came to him to be married, visited J.R. He performed the wedding at his house (Lincoln County, Tennessee Bible Recordings, p. 169).

This next letter to the *Advocate* demonstrated his love and appreciation for the brethren also. The entire letter is included because it bears the very soul of a man who loves God and his people. It began:

I am glad to be permitted to inform the brethren and sisters that the interest spoken of in my last letter has been paid. Since my last letter we have received quite several letters, some containing gifts and some not. For all these we are certainly thankful. Some are signed "A Brother and Sister"; some "A Brother"; others, "A Sister"; and some signed their names. We now believe that enough will be given to pay the other bills also.

On March 29 we had a very pleasant surprise. Several brethren and sisters visited us, with a nice dinner, some groceries, and money. On the second Lord's day in April others came to partake with us of the Lord's Supper. They brought us nice presents, dinner, and several dollars in money. I tell my wife that a few more such surprises may cure me but may make her sick. May God bless them all.

I am glad to say that my improvement has been very perceptible since my last letter. I have gone to town (three miles) with a good brother three times since my last report. It seemed to worry me very little. On the strength of my improvement, I have agreed to be present at the opening of the new house of worship at Taft, Tenn., some time in May. Brother C.L. Talley, of Bidwell, Tenn., is expected to be with us there.

Brethren and Sisters may the dear Heavenly Father bless you all and help us to be thankful and worth of his and your kind and much appreciated favors.

J.R. Bradley, Fayetteville, Tenn.
(G.A., May 5, 1904, p. 285).

J.R., by the time he wrote this letter, was cheered for at least two reasons. First, his debt had been reduced. This no doubt eased his mind, so he could begin healing. That was the second reason J.R. was cheered. His health, seemingly, had improved greatly. This, however, proved to be very temporary. As a matter of fact, when the above letter was printed in the *Advocate* on May 5th, J. R's condition had already worsened very much.

In his next letter he sadly wrote:

> I wish to say to the brethren that I was taken much worse on
> May 2. I went to church twice in the beginning of brother
> Klingman's meeting. The fatigue may have been the cause. I
> have been in the bed most of the time since then. It seems as
> if the efforts of my physicians will prove futile. I am sure they
> are doing all they can of me. I am very much discouraged; I am
> too easy to become so, I think. I was much encouraged and
> hopeful when I wrote the last letter. Brethren allow me to still
> beg to be remembered in your prayers. The Lord chastens
> those he loves (*G.A.* June 9, 1904 p. 363).

J.R. admitted that he was prone to being easily discouraged with
his disease. He also let us know that he was a man of prayer. He
always solicited the prayers of his brethren. He, seemingly, believed that maybe he was being chastened by God. J.R. took this
as a sign that God loved him. His faith was still unwavering, even
with the terrible backset in his health.

With his deteriorated health, he had to change plans that he had
made. In his letter in the *Advocate* of May 5th, he had expressed
his intentions to be present at the opening of the new house of
worship at Taft, Tennessee. He was looking forward to being with
Charles L. Talley and the brethren at Taft. Taft was a station on
the Tennessee and Alabama Railroad and J.R., some years before,
had established the church at this place. The dedication was May
5th; just three days after J.R. became bedridden again. Apparently, Talley and his wife, Miriam stopped to visit J.R. and Mary,
while they traveled from Bidwell, Tennessee to Taft. Talley
wrote: "I recently saw Brother J.R. Bradley on his way to Red Boiling Springs, Tenn. Brother Bradley's friends and brethren are
assisting him in this needed trip. Brethren or Sisters fellowship-
ping him in his affliction will be lending to the Lord" (*G.A.*, June
16, 1904, p. 381). Red Boiling Springs was a health

resort, which was located just below the Kentucky-Tennessee line just west of Gamaliel, Kentucky. It was believed that drinking and bathing in these mineral waters could improve, maybe even cure, J.R.'s disease. His friends and brethren had persuaded him to go and they helped him financially to make the visit possible. This demonstrates the love and respect that J.R.'s community had for him.

Reports on his health began to trickle in to the *Gospel Advocate*. The first reported that J.R. was at Red Boiling Springs. J.R. wrote that he thought he should remain there through July, but his money was running out. He said, "I think I have improved very much since coming here." He also noted that there were "four members "of the church of Christ" there. He further noted that he desired to remain there long enough to get full benefit of these springs, but his money would be gone after the end of the month. McQuiddy wrote: "Who will help Brother Bradley to remain another month?" (*G.A.*, June 30, 1904, p. 405).

Another appeal for J.R. was made in the *Gospel Advocate* of June 7, 1904. It read as follows:

> Brother J.R. Bradley has been much improved by his stay at Red Boiling Springs, Macon County, Tenn. He desires to remain about three weeks longer and will need about thirty dollars in order to do this. We hope his friends and the brethren will see that this necessity is supplied (*G.A.* July 76, 1904, p. 421).

It was perhaps McQuiddy who wrote this on J.R.'s behalf, since he usually handled this section of the *Advocate*.
McQuiddy made another appeal on J.R.'s behalf two weeks later. His appeal went thus:

> Brother J.R. Bradley stopped over and spent several days with us as he returned home from Red Boiling springs, Tenn. He is

much improved but is aft from being well. Brother Bradley is anxious to be in the field and at work preaching the gospel of Christ. He is very grateful for the help and encouragement he has received since he has been sick. In helping the preacher of the gospel, the Christian should remember that "it is more blessed to give than to receive." Address Brother Bradley at Fayetteville, Tenn. (*G.A.* July 21, 1904, p. 457).

J.R. was anxious to put his ailment behind him and get to the task at hand—preaching the gospel of Christ—saving souls. That was his heart's desire. Just maybe he would be well enough to preach very soon.

13

THE AUTHOR

Even though he had been sick, he had not been idle. He had written articles for the *Gospel Advocate*. The previous year he even carried on a written debate with a Primitive Baptist preacher by the name of Archie Brown, who preached in his neighborhood. J.R. decided to have the debate published as a tract by the *Advocate*. McQuiddy may have encouraged Bradley to print this when J.R. stopped over in Nashville on his way home from Red Boiling Springs. The report in the *Advocate* concerning J.R.'s decision was as follows:

> Brother J.R. Bradley is anxious to have published a corre-
> spondence between himself and a Primitive Baptist preacher.
> The doctrine of unconditional election to eternal life or death
> is considered. The proceeds of the tract will go to help Brother
> Bradley to meet his living expenses after the cost of publica-
> tion is paid. Brother Bradley is sorely afflicted, not able to
> preach and feels grateful to the Lord and the brethren for the
> help that has already been extended to him. One brother has
> already given him ten dollars to have the tract published. A
> friend suggested to Brother Bradley that he ask if forty other
> brethren would not send one dollar each to be placed to the

credit of J.R. Bradley. Every brother who sends one dollar is to receive one dozen tracts so soon as the tract is from the press. In this way the brethren can help Brother Bradley and also do a good work. Send your contributions direct to the McQuiddy Printing Company, stating that it is to enable Brother J.R. Bradley to publish his tract. Prices: Single copy, fifteen cents; per dozen, one dollar and twenty cents (*G.A.*, July 28, 1904, p. 460).

The *Advocate* continued to publish statements of endorsement for Bradley's tract and to encourage the brethren to buy the tracts so that J.R. could be helped financially.

The first issue of the *Advocate* for the month of August bore the following:

Do not forget to send us one dollar to assist in the publication of Brother J.R. Bradley's tract. One dozen tracts will be forwarded you so soon as the tracts are from the press. One brother has already contributed ten dollars for the publication of the tracts (*G.A.*, August 4, 1904, p. 485).

One week later another appeal appeared in the second August issue with a very strong plea to get brethren to donate money to help publish the tract. Remember that the original plan was to get brethren to contribute enough money to pay for the publishing cost and then J.R. would receive all the funds brought in by the tract. In the second August appeal we read:

Several persons have already sent in one dollar to enable Brother J.R. Bradley to bring out his tract. We hope others will respond at once. Remember, one dozen tracts will be forwarded you so soon as the tract is published.... send whatever amount to us you feel disposed to give, and we will place the amount to the credit of Brother Bradley's tract fund. The tract will do good and should have a wide circulation. We should be active in circulating good tracts (*G.A.*, Aug. 11, 1904, p. 501).

By this note we see that the brethren had not responded as had been wished. Maybe this second plea would get results. McQuiddy and Bradley were anxious to get the tract published and circulated. The tract would be very useful for those studying with the Primitive Baptist or any other Calvinistic group.

J.R.'s next correspondence, which continued a short note of thanks to the brethren and sisters for their aid to him in his visit to Red Boiling Springs, began by saying:

> Brethren and sisters in Christ, allow me to thank you all for your kindness to me in helping bear my expenses at Red Boiling Springs. I drank the water just six weeks, and I think I am very much benefited; my physician also thinks so. All my brethren and sisters here say that I look very much better. They say that I must go back to the springs and have already given me thirty dollars to help pay my expenses. The McQuiddy Printing Company is at work on a tract for me. It is a written discussion between a Primitive Baptist preacher and me. If you desire to help me spend another month at the springs, you can do so by sending for these tracts. I think the tracts will cost about ten cents each; however, Brother McQuiddy will state the price. The tract will be ready in a few days. I think it will be interesting to you, and a good thing where Primitive Baptist doctrine is preached. You will certainly help me greatly in my affliction by getting the tract (*G.A.*, Aug. 18, 1904, p. 522).

J.R. also included the address of the McQuiddy Printing Company, which this writer found interesting. It was at that time "232 North Market Street, Nashville, Tenn." J.R. concluded his letter by saying: "I feel sure that it will aid the cause. Pray for me" (*G.A.*, Aug. 18, 1904, p. 522). J.R. knew from years of experience in preaching, and from his early family experience, that the brethren would encounter difficulties with the Primitive Baptists. They were in nearly every southern community, and very active. That is why he originally conceived the idea to publish the tract. The extra money it would bring him, if any, would help him in his finances, but that was an afterthought. His original purpose was just simply to educate the brethren in Primitive Baptists' doctrine.

By August 25th, the last August issue for the year tells us that the tract still was not published. J.C. McQuiddy wrote:

> Several brethren have sent one dollar each to assist Brother J.R. Bradley publish his tract. Will not others respond at once, so we can complete the work? The proceeds derived from the sale of the tract will help Brother Bradley considerably. Send us one dollar and we will mail you one dozen tracts so soon as published (*G.A.*, Aug. 25, 1904, p. 533).

It was very hard to get the brethren to buy tracts as we have seen by following the progress on the printing of J.R.'s tract.
By September it still was not published. McQuiddy wrote of Bradley and his tract:

> Brother J.R. Bradley has returned to Red Boiling Springs, Macon County, Tenn. Correspondents will note the change. Brother Bradley says "When the tract is ready, please mail some copies to me. I hope I can sell them," While we are at work on this tract, we have not received nearly enough to pay the actual cost of publication. We hope the brethren will contribute enough to pay the entire cost of printing, so that all the proceeds of the sale may go to Brother Bradley. We lack about twenty-five dollars after donating five dollars ourselves. Who will send one dollar (*G.A.*, Sept. 1, 1904, p. 549).

It now seems that J.C. McQuiddy was really trying to make amends for his harshness a few years before toward J.R.; when J.R. had made an appeal to the brethren; and especially after Sister Mollie DeFord's appeal, in 1889, brought the thunderous pen of McQuiddy's disapproval. During this period of illness, McQuiddy had demonstrated genuine concern toward J.R. and his illness. The next report on J.R.'s tract came from McQuiddy once more. It began with the title:

> "Can the Sinner Do Anything to Be Saved?" This is the title of a tract of forty-one pages, being a discussion by J.R. Bradley, of the church of Christ, and Archie Brown, of the Primitive Baptist Church. The discussion is conducted in a dignified and courteous manner. The tract should have a wide circulation. We think it will do good. The truth covets investigation (*G.A.*, Sept. 15, 1904, p. 581).

By McQuiddy's backing the sale of the tract, yet complimenting Bradley on the way the debate was conducted, this shows his confidence in J.R.'s ability to debate and get results. You may recall that J.R. had converted several Baptist and Methodist preachers.

J.R. was at Red Boiling Springs for the second time, and it appeared that the water was helping him. Remember that the "cystitis" was a urinary infection and the minerals in the water at Red Boiling Springs may have helped his problem. His doctor back in Fayetteville believed that the water helped his situation (*G.A.*, Aug. 18, 1904, p. 522). With J.R. back on the right track health-wise, he was looking forward to getting back into the pulpit. That was J.R.'s passion. It grieved him very much to not be able to preach. He was an evangelist at heart. His progress was given in a letter to the Advocate of the last week of September. J.R. had returned home from Red Boiling Springs, after a month's visit to the mineral springs, "in search of health" as McQuiddy had written (*G.A.*, Aug. 18, 1904, p. 522).

By the end of September Bradley was home from the springs and "much improved in health" (*G.A.*, Sept. 29, 1904, p. 618). The *Advocate* was still strongly advertising J.R.'s tract. It is apparent that J.R. stopped over again in Nashville on his way home from Red Boiling Springs. McQuiddy reported that J.R. made a visit to Nashville. He wrote: "He made a short talk for the brethren at Tenth Street church of Christ on the fourth Lord's day in September. His health is much improved, but he is far from being a well man" (*G.A.*, Oct. 6, 1904, p. 629). This may have been the only sermon that J.R. preached in 1904. His health was on the mend, but as McQuiddy said, "he was far from being a well man." This stop in Nashville did wonders for J.R.

While in Nashville, he discussed a new price for the tract. J.R. was willing to sacrifice some of the money he might receive to get the tract in the hands of the brethren. The new price would be ten cents per tract, or one dollar per dozen. His tract had begun to get favorable reviews from the brethren. The *Highland Preacher* said: "The question is well discussed and is worth a large circulation" (*G.A.*, Oct. 6, 1904, p. 629). By the end of October, the *Advocate* was advertising his tract under "Publishers Item," which was the *Advocate*'s main advertisement for the McQuiddy Printing Company (*G.A.*, Oct. 20, 1904, p. 661). By the first of November, J.R. had written an article about one and one-half columns in length, under the title of "Faith and Live or Live and Faith—Which?" In this article, he reviews the Primitive Baptists' doctrine of election. Do you have eternal life before faith or after faith? The Baptists' position of election has one being born from the natural birth with eternal life. J.R.'s position was simply that one receives eternal life after faith and obedience; therefore, faith comes before eternal life. His position was totally opposite that of the Primitive Baptists' teaching.

J.R. let it be known that he was not trying to be unkind to the Primitive Baptists. He stated:

I have a kindly feeling toward Primitive Baptist people. My dear old father, who has long since crossed the "silent river," was a zealous member of the denomination. While I often heard them in his day, I was too young and unthoughtful then to catch their teaching on these things. I am now fifty-eight years of age and have been closely engaged in the study of God's word for about thirty years. For four years I been living within a short distance (in sight) of a Primitive Baptist Church that has a strong membership. I frequently hear their preachers who are called "strong men," Especially have I heard them since I have been afflicted and confined at home. I am certainly astonished when I hear any preacher of fair attainments misquote or misapply our Father's holy will as this dear people do (*G.A.*, Nov. 10, 1904, p. 719).

J.R. and McQuiddy used this article as an advertisement for J.R.'s tract. This is apparent with the footnote at the article's ending. J.R. wrote: "In this tract of forty-one pages the question at the head of this article, I think, is well discussed by myself and Brother Archie Brown of the Primitive Baptists Church" (*G.A.*, Nov. 10, 1904, p. 719). The tract was gaining in circulation. By the end of November Brother J.W. Atkisson, of St. Louis, Missouri, had read the tract and wrote the following assessment of J.R.'s work:

I have received a copy of Brother J.T. Bradley's tract, "Can the Sinner Do Anything to Be Saved?" This a debate between Brother Bradley and a very able debater of the Primitive Baptist persuasion; and I can truly say it is the best tract of the kind I have ever seen, and I have read a great many debates. Brethren send ten cents to the McQuiddy Printing Company and get a copy of this able debate (*G.A.*, Dec. 1, 1904, p. 766).

That was the best compliment on the tract that anyone could get. This is the kind of recommendation J.R. needed to sell his tract.

His final communication to *Gospel Advocate* for the year was another article reviewing more Primitive Baptist doctrine. This article reviewed the doctrine that there were "elect infants" and "non-elect infants" and what would be the destiny of each class of infants. This had also been covered in the debate with Brown. Again, this article was about one and one-half columns in length.

The last paragraph of this communication was a report on J.R.'s health and the health of the Fayetteville church. His report ended by writing:

> Dear brethren and sisters in the faith, please think of your afflicted brother when you engage in prayers and the worship of our God. Many of my near and dear friends hold to the doctrine of the creed as above quoted, though they are kind and good to us. I get to meet occasionally with our brethren and sisters in Fayetteville. Our members, or most of them, are loyal and true. No organ, no societies, creeds, fads, and fancies of men bother us, only as we know of the fact of their adoption by others. I can only get out in pretty weather. I am sure that I can never get well. Pray that I may hold out faithful to the end. I grieve over the fact that I am deprived of preaching the "glorious gospel of Christ," It seems that I cannot help it.
>
> J.R. Bradley
> (*G.A.*, Dec. 29, 1904, p. 819).

With this correspondence, J.R. closed the very worst year of his life up to that point. He only preached once, as far as records show, for the year. That was at Tenth Street congregation in Nashville, when he returned from his second visit to Red Boiling Springs, Tennessee (*G.A.*, Oct. 6., 1904, p. 629). It is little wonder that J.R. thought his life was near the end. During this year he had made two trips to Red Boiling Springs. He had worried over the possibility of losing his farm. He was also stressed over getting enough money to pay his medical bills. Where would food come from? He and Mary had sold what seemed to be surplus. At the time there seemed to be a surplus of corn, lard and bacon in March. But with winter upon them that was now needed. He was anxious over getting enough money contributed to print his tract, which he and others felt was much needed to teach the brethren. Would he and Mary go through another winter with no winter clothes? That is what happened the previous winter. Despite all of his earthly concerns, J.R. never flinched in his faith toward God. He was always looking forward to being eternally with the Lord in heaven. Deep down J.R. felt that God's people would care for him and Mary. Maybe 1905 would be a happier year. Maybe he would improve in health and get to preach again; just maybe. God only knew; and after all, He knew what was best.

14

OPERATION AND RECOVERY

J.R. was not well enough to write until February of 1905. The *Advocate* published the letter with the following comments at the head of this letter:

> Brother J.R. Bradley, of Fayetteville, Tenn. has not improved much of late. His disease is troubling him considerably, both day and night. He says: "We are having a hard time this winter. We could not, nor can we now, see how we will get through the winter; but we both are doing all we can, we think, to be cheerful and to patiently bear our hard lot. Some friends have sent once and again to our help. God knows we are thankful first to him and then to them for their gifts." We trust the brethren will remember Brother Bradley and wife in their affliction. Make them a gift that will relieve their minds (*G.A.*, Feb. 16, 1905, p. 101).

No doubt, J.C. McQuiddy penned the "fore and aft" notes to J.R.'s letter. It is now noticeable that J.R. never mentions the note on his farm. It seems that he has resigned himself to the fact that the farm was lost. J.R.'s and Mary's health were the major issues in the beginning of this New Year, just as the previous year which was a total disaster, health wise.

One week later, the *Advocate* published an article by J.R. titled, "What Grace Is Meant?" This was a study on Ephesians 2:8: "for by grace are ye saved through faith." He also gives the American Revised Version's [American Standard] rendering of that part of Eph. 2:8. This shows that J.R. was open-minded on translations of the Scriptures. Remember that the American Standard Version was a new translation. It was published a little less than four years before. His arguments were constructed to show fallacies in the Baptists' arguments, and especially that of the Primitive Baptists. He referred to the way he had heard the test used to support the idea that man had nothing to do with his salvation (*G.A.*, Feb. 16, 1905, p. 101).

He argued that grace is the thing given. Christ is given to save us. We are saved by grace. Christ saves us. Therefore, he is grace. You can see that J.R. was still studying the subject he covered with Archie Brown in his tract. Writing is all that he could do until he was well. He was pained very much to have to depend upon gifts of money from the brethren. But what else could he do with his illness?

The first week in March he wrote, thanking two sisters for sending a dollar each to aid him and Mary. A brother and sister Darnall of Corinth, Mississippi, sent him five dollars. The church at Totty's Bend, Tennessee, through Brother D. L Martin, sent him five dollars. Sara Molloy of Spencer, Tennessee, sent a dollar. He asked God to bless those kind-hearted people. He wrote: "May our dear Father bless them all. He knows that we are thankful to them all for this help. I am not yet able to do anything at all. My dear woman has both my part and her part of our work to do. She suffers some with rheumatism this bad weather. Pray for us" (*G.A.*, Mar. 9, 1905, p. 149). His disease and need for help were prolonged for a much longer period.

A month later he had written about a lost check from the brethren at Iron City. Brother C. E. Holt had sent the check to J.R., on behalf of the church in that place. The amount was twelve dollars.

Somehow it had been lost in the postal system. The church sent another check. J.R. wrote:

> ...those frightful hemorrhages have ceased, and I am sitting up
> I thought if going down town today. Several of the brethren
> and sisters came to see us yesterday (Lord's Day) and brought
> a nice dinner and some presents. They also brought the em-
> blems, and we partook of the Lord's Supper and had a nice
> service. May our dear Father bless them all. Pray for us (*G.A.*,
> April 20, 1905, p. 245).

During this period J.R.'s condition worsened. His hope of ever being able to preach again was gone. Those were dismal times. Sometime between April and October, J.R. had an operation. His physician finally decided that surgery was his only chance at get-ting well again. The second week of October he wrote a letter to the *Gospel Advocate*, which was published in its entirety. It read as follows:

> I feel that I should write a few words, after a silence of quite a
> while. I have tried to preach three sermons since I was oper-
> ated on.
>
> I was with Brother A.L. Rozar three or four times in a recent
> meeting at the George Schoolhouse and preached one time.
> They had a good meeting, which continued for about eight
> days and resulted in five additions to the Lord's army. I am
> persuaded that Brother Rozar and the few faithful ones there
> are doing a grand work. Brother Rozar has about all his time
> engaged with poor congregation and at schoolhouses and is
> one of those faithful characters who works on the farm during
> crop time for support for his family.
>
> I was at Booneville, this county, on last Sunday and Sunday
> night (October 8). Our home in days gone by was with these
> dear people. Brethren Talley, Cambron, Dixon, and possibly
> others, have been preaching at this place some during the last
> two years. We trust that much has been done by the joint

labors of these brethren toward the establishment of Christ's blessed cause and the salvation of souls at that place.

I am expecting to visit some of the congregations—and not only the established congregations but the schoolhouses and mission points as well—if my improvement continues. The brethren and sisters say that I speak with almost as much clearness and earnestness as I did, although I have been practically silent for more than two years.

I shall go to Stoney Point on the third Sunday, and on the fourth Sunday I will be at Chestnut Ridge. On the fifth Sunday I expect to be at County Line, and in the near future I expect to be at Molino and Taft. I cannot go out in bad weather. My wound has not entirely cured up yet, and my physician says that I should be careful and not expose myself for quite a while yet. I have had the encouragement of all the faithful in Christ since my disability. May our dear Father bless them all. Our Fayetteville congregation has in a special manner been kind to us.

J.R. Bradley (G.A., Nov. 3, 1905, p. 699).

There are several revealing things in J.R.'s letter. Number one is that he had improved greatly. Secondly: It took an operation to make him better after more than two years of chronic illness. Thirdly: He wasted no time getting back into the pulpit. Fourthly: He made it clear that he was still intending to work with the poorer churches and mission points. That was just J.R. He had been poor all of his life and his heart was with those kinds of people. Finally, he showed his love and appreciation towards his fellow preachers. He never ever exhibited any kind of jealousy toward his co-laborers, unlike many preachers of modern times. He truly loved the Lord, his church and his laborers. Some of these men mentioned by him had also been baptized by him also. The year ended, leaving J.R. with more hope and cheerfulness than he had had in several years. He had, however, endured his affliction, like Job, and now had overcome. He was looking forward to the coming of the New Year.

J.R. and Mary welcomed the New Year with much joyous and hopeful expectation. During the winter months of 1905-06, he had been sick, and still recovering from an operation. His first communication to the *Advocate*, which was probably written on January 1 as follows: "Since December 13, I have been laid up with la grippe. My health otherwise is much improved. I have preached six times since I was operated on last June" (*G.A.*, Jan. 18, 1906, pp. 37-38). He was just looking forward to getting better from his old problem, which had lingered so long, but now was on the mend since the operation. The la grippe (a type of chest and lung infection) was just a temporary thing. Someone in the Advocate addressed J.R.'s state of health during the winter by simply stating: "Brother J.R. Bradley, of Fayetteville, Tenn., has been in a very poor state of health during the whole winter." (*G.A.*, March 15, 1906, p. 165). Thus, we know that winter was not kind to the Bradleys.

15

THE MISSIONARY SOCIETY

During the time that J.R. had been "laid up" he read all of the *Gospel Advocates* he could get into his hands. He loved reading after Lipscomb, Sewell, McQuiddy, and other old acquaintances. He especially loved Sewell's writings: so, apparently, along with his report on his health, he sent Sewell a question to be answered through the pages of the *Advocate*. He wrote concerning the Apostles and the lack of biblical information on some of them. He couldn't understand why the New Testament did not contain work by all of them. Sewell wrote back:

All these things are of divine wisdom. So, the New Testament, as given, is a marvel of divine wisdom, and show the whole to be a matter of divine origin. Uninspired men could not possibly produce such a volume (*G.A.*, Jan. 18, 1906, p. 41).

Apparently, Sewell's explanation satisfied J.R.; he never responded. This was typical of him. Once someone gave a valid scriptural explanation of a problem, he accepted it.

In the same letter (dated Jan. 1, 1906) he also asked E.A. Elam a question concerning whether the wine was fermented that was used in the Lord's Supper. Elam and Bradley knew one another from their Mars Hill days and had remained friends through the years.

J.R.'s question was:

> Brother Elam: Ever since I read your article in the Gospel Advocate of December 7 upon the Lord's Supper, I have been anxious to have another [article] from you, showing the kind of "wine" or "fruit of the vine," whether fermented or unfermented, we should use. At the time of the Lord's Supper, as stated in 1 Cor. 11:21, we see that they so abused this sacred ordinance as to become "drunken," Will the original word for "drunken" here be correctly translated if we use the word "filled" instead of the word "drunken?" I, from my view of it, would be perfectly willing to use unfermented wine all the time, if in this way we could have perfect harmony and agreement among the faithful in this part of our worship. I am sure that in the unfermented state it is "the fruit of the vine" as well as in the fermented state. And to adopt the use of unfermented wine we avoid the idea of drinking intoxicating liquors (*G.A.*, Jan. 18, 1906, p. 33).

This question had been prompted by Selina Holman, who was a member in Fayetteville, and who had written several articles in *Gospel Advocate* during the 1880's-90's. J.R. favored her position of opposing the use of fermented wine for any reason. However, some churches, such as the Petersburg Church of Christ, continued to use fermented wine for communion on into the early 1900's (from receipts to the Fayetteville Liquor store, found in the Petersburg records). This question was causing problems in the churches in the Fayetteville-Lynchburg area. J.R. thought that maybe Elam could help end the confusion.

Elam was gracious to J.R. and published an answer to J.R.'s question. It began by pointing out that the word "filled" could not be substituted for "drunken," since that called for two different words. Elam pointed out that drunken was from "methuo" and filled was from "chartazo." He wrote:

While this is true, there is a vast difference between the fiery, intoxicating poisonous wine which some buy at drug stores and saloons to be used on the Lord's table; and the pure, wholesome "fruit of the vine" of Palestine, an abundance of which one could drink without becoming intoxicated. There is no excuse for not having the pure "fruit of the vine" on the Lord's table.... Since Jesus speaks of "the fruit of the vine," all Christians should be satisfied with that, as Brother Bradley suggests. The pure fruit of the vine, if there be some fermentation is it, or if there be none, I can drink with a clear conscience. There is a mild, pure wine which the good sisters in many congregations prepare for the Lord's table, or which can be obtained from different men who prepare it, and it is safe and wise to use this kind. Certainly, one should not raise trouble in a congregation over this question (*G.A.*, Jan. 18, 1906, p. 34).

Elam and Bradley both used similar thinking to solve the problem. This question spread all over the southeastern part of the United States. During this period a brother who had overseen preparing the communion at Hopewell Church of Christ in Colbert County, Alabama, failed to show with the communion one Sunday morning. When some of the brethren went to check on him, they found that he had drunk all the communion wine and had become drunk. In a similar frame of time, an elder at one of the churches in Huntsville, Alabama oversaw making the communion wine in the basement of the church building and became an alcoholic from continuously tasting the wine for readiness. This happened over a period of several years of test tasting. You can understand J.R.'s and Elam's concern over using fermented wine. Now we can understand why J.R. explored the ways to oppose the use of fermented wine in the Lord's Supper. He was concerned over what either was already happening or might happen in the future.

He turns his attention to the subject of "Evangelizing the World" in February. He sent a sermon and it was published in the *Advocate*. He showed the urgency of preaching, since it was the subject of the "great commission"; since it was preached on Pentecost by Peter; since Paul preached immediately after his conversion; it was necessary to evangelize. In his summary remarks he wrote:

> Allow me to ask: How does it look, in the face of Paul's plain statement regarding himself, for our preachers now to be too clean and nice to do anything with their hands: he says to the elders of the church of Ephesus: "Ye yourselves know, that these hands have ministered unto my necessities, and to them that were with me" (Acts 20:34.). Are preachers to-day better than Paul was? Why not work with their hands some to help sustain themselves (*G.A.*, Feb. 15, 1906, p. 99).

Many of the older preachers felt betrayed by the younger generation of preachers. J.R. was not alone in these kinds of feelings. Mansell W. Matthews wrote his concerns for the same thing:

> ...I realize that the churches in this country in the main are disposed to ignore the old pioneer preachers that wore the copperas or jeans pants, tread down the grass and swam water courses for the love of truth. They are made to stand aside, and the young and stylish with their hair parted in the middle, who can sport a massive chain, charm and diamond ring on the finger are those who are first to advocate the cause of Him, who, while the foxes had holes and the birds' nests, had nowhere to lay his head" (*G.A.*, Aug. 22, 1888, p. 14).

Matthews, like J.R., was concerned about the way the work of the church had turned because of the youthful preachers having different mindsets about what kind of service the church needed from them. This was being done at the expense of all the labor accomplished by earlier preachers. The trend continues today (2019).

In April, J.R. turns his thoughts away from preachers, whom he thought were too good to work some with their own hands, to the subject of the proper name by which the church should be called. J.R. wrote a lengthy question and proposition under the title: "What Name Is It?" In the outset, he makes it clear that he only wanted to follow the Bible and not his own will. He presented his question in the following way:

> Then to sum up, we have: I. Zion is promised "a new name" to be given by "the mouth of the Lord" when the "Gentiles shall see thy righteousness, and all kings thy glory." (Isa. 62:2) II. Paul chosen by the Lord to bear his Name: before the Gentiles, and Kings and the children of Israel." (Acts 9:15). III. The Gentiles do see the righteousness of Zion in their conversion to Christianity (Acts 10). IV. The name borne to them by the apostle Paul and Barnabas, his companion (Acts 11:25, 26), at Antioch. V. The name is "Christian," "And they [the disciples] were called Christians first in Antioch." (Verse 26). VI. These disciples are called "the church." (Verse 26) VII. All in the church are "Christians" so named by the mouth of the Lord"; and one cannot truly be in the church and not be a "Christian," Then why not "Christian Church?"
>
> Brother Lipscomb, will you please show the mistakes that I make (if any) in my effort to connect the above scriptures? I certainly wish to be with the Bible regarding the "name," as well as I do upon all other Bible subjects (*G.A.*, April 5, 1906, p. 217).

Lipscomb wrote in response to Bradley:

> Brother Bradley's reasoning seems to be close, and I do not feel enough interest in the question to give much attention to it. It is very safe to follow the Scriptures, and I have found no example of the church being called the "Christian Church," so I cannot contend for it. Nor do I find any name given as a distinctive name, so I cannot contend for a distinctive name (*G.A.*, April 5, 1906, p. 217).

Lipscomb was strictly to the point and a little confusing. J.R. wanted to know why the church could not be called "Christian Church" and Lipscomb said that Bradley was close. How could he turn around and say he could not contend for the church to be called the "Christian Church" or by any other distinctive name? Was J.R.'s thinking close or totally wrong? From Lipscomb's response it is difficult to tell.

J.R. was cautious as to what was transpiring in the churches of his region. Some people were beginning to advocate the use of the Missionary Society for evangelistic work. Those who advocated a society usually tended toward the use of the name "Christian Church" for a distinct name. In the above article, J.R., who was totally against the use of a missionary society, still thought "Christian Church" was a proper biblical use of the word. He would later abandon that thinking totally, after seeing the trouble caused by those "Christian Churches," so called. To highlight the concern for coming problems over the societies, T.C. Little sent the following letter to Lipscomb:

> Brother Lipscomb: In response to your letter in regard to the churches in Lincoln County, I will say: We have twelve congregations and about that number of houses for worship. Before the war [Civil War] there were two congregations who met occasionally and had preaching – one at Fayetteville and one in the western portion of the county [the one in "the western portion of the county" is unable to be identified]. After the war they took on new life, soon began meeting on every Lord's day, and had more preaching, going into other neighborhoods as opportunity offered. The demand for preaching increased, and soon a number of preachers were making regular visits to the county. Among these were Jesse Sewell, T.W. Brents, W. H. Dixon, and G. Lipscomb. Especially did Brethren Dixon and Lipscomb devote much of their time to this county, and, as a result, a number of congregations were established. To brother Dixon, more than any one is credit due for this work. He was constantly in this work until his death.

In November 1881, I was set apart by the church at Fayette-ville to preach the Gospel. My labors have been mostly in this count, and I have been for years doing mission work in this county without any stipulation for support with anyone. There are a number of congregations which are not able to employ a preacher. My throat prevents my preaching as much for them as they want or that I would like. Brother Rozier, Brother Bradley, Brother C.L. Talley, and myself are the preachers living permanently in this county. The work has been carried on entirely without the aid of any society, only one congregation ever having affiliated with them, and it is free from them now. So, at present we have none; only a few individuals in this county are that way (*G.A.*, April 26, 1906, p. 265).

Lipscomb had been gathering reports on all the Tennessee churches of Christ to show that more Christians in Tennessee were against the societies than were for them. Little stressed the non-use of societies in Lincoln County, Tennessee. Little, Rozier, Bradley, and Talley were all opposed to the missionary society. As poverty stricken as J.R. was, he would never even entertain the idea of seeking aid from the societies. It was men like J.R. and the other men mentioned by Little that kept the society out of South-central Tennessee.

16

TAFT, TONEY, AND WEST TENNESSEE

One of those churches that had been established without the aid of a society, which Little included as part of his number, was Taft. J.R. had established this work in the summer of 1902. It was first begun as a brush arbor meeting. That same year they began work on a house of worship, which was not completed until nearly eighteen months later in 1904. He also held a meeting at Bonner Schoolhouse near Taft. In those two meetings he had baptized nine persons. He was supposed to hold another brush arbor meeting in 1903 but could not keep the appointment due to illness. C.L. Talley, one of the men Bradley had baptized, preached in that meeting. A.H. Rozier, whom Bradley had also baptized, aided Talley. The meeting house was completed in 1904 and J.R. was supposed to preach the first sermon in it, but again his illness intervened, and Talley preached instead (*G.A.*, May 31, 1906, p. 352). Taft was located on the Nashville, Chattanooga, and St. Louis Railroad, between Fayetteville, Tennessee, and Jeff, Alabama. It was very near the Alabama-Tennessee state line. In 1905, J.D. Floyd held a meeting at Taft and, during his series of lessons, preached a sermon on the Sabbath and the Lord's Day – "contrasting them," A Mr. Haysmer, a Seventh-day Adventist, was there and took notes. He did not challenge Floyd that night but waited until Floyd had gone back to Flat Creek. J.R. followed

Floyd the following Sunday and Mr. Haysmer was present. He
rose and said that he was going to begin a review of Floyd's lesson
that afternoon at four o'clock. J.R. went and heard his review and
said that Haysmer never touched any of Floyd's points. J.R. challenged him to debate one of our brethren in debate. After much
persuasion on J.R.'s part, Haysmer agreed to debate. J.R. con-
tacted L.R. Sewell and Sewell agreed to debate him in September
(*G.A.*, May 31, 1906, p. 352).

On May 19, J.R. went to Estill Springs in Franklin County, Tennessee, and preached. That was a Saturday night. He stayed
overnight with the Mason family. He then preached Sunday
morning and night before returning home. He had held a meeting
there thirteen years before (*G.A.*, May 31, 1906, p. 352).

By the end of June, J.R. announced the date for the debate at Taft
between L.R. Sewell and A.J. Haysmer. It was set to begin on September 11, 1906. The debate was to run for four days (*G.A.*, July
5, 1906, p. 421). On the fourth Sunday in July, he was back at Taft.
He wrote: "They are looking forward to the discussion which is to
begin there on September 11, next, between Brother L.R. Sewell
and a Seventh-day Adventist" (*G.A.*, July 5, 1906, p. 421). For
some reason the building at Taft was still not finished in the summer of 1906. J.R. wrote: "they have a nice new house, which was
built at a great sacrifice, and though it is not yet completed they
can use it" (*G.A.*, August 23, 1906, p. 540).

Earlier in July (July 8th), Bradley had preached at County Line,
Moore County, Tennessee. From there he went to Toney, Alabama to hold a seven-day meeting. He began on the third Sunday
in July. He only got to preach four times because of excessive
heavy rain. He remained there the entire week hoping to complete the week but could not. Toney was not very far south of Taft,
Tennessee, thus making it convenient for him to wait the entire
week at Toney and then speak at Taft on the following Sunday.
From there he traveled back home to Fayetteville for a week of
rest and home work. He then went to Molino and preached one

sermon and baptized one young man. This was the first time J.R. had been able (health-wise) to be with the brethren at Molino in three years (*G.A.* August 23, 1906, p. 540).

He continued to fill his regular preaching appointments until the third week in August. On August 19, he went back to Toney, Alabama, and tried for a second time to conduct a meeting of six nights. Due to the fact they were using a school house for a meeting place, Sunday was the only time they could meet both day and night. The remainder of the meeting was at night because school was in session during the day (*G.A.*, October 11, 1906, p. 652). He had two baptisms. Toney was another work established by J.R., and he was fond of these people.

From Toney he went home for a few days and then began a meeting at County Line in Moore County, near Lynchburg. The meeting began on the first Sunday in September. It ended on the second Sunday of September, with one baptism and three from the Baptists (*G.A.*, October 11, 1906, p. 652). County Line had been a regular preaching point for J.D. Floyd, A.H. Rozier, and J.R. The congregation is still a strong one, over one hundred years later (2019). J.R. had a special relationship with this congregation. He ended his report, dated October 3, 1906, by giving an account of his regular work as follows:

> I am preaching now almost every Lord's Day and Lord's Day night. My health is very much improved, though I am not entirely well. My preaching is done nearly all the time at destitute places and hence I do not get traveling expenses. This is exceedingly hard for one who has spent so much and for so long, trying to get well (*G.A.*, Oct. 11, 1906, p. 652).

With the struggle to recover from extended illnesses and to survive, everything was slowly taking a toll upon J.R. He continued to have the very same struggles the remainder of his life. To add to his woes, Mary was staying ill longer and even more seriously with each bout of her discomforts.

J.R.'s next report to the *Advocate* was on the Sewell-Haysmer debate at Taft. It had begun on September 11 and had continued four days. The debate is probably why J.R. never reported any meetings for the month of September. He only kept his weekly appointments to attend the debate. J.R. loved a good debate, especially this one, as it was on behalf of one of the congregations he had established. The people at Taft were being confused by Haysmer, who kept chiding them when J.R. was away in other work. J.R.'s report is given in full, for the reader to understand the entire situation at Taft. It read:

> The discussion between L.R. Sewell of the church of Christ, and A. J. Haysmer, Seventh-day Adventist, at Taft, Tenn., is past. They began on September 11 and continued for days. The Sabbath question was the only subject discussed. I am sure that Brother Sewell's arguments were strictly scriptural. His arguments were to show what the "old covenant" contained, with whom made, and when abolished; and that the Ten Commandments being the heart of the Old covenant, and the only covenant containing the Sabbath, that, of course, the Sabbath was done away too. To put it in the language of one who was a close observer:
>
> Sewell made the Bible arguments, and Haysmer made the thunder. Brother Sewell remained a week with us and preached some very fine sermons. Our crowds were large during the discussion and did fairly well of nights during the meeting. Elder Haysmer broke over the rules of "honorable controversy" at least twice. One time he insinuated that Brother Sewell was an agent of the devil, and in his closing speech he brought up new material to which Brother Sewell could not reply. He is certainly as fine a dodger as I ever heard (*G.A.*, October 18, 1906, p. 671).

J.R. and the people at Taft were pleased with the way Sewell defended the truth, and the gentlemanly way he conducted himself during the debate. Sewell had won the hearts of the Taft congregation and made a lifelong friend of J.R.

His last report for 1906 was an obituary of a dear friend of his, Brother R. H. Bryan, who was a member at Toney. It was Bryan who was partly responsible for J.R. ever going into the Toney community and preaching. J.R. had known Bryan ever since he had been in the Fayetteville area. Bryan was the first person ever baptized by Grandville Lipscomb. That event took place on Swan Creek, Lincoln County Tennessee, in the mid-1870's. J.R. conducted his funeral at the Old Bryan Family Cemetery in Lincoln County, Tennessee, on October 23, 1906. J.R. stated that there was "a large concourse of relatives and friends." He described Bryan as being "true to the cause of Christ" and that he "seemed to enjoy gospel preaching as much as any man I ever knew" (*G.A.*, Nov. 22, 1906, p. 748).

With the publishing of this obituary J.R.'s work for the year was closed, except his regular Sunday appointments. It had been a very productive year for his work in the Kingdom of God, and J.R., for once, seemed to be pleased with the results.

1907 began with J.R.'s health so much improved that he was regularly engaged in the ministry of the word (*G.A.*, Jan. 17, 1907, p. 37). At some point, either during December of 1906 or January of 1907, someone requested J.R. to give full details of the Sewell-Haysmer debate at Taft. It may have been the editors at the *Advocate*. J.R. complied and his first part of the report was published in the *Gospel Advocate* on February 7, 1907, on page 96; the second was February 28, 1907, on page 141; the third was March 28, 1907, on page 203; and the final report was on April 25, 1907, on page 266. These reports were a summary of the arguments made by Sewell and by Haysmer. With the end of the final report, J.R. wrote: "This closes what I shall say of the discussion, I have tried to do justice to both" (*G.A.*, April 25, 1907, p. 266).

Early in the month of May, the news had made its way from Iron City, Tennessee to J.R. and Mary that Sister Sarah Ann Wade had died. She was John Dickie Wade's second wife, and Chappell Wade McQuiddy's mother. She had lived the last fifteen years of her life in almost total blindness. She and John D. had been chartered members at Wades Chapel (Antioch, later Iron City Church of Christ). Her memories were precious to the Bradleys, as they were in her home many times. C.E. Holt of Iron City sent the report to the *Gospel Advocate* (*G.A.*, Feb. 28, 1907, p. 142). She was buried beside her beloved husband in the old Wade Family Cemetery, in sight of the house where she had lived most of her life. This ground was sacred to J.R. because so many of his friends were buried there. One may remember that in September of 1902, when J.R. was engaged in a meeting at Iron City, he made a visit to the old cemetery and was greatly disappointed in the local people for not taking good care of the place (*G.A.*, Oct. 22, 1903, p. 687). He got them to help him clean it up and made them promise to keep it clean. J.R. loved visiting the cemetery to reminisce about old times with old friends.

His meeting schedule was underway by the end of July. His first reported meeting was at Toney, Alabama. The meeting was conducted by J.R. and A.H. Rozier of Fayetteville. There were three baptisms and one restoration, and another placed membership. Bradley reported large audiences were in attendance. The meeting was in progress from the fourth Sunday of July and ended on the first Sunday night of August. While the meeting was in progress, a Brother A. L. Dixon was conducting a small singing school for the Tony brethren. Anybody who loved singing was a friend of J.R.'s. J.R. said the singing school and Brother Dixon were "a help to our meeting" (*G.A.*, Sept. 5, 1907, p. 557). From Toney, J.R. would travel to Wells Hill, which was northeast of Toney a few miles.

Bradley had written that the meeting at Toney had ended on the first Sunday night of August (August 4th). The only way that this was possible, was for either Rozar, who was engaged in three meetings with J.R., to begin the meeting at Wells' Hill and be joined by J.R. later; or J.R. began at Wells' Hill and Rozar finished at Toney. That is the only explanation that works chronologically. At Wells' Hill there were six baptisms reported. The meeting was finished there on Sunday morning and then Bradley and Rozar traveled nearly fifteen miles to Molino, which was north of Fayetteville (*G.A.*, Sept. 5, 1907, p. 557). A note of explanation is needed concerning the spelling of A.H. Rozar's name. It appears, very often in the Advocate with the spelling "Rozier," However, when J.R.'s reports include something about Rozar, it is always spelled "Rozar," It seems that either spelling was used by the people around Fayetteville. T.C. Little spelled the name "Rozier" (*G.A.*, April 26, 1906, p. 265). This writer knows of a case where two brothers spell their name differently. One spells his name "Green" and the other spells his "Greene," Maybe this was the case with A.H. since J.R. had baptized him out of the Baptist, and immediately began work with him; surely J.R. knew how to spell the name. The two working friends found no rest upon leaving Wells' Hill but began their next meeting at Molino.

The report on the meeting at Molino was very short and to the point. It read as follows: "Brethren J.R. Bradley and A.J. Rozar closed a meeting at Molino, Lincoln County, Tennessee, on Monday night, August 19th, with four baptisms" (*G.A.*, Sept. 5, 1907, p. 549).

On this same page of the *Advocate*, J.R. learns of the death of the widow of one of his old Mars Hill teachers. Belle Gresham Ott was the sister to T.B. Larimore's wife Esther and the wife of J.C. Ott. Sister Ott was well known by J.R. and all the "Mars Hill boys," That was two of J.R.'s friends from his early days which had crossed the cold river of death (*G.A.*, Sept. 5, 1907, p. 549). He would stop at times and remember the "good old days" and then get back to the task at hand. Throughout September he would hold meetings and fill regular appointments. J.R.'s preaching field was getting spread over a wider area by the end of the third quarter of 1907.

In October J.R. deviated from his usual pattern of work to travel near Corinth, Mississippi. On October 11, he boarded a train in Fayetteville and headed for Corinth, Mississippi, the nearest station to his destination. He arrived in Corinth on Saturday morning the 12th. His brother-in-law met him at the station. J.R. had two sisters living north of Corinth, just over in McNairy County, Tennessee, and only about five miles apart. His oldest sister was Lucy A.F. Bradley (Lawrence Co., Tenn., census Records-1860, p. 113). She was nearly two years older than J.R. and was the oldest child in his family. His youngest sister was Mary. It had been nearly 25 years since J.R. had seen these two sisters. They had married and moved to west Tennessee several years before. With J.R. living at Fayetteville, they lived more than one hundred miles apart. This explains the reason they had not seen one another in so long.

It appears that J.R.'s sisters had invited him to come to McNairy County and preach. His oldest sister, Lucy, had not obeyed the gospel. It could have been upon Mary's invitation that J.R. traveled so far to preach.

On Sunday morning, October 13th, he preached in a new meetinghouse and schoolhouse nearby, in a little village called "Tula," He preached two sermons with dinner on the ground (*G.A.*, Nov. 21, 1907, p. 752). At the end of the evening sermon Lucy came forward and made the good confession and was baptized on Tuesday, October 15. J.R. wrote: "I was certainly much rejoiced to see this" (*G.A.*, Nov. 21, 1907, p. 752). He preached three more times after Sunday, and only then at night. He then traveled about two miles from Tula to Michie, Tennessee. It had been named after the Michie family. There were several Michie families living in the vicinity. He preached twice on Sunday, October 20th. They also had dinner on the ground. The services at Michie were largely attended.

Between services at Tula and Michie, J.R. was taken to visit the Battlefield at Shiloh. That was a very moving experience to him, especially when he read some of the inscriptions on the monuments. He was very saddened when he learned that more than twenty-three thousand men died in that two days' battle. His mind wandered back to that fateful day of April 6, 1862, to a bluff top in Lawrence County, Tennessee, near Iron City, where he and his two younger brothers sat and listened, all day, to the distant roar of the cannon from the fields of Shiloh. He said that he and his brothers missed dinner to listen to the thunderous roar in the distance. After he finished at Michie, he boarded a train on October 21st, and began his long journey homeward to Mary in Fayetteville (*G.A.*, Nov. 21, 1907, p. 752). Before leaving, he promised the brethren at Tula and Michie, that he would come back next year and hold meetings for them. He wrote:

> I have promised to visit those people next year, if I am living and am able to preach, and hold several meetings in that country, beginning on the third Sunday in July. It is left with Brethren Wade, Michie, Springer, and possibly others, to arrange for the work. I am to spend a month or longer, if necessary, in that country. My sister was the only addition I had while there. They think of erecting a house of worship there in the near future (*G.A.*, Nov. 21, 1907, p. 752).

The new house of worship J.R. mentioned was no doubt for the brethren at Michie, as Tula already had a "new church and schoolhouse," or maybe they wanted their own house of worship, so they would not be hindered by school schedules. It was common in many communities where schoolhouses were used by churches also. Usually daytime school interfered with gospel meetings when preaching was done daytime as well as nighttime.

17

Deaths and a Debate

We have no record of J.R.'s work for the year of 1907 after he returned from west Tennessee. We can assume that he continued his regular appointments, and perhaps other gospel meetings before the year ended. There was no indication that J.R. had any illness. He did, however, write an article for the Advocate entitled "Led By The Flesh Or The Spirit-Which?" (*G.A.*, Nov. 28, 1907, p. 755). He also moderated a debate for A.H. Rozar and reported it in the first issue of *Gospel Advocate* for the year 1908. J.R.'s report was as follows:

> Brother A.H. Rozar of the church of Christ and Elder B.L. Towery, of the Primitive Baptist Church met in debate on Monday, December 16, at Pleasant Grove, a Primitive Baptist Church, in Lincoln County, Tenn. The discussion continued for four days. Each affirmed for two days the church of which he is a member is "apostolic in origin, doctrine, faith, and practice." Brother Rozar made about the usual arguments made in discussion by the brethren. It was my pleasure to be present and act as Brother Rozar's moderator. I certainly believe that his arguments were invincible. Elder Towery had a lot of papers published by his brethren and a Primitive Baptist history, and read very freely from them on "Baptist succession," as it

is called. Brother Rozar reminded him and the audience of the fact that he had agreed to prove his church to be "apostolic" in origin, doctrine, faith and practice, and not "historic" in these or any other respect. Elder Towery was very nervous and hard to please all through the debate. Brother Rozar proceeded to ask several questions, and Elder Towery stopped him at once, claming that moderators should not allow Brother Rozar to ask them. We thought then, and still think, that Elder Towery objected because the questions were such that he could not answer them (*G.A.*, Jan. 2, 1908, p. 13).

J.R. gave several questions that Towery would not attempt to answer. Rozar and Bradley consented to let Towery off the hook and not answer them. Towery's efforts to manipulate the debate continued. He even interrupted Rozar while Rozar was speaking (which was against the rules for debating) and asked him a question. J.R. wrote this interruption in its entirety:

He asked Brother Rozar, while Rozar was speaking, if God ever said a thing should be done and still it was not done. Brother Rozar answered, "Yes," but that he could not just then remember where the passages were and asked if anyone present could give chapter and verse of such a passage. I at once called out: "Yes; Jonah 3:1-10," To this Elder Towery objected. He reproved me for giving the passage to Brother Rozar, and sharply said to me: "I am not debating with you, am I?" At the same time his son was getting him passages and had been helping otherwise all the time. I trust that the discussion will do good. A Methodist preacher, named "Brown," who heard it all, said more than once that Towery was defeated. (*G.A.*, Jan. 2, 1908, p. 13).

J.R. thought fairness was each man having an equal advantage. Towery, however, thought otherwise.

From the foregoing discussion, we can see that Bradley was well versed in scripture. Towery was probably glad that he was debating Rozar instead of J.R. With the close of this debate, we know nothing else of J.R.'s activity in 1907. The year had been one of the better years for J.R., but Mary's health was slowly deteriorating. This remained a constant concern for J.R., and it did affect, to some degree, the distances that he would travel away from home and his beloved Mary. The Rozar-Towery debate occurred not far from his home, thus he was able to attend the entire debate and serve as Rozar's moderator. Even though J.R. had sent the report in December, it would not be published until January 2, 1908. J.R.'s first correspondence to be published in 1908 was, as we have already seen above, the Rozar–Towery debate that occurred during December 1907. His next correspondence was a short tribute to his old friend and preaching companion, Thomas L. Weatherford of Limestone County, Alabama. He wrote:

> In a recent issue of the Gospel Advocate, Brother W. Derryberry, of Athens, Ala., made the announcement that Brother T.L. Weatherford had died suddenly. Brother 'Tom,' as he was familiarly called was a good man, a faithful preacher, and an earnest Christian. He boarded with us at Mars Hill during the term of 1878. He assisted me in several meetings after we left school, and he was certainly a companionable man and a true yokefellow. May our Father bless the surviving members of his family (*G.A.*, March 26, 1908, p. 197).

Weatherford and J.R. had held several meetings together in Limestone County, Alabama, and Giles County, Tennessee, especially at Shoals Bluff. Weatherford's death was a great loss to J.R. and a reminder of his own advancing age. Weatherford was a little more than eight years older than J.R. These two men had baptized many people in their work together. When J.R. would visit Limestone County, he would visit his old friend's grave at the Pleasant Point Cemetery in the western part of the county.

J.R.'s first report on his evangelistic work since November of '07 did not come to the Advocate until the latter part of March of

1908. The reason for so long a gap in his reporting is unknown to us. He may have been recovering from some illness he suffered during the winter months, or he may have intentionally not reported on his preaching appointments because he believed the work was just not worthy of a report. That would not have been the first time that J.R. had felt that way. That type of behavior usually came from J.R. when he was depressed; however, he had not shown tendencies for depression that year. From J.R.'s past track record, we know that he preached somewhere every chance he got. We can safely assume that he was preaching, even though he did not report it.

His first actual report of his evangelistic work was, however, not on what he had done, but rather what he planned to do in the future. He wrote concerning his plans:

> I hope to begin a meeting in the Lincoln County tent on the first Lord's day in July, at or near the State line, on the Huntsville—Fayetteville road, about twelve miles from Fayetteville, Tenn. This meeting will likely continue for about two weeks. On the third Lord's day in July I am to begin a meeting at or near Michie [pronounced Mickey], McNairy County, Tenn., and will conduct meetings in that part of the country for a month or six weeks, at such places as may be arranged by Brethren Michie, Wade, Springer, and Rogers, who live in that district. After those meetings I hope to begin a meeting at Gnat Grove, near the corners of Lincoln, Giles, and Marshall Counties, to continue for a week or ten days. I can arrange to hold some other meetings after the close of this meeting. I would be glad to hear from brethren who desire my assistance. Address letters to me at R.F.D. Fayetteville, Tenn. (*G.A.*, April 2, 1908, p. 213).

These were J.R.'s projected plans for the meeting season of 1908. Most of them would be in his immediate vicinity, except for his projected work in West Tennessee; but that would be after his work near the Alabama – Tennessee State Line.

He began the tent meeting at the State Line Community at the Quick Schoolhouse. The following report was written by J.R.:

> Beginning on Saturday night before the first Lord's day in July and closed on the second Lord's Day night. I held a meeting with a very faithful little band of Christians, and their neighbors and friends, near the State Line on the Huntsville – Fayetteville road and near the Quick schoolhouse, in Lincoln County, Tenn. In this meeting we used the Lincoln County gospel tent. We are sure that the success of this meeting is largely due to the faithfulness of the small congregation of earnest brethren and sisters who worship 'as it is written' in God's Book and who let their light "so shine" in that community. Brother Tom Petty led the singing and did it well. This is my first protracted meeting this year. During this meeting I preached sixteen sermons, and I think I stood the work well (*G.A.*, Aug. 6, 1908, p. 508).

This work at the State Line soon became an established work and they now had their own meetinghouse. The congregation is still a viable congregation in 2010. The meeting, for some reason, did not last the full two weeks as J.R. had announced in the April 2 issue of the *Advocate*, but J.R. was pleased with the results. He had baptized seven persons at that place.

Another observation is here worthy of mention. J.R. had written in this report that he thought he had stood the work well, which possibly indicates that he had been sick earlier in the year. That may be the reason that his reports did not mention evangelistic work between October of '07 and July of '08, which was his State Line meeting.

From the meeting near Quick Schoolhouse, near the State Line, J.R. went to Toney, Alabama, for a meeting (*G.A.*, July 30, 1908, p. 485). Toney, Alabama, was situated just a few miles south-west on the Pulaski-Huntsville road. J.R. was aided in that meeting at Madison's Cross Roads, Toney, Madison County, Alabama, by A.J. Rozar (*G.A.*, Aug. 13, 1908, p. 517). J.R. had announced that Rozar was going to work with him in six meetings after the State Line meeting (*G.A.*, Aug 13, 1908, p. 506). They had two persons. They had the largest attendance during that meeting they ever had at that place.

From that meeting Rozar and Bradley went to Molino, Lincoln County, Tennessee (*G.A.*, Aug 13, 1908, p. 506). They gave a report of the results at Molino, which was in the August 27 issue of the *Advocate*. It read as follows:

> Our meeting at Molino, which began on the first Sunday in this month [August], closed on the second Sunday night. We had splendid audiences all the time, not withstanding the excitement over the election, with much rain and mud to hinder. I have been in several meetings at Molino in a period of about twenty years, sometimes by myself and sometimes with other preachers. This is the only one during which we had no additions at all. I hardly think the preachers and the preaching were the only cause of having no additions this time. Brother A.H. Rozar, of Fayetteville, assisted us in this meeting, and his sermons were strong and scriptural. The brethren, and also some of the outsiders, expressed themselves that the efforts of the writer were passably good. This congregation, as a whole, is not working as it should (*G.A.*, August 27, 1908, p. 559).

It is interesting that J.R. devoted so many lines to the Molino meeting with no visible results. It was disappointing to him since he had helped establish that congregation years before.

In August he had written to the *Advocate* in a kind of tribute to M.N. Moore, formerly of Lynchburg, Tennessee and sent a copy of a letter that he had sent to Bradley. He wrote:

> The accompanying letter was written to me by that venerable soldier of the cross, M.N. Moore, just before he died. Please publish it in the Gospel Advocate. I did certainly love him for his work's sake and for his pure and almost spotless life. I feel

sure that I have been a better man by my association with him (*G.A.*, Aug. 6, 1908, p. 507).

Why J.R. waited so long in writing this tribute is unknown. Moore had died on January 5th, 1906 (Inscription on his tombstone in the Lynchburg Cemetery). M.N. Moore had been preaching in the Lynchburg area when J.R. first came to that part of the country. Moore had been a charter member of the Lynchburg Church of Christ. J.R. had befriended him and co-labored with him in Lynchburg. Moore's remains rest on the hillside, by his old friend T.J. Shaw, in Lynchburg, Tennessee.

J.R. also wrote in the same issue of the *Advocate* to E.G. Sewell. The occasion was an article entitled: "Those White Robes, What Are They?" Bradley said if there were more writers who wrote upon themes, instead of theorizing and faultfinding, the cause of the Kingdom of God would "be more appreciated by the people of God, and sinners would have by far greater inducements in putting on these beautiful garments" (*G.A.*, Aug. 6, 1908, p. 511). J.R. wrote the conclusion to the article as follows:

> Dear brother, allow me to say in this connection that I have always greatly admired your style, both in preaching and writing. May our dear Father spare you yet many, many more years, to your brethren and to the work of preaching "the unsearchable riches" of the cross. I would so much enjoy to again be permitted to meet you and hear you preach (*G.A.*, Aug. 6, 1908, p. 511).

It had been more than twenty years since J.R. had heard Sewell preach in a meeting at Campbell's Station, Giles County, Tennessee. From that time forward Bradley had admired Sewell's work, and highly regarded Sewell's studies of the Bible. This article and the tribute to M.N. Moore had been written before he left Molino. His next meeting was at Taft, Tennessee. (*G.A.*, Aug. 20, 1908, p. 533). Taft located on present day (2019) old Railroad Bed Road, about two miles north of the state line and about three miles north of Elkwood, Madison County, Alabama. Taft was also about six miles southwest of Molino. Thus, all of J.R.'s meetings for these protracted meetings had been preached in about a twelve to fifteen-mile circumference of one another.

From Taft, J.R. and Rozar traveled seven or eight miles northeast back toward the south rim above Fayetteville, to Wells' Hill, also called "Skinnem," Brother W. J. McAllister sent the following report:

> Brother A.H. Rozar, of Booneville, began a meeting at Well's Hill on the fourth Sunday in this month, and continued it day and night, except on last Saturday at eleven o'clock, until the fifth Lord's day night, with extra good crowds and good attention. There were only three additions, but we consider it a good meeting indeed. Brother J.R. Bradley assisted Brother Rozar in the meeting. Brother J.J. Bedwell conducted the song services, and he is a good leader (*G.A.*, September 10, 1908, p. 588).

By Rozar seemingly having taken the lead in the Wells' Hill meeting this may indicate that J.R. was growing fatigued from constantly being on the road and without rest for the past six weeks. He may have also been saving his strength for the trip to west Tennessee, which would occur just a few days after Wells' Hill. He began a meeting at Corder, Lincoln County Tennessee, on the fifth Lord's Day in August and continued until Wednesday, when he left for Oak Hill, Mississippi. Rozar finished the meeting (*G.A.*, Sept. 17, 1908, p. 597).

18

OAK HILL AND MALARIA

On September 7th, J.R. was reporting from Kendrick, Mississippi, near Corinth. Kendrick was just below the Tennessee-Mississippi state line. This is the area of Tennessee and Mississippi that J.R. would work for the next few weeks was just north and east of Corinth. He wrote:

> I am now at Oak Hill, near Kendrick. Prospects are fine for a good meeting. Only two sermons have been delivered. Two persons came forward at the first sermon. We aim to close the meeting on next Sunday with two sermons and dinner. There is a large membership here, but I am informed that they are not doing the work as they should (*G.A.*, September 17, 1908, p. 608).

Kendrick was the community established by Allen Kendrick and his family. His son Mansel had established the Oak Hill congregation at the old Kendrick home place. The home place sat about a hundred feet north of the Tennessee–Mississippi state line, and the church building sat about twenty-five or thirty feet south of the line. J.R. had preached there on his first trip to Michie, Tennessee the previous year. He loved the Kendrick family and the contribution they had made to God's Kingdom. One wonders if nostalgia and his respect for dead saints took J.R. to the cemetery behind the old meeting house. If so, there he found the graves of four gospel preachers who had pioneered the work in that community. They were Allen Kendrick; his two sons, Mansel and Allen R.; and Allen, the son of Mansel.

At the close of the Oak Hill meeting, a Brother J.R. Splann wrote: "Brother J.R. Bradley, of Fayetteville, Tenn. has just closed a week's meeting at Oak Hill with four baptized and three restored. Brother Bradley presented the truth faithfully, which so aroused the brethren to a sense of their duty that they will meet on the first day of every week here after" (*G.A.*, Sept. 24, 1908, p. 618). As was the case of many of the congregations of that period, Oak Hill had grown lax in their meeting every Sunday for worship. That may have been because they did not have regular preaching. It could have been just plain complacency, which seemed to be the case at Oak Hill, due to the remarks by J.R.: "I am informed that they are not doing the work as they should" (see the above). The thing that seems strange about the Oak Hill situation is that Allen Kendrick's son, Dr. Carroll Kendrick, was living at Kendrick, Mississippi, which was just a mile or two down the road from Oak Hill. He was a preacher, but of the more liberal type. He favored the use of the instrument in worship and the missionary societies. Why had he allowed the congregation, which was established by his brother Mansel, to drift into such a shameful state?

A week after returning home from Mississippi, Bradley developed malaria. He wrote: "I have been confined at home since September 22. My physician tells me that I contracted Malaria while in a meeting at Oak Hill, Miss. I have had about a dozen hard chills and as many fevers, but for three weeks I have been improving and hope to be at work again soon" (*G.A.*, Dec. 10, 1908, p. 789). The irony of all of this is that J.R. was holding the meeting at Oak Hill in the vicinity where Dr. Carroll Kendrick was living. Dr. Kendrick was, at that time, one of the world's leading authorities on the study and treatment for malaria. Kendrick had published several articles in various medical journals of his day on the subject. He wrote especially about the strain called "Tennessee River malaria," which was rampant in the Oak Hill area (*The Medical World*, February 1889, p. 65). It was in this very community that J.R. contracted the malaria. The malaria may explain why J.R. only held one meeting in the Mississippi–West Tennessee region. Back in April, J.R. had said that he would hold meetings in that region for four to six weeks (*G.A.*, April 2, 1908, p. 213). Even though his time table was off about two months from what he had originally planned to do, he would still have stayed the full length of time, if something had not hindered him. His symptoms could have been showing up in his preaching at the end of a hard week of preaching. That may have been what ended his trip to the west.

He did say in that same report that he had to cancel some appointments. He continued: "During this year I have been in seven meetings. In five of these meetings, I was assisted by Brother A.J. Rozar. I had to call in the appointments for four meetings, which I had agreed to hold" (*G.A.*, Dec.10, 1908, p. 789). A year that had started out with so much promise ended with desperation and winter. The cold winter was bleak and so were J.R.'s hopes. What would the New Year bring to J.R. and Mary? He could always write articles to be published in *Gospel Advocate*: that, however, was not what J.R. preferred. He loved preaching and that was his hope for the New Year.

1908 had ended with J.R. battling malaria, which he had contracted while in a meeting at Oak Hill, near Corinth, Mississippi. His doctor had partially confined him to his house. Obviously J.R.'s doctor did not have the knowledge concerning the malarial disease that Dr. Kendrick of Mississippi had. The good doctor in Fayetteville did not seem to help J.R. all that much; thus, his meager schedule for 1909 was totally centered on his illness. The malaria, coupled with J.R.'s other maladies, nearly incapacitated him for the entire year. He only reported two efforts at preaching for the entire year.

His first meeting was a one-day meeting at Ostella, near Cornersville in Marshall County, Tennessee. It was reported in the first May issue of the Advocate for 1909. It read as follows: "Brother J.R. Bradley, of Fayetteville, Tennessee will preach at Ostella, Tenn., on the fifth Lord's day in May. There will be two sermons and dinner on the ground" (*G.A.*, May 6, 1909, p. 561). It seems that Bradley sent the report, but it is highly possible that someone at Ostella sent the report. Nothing was reported after the meeting by anyone. We, therefore, do not know if J.R. had been well enough to meet the appointment.

His second appointment was not reported until much later in the year, in October. This report read:

> Brethren J.R. Bradley and A.H. Rozar recently closed a tent meeting at Stateline, Lincoln County, Tenn., with two baptized. There is a small congregation at Stateline meeting regularly at Quick Schoolhouse (*G.A.*, Oct 7, 1909, p. 1264).

The church at Stateline became one of J.R.'s best works. He always had a soft spot in his heart for the brethren at that place.

Most of the summer between these two reports, J.R. suffered many chills and fevers. They nearly stopped his work for that year completely. He was unable to farm. He could not hold meetings and Mary's illness was becoming much more aggressive. He must have felt completely useless during that time. He could not stay in the house very long at a time. When he came outside, his disease was troublesome to him, so he must have been very miserable during that summer. The season for protracted meetings came and went. Any meetings he had promised the previous year had to be cancelled or rescheduled until he was in better health. These were things that tested his patience. His Scotch-Irish blood made him restless, yet his faith in God gave him stronger patience.

He never ever doubted God's workings and in his simple faith he believed that God had better things for him.

In November of that year on a cold winter day, he received a visitor requesting that J.R. come to the house of G.L. Rogers, who lived in J.R.'s community. G.L.'s wife, Addie, had been suffering with consumption (modern day T.B.) for a long period. She had determined that she would be baptized, thus the reason for J.R.'s visit. She had been bedfast for a long time; therefore, her strength was very low. It would be difficult to baptize a bedridden person. J.R.'s farming came in good for something beside growing corn. He came up with the idea she could be baptized in a container much like a feed trough, only deeper. He wrote: "The writer baptized her in a box of warm water at her request on the date above mentioned (November 8, 1909). She had for some time contemplated obedience to our Savior's demands and had spoken of it to her friends often." (*G.A.*, May5, 1910. p. 566).

She lived until December 25, 1909. On Christmas day she was promoted to eternal life with her Savior. J.R. was well enough on the 26th to travel from home to the Rogers' house and there he preached Addie's funeral. J.R. expressed hope that Mr. Rogers would obey the gospel soon.

19

EVANGELISM AND FAMILY IN ARKANSAS

It appears that J.R. was not feeling much better until spring of the new year. His first report was the obituary of Addie Rogers, who had died December 25th and was not published until May of 1910. This means that for some reason J.R. had not sent the report until a few weeks before publication. This, also, may indicate that he was not feeling well until sometime in April of 1910. Whatever the reason, his work for 1909 ended with very little to report.

As has just been pointed out to the reader, J.R.'s first report in 1910 related to a funeral he conducted in December of 1909. His first report on his work for 1910 did not come until the first August issue of the *Gospel Advocate* for 1910. It seems that the summer had been kinder to J.R. than previous summers. He now seemed to be back to his "old self," He was enjoying preaching again.

His first reported meeting was at Molino, Lincoln County, Tennessee. A.H. Rozar helped J.R. in that meeting. It lasted from July 24th until July 31st, the fourth Sunday through the fifth Sunday. The results were seven baptisms (*G.A*, Aug. 4, 1910, p. 901). One could almost sense the excitement as he gave this report. He continued with the following words:

I am now in a meeting at this place (Elora, Lincoln County, Tennessee), with good audiences at night. This is the home of Brother J.J. Horton, who is assisting me in the meeting. Brother Rozar is now in a tent meeting at Mount Hermon, Bedford County, Tenn. Brother Horton and I will be in a meeting next week at Corder's Cross Roads (*G.A,* Aug. 4, 1910, p. 901).

Elora would become very special to J.R. in the future. That is where he eventually moved to live out the rest of his earthly sojourn. He and Brother Horton would soon become the best of friends and co-laborers.

J.J. Horton also reported on the meeting at Elora, but it was September before it was finally printed in the *Advocate.* It read as follows:

Brother J.R. Bradley closed on last Tuesday (August 2nd), a ten days' meeting (assisted by the writer), which resulted in eleven baptisms and one by membership. The church was greatly encouraged as a result of the meeting. Brother Bradley did some fine preaching. During the meeting Brethren H.A. Smith and J.S. Robertson were appointed elders to oversee the flock at this place, they both having proven themselves to be faithful and worthy of the trust imposed in them (*G.A.,* Sept. 1910, p. 1024.)

Horton's report shows that J.R.'s preaching had not been hurt much by his continuous illnesses. He could still do "some fine preaching" and the results prove it.

His next meeting would take him to the most distant point he would ever travel. Some thirty years before, his two youngest brothers, William and Alexander, had moved their families to Arkansas. J.R. had not seen either of them since that move. By the year 1910, both brothers had died. Their families, however, had invited J.R. to come to Arkansas and hold meetings in their neighborhoods. He accepted the invitation.

His intended plans were published in the Advocate, August 1, 1910, as follows:

> Brother J.R. Bradley, of Fayetteville, Tenn., is to begin a meeting at Hattieville, Ark., on Wednesday, August 21th. Thence he goes to Atkins, Ark. And after this meeting closes, he is to hold a meeting at a schoolhouse near Hattieville. It is expected that Brother A. Douglas, of Walnut Ridge, Ark., will assist in the meeting at Hattieville (*G.A.*, Aug. 18, 1910, pp. 948-949).

He followed through with his plans. On August 18th, after posting the above notice, he boarded a train in Fayetteville, Tennessee, and began his long journey westward to Arkansas (*G.A.*, Nov.3, 1910, p. 1221). After riding all night, he arrived the next day (which was Friday, Aug. 19th) at Atkins, Arkansas. He was met at the station by friends "according to promise," as J.R. had written.

While engaged in his series of meetings, J.R. wrote back to the *Advocate:*

> Our meeting here (Hattieville) closed last night with six baptisms. Brother A. Douglas, of Walnut Ridge was with us during the meeting. He has been preaching for this congregation for two years. He is held in high esteem by the Hattieville Brethren and sisters. My next meeting will begin next Sunday (11th) at Atkins, Pope County; next at Hale, beginning on the fourth Sunday in this month. Our people are greatly persecuted in this country. The congregations in this part of Arkansas are loyal to the truth. They meet every Lord's Day to worship, with or without a preacher (*G.A.*, Sept 29, 1910, p. 1096).

This report gives a view into what was happening in Pope County, Arkansas in J.R.'s day. The picture was not pretty, but there was a ray of light. Some souls were being converted and some saints were worshipping regularly as they should worship. From the report you can see that much work was needed in this section of Arkansas.

J.R. ended his reporting to the *Advocate* for the year with a letter entitled "My First Visit to Arkansas" which appeared in the November 3rd issue for 1910. Even though it repeats a few items from the previous report we endeavor to give his letter in full. It read:

On August 18th, I boarded the train at Fayetteville, Tenn., and on Friday Following arrived at Atkins, Ark., where friends met me, according to promise, and accompanied me over to Hattieville, a distance of fifteen miles, where on the night of August 23rd, we began a meeting. Brother A. Douglas of Walnut Ridge, Ark., assisted in this meeting. We closed the meeting on the first Sunday Night in September, with six baptisms. The church at Hattieville is strictly loyal to the truth. Brother Douglas has been preaching to this congregation for about two years, and is a good, plain gospel preacher. These brethren are strongly opposed by the denominational sects and prejudice. I have many relatives at Hattieville and at Atkins, who for years have been soliciting me to visit them and assist them in meetings, but this was my first visit. Many of these relatives I had never seen.

Our next meeting was at Atkins, beginning on the second Sunday in September. We continued it till the night of the third Sunday and closed with one baptism; but Brother Montgomery, one of the elders, baptized another person after the meeting closed. Here we had fine attendance and attention, and I feel sure that good was accomplished not measured by the number of additions. The Atkins congregation also is persecuted by strong denominational prejudice, but they seem fully confident that a "faithful continuance in well doing" will in the end win, as also do the brethren and sisters of Hattieville.

Our next Meeting as at a church called "Zion Hill," about halfway between Atkins and Hattieville, which began on the fourth Lord's day in September and closed on the first Sunday in October without a single addition. Here we had preaching only at night except Sundays. The crowds attending these services were large and attentive. The church here is small, but strong in faith and good works. They are sure to conquer if they continue faithful.

While I had three chills and fever while in Arkansas, I certainly enjoyed the time spent with these faithful Christians and relatives. I had two brothers in the flesh to move into Arkansas about thirty years ago. Both of them are dead. One of them left a large family. Some of them I had never seen. I agreed to return to Arkansas next year, if the Lord wills, and assist in meetings at those same places and at three others. We have announced to begin at Hattieville on the second Sunday in August. Brother Dr. J.J. Horton of Elora, Tenn., has conditionally agreed to go with me next year. I arrived at the Fayetteville depot on October 5th on my return home, and found my wife there with horse and buggy, ready to take me home (*G.A.*, Nov. 3, 1910, p. 1221).

Unbeknown to J.R., that was the last time he would be greeted by Mary's sweet face at the depot after an extended preaching tour. His next trip homeward from Fayetteville Depot would be a lonely one. J.R. and Mary always made good with the time they shared together. She would get excited listening to him as he told of the meetings, the souls saved, and of course of relatives who lived in distant places. Mary was always a great encouragement to J.R. She was always "glad in her heart that she could manage the worldly affairs of their humble home while Brother Bradley preached the gospel to a dying world" (*G.A.*, April 27, 1911, p. 495).

20

MARY'S DEATH AND BACK TO ARKANSAS

The year 1911 began with Mary's health constantly declining. This was the year J.R. had dreaded for so long. His health had improved considerably after his operation, but Mary's had continued to decline. For the past two years, she had gradually grown weaker and weaker. J.R. remained close by her bed through the bitter cold winter of 1910-1911. He knew the end was in sight for Mary. She died at home, in her own bed, on April 4, 1911, of cirrhosis of the liver. She had been on various medications for so long because of her illnesses that her liver finally stopped functioning properly. She had been attended by two brothers-in-Christ, who were good physicians. They were B.E. Noblitt, M.D. and A.L. Yearwood, M.D., both of Fayetteville, Tennessee. These men were not only doctors and brethren to J.R. and Mary, but they loved and respected the Bradleys.

Mary's obituary was written by the most unlikely persons; not just ordinary friends, family, nor a preacher, but her two physicians. Noblitt and Yearwood wrote of her:

> It has been our pleasure to know Sister Bradley several years and we have always found her kind, gentle and good in every way. She was left alone a great deal on account of Brother Bradley's work being away from home. She bore this patiently

and bravely and seemed glad in her heart that she could manage the worldly affairs of their humble home while Brother Bradley preached the gospel to a dying world (*G.A.*, April 27, 1911, p. 495).

This was a testimony to both—Mary's being supportive of J.R.'s work and to J.R.'s determination to try to reach as many souls for the Lord as he possibly could. The good doctors knew them intimately and saw these things in the lives of J.R. and Mary every day. They continued:

> Ordinarily it is not a difficult matter to write a biographical sketch. Here are the dates, one in faded ink in an old bible, the other glistening in the morning sun or evening stars on the cold gravestone. At little scrap of paper and there is no difficulty in grouping those things, throwing in a word of eulogy here and there, and sympathizing in a formal way with the friends and relatives and the community in general: but to give an adequate shape to even the slightest sketch of the submissive personality of Sister Bradley as, she would kiss her husband goodbye as he departed, and turn to go alone into the solitude of her own home, there to work, watch, and pray for the safe return of her beloved, not for one time only, but for year after year, with all its responsibilities- to express that is more than we can do: but we feel that in the language of Paul, she has "kept the faith," she has "fought a good fight" and has gone to receive her crown of glory.
>
> B. E. Noblitt, M.D.
> A.L. Yearwood, M.D.
> Her Physicians
> (*G.A.*, April 27, 1911, p. 495).

Her funeral was held in the Fayetteville church building. Brethren G. Dallas Smith and T.C. Little did the service. Brother Smith read the "Epistle of Paul concerning the resurrection." Brother Little having known Sister Bradley intimately for several years, spoke at length of her noble Christian life, her devotion to her husband, the difficulties necessarily encountered, and the inconveniences suffered from being a preacher's wife, having the care and responsibilities of the household matters during her husband's absence (*G.A.*, April 27, 1911, p. 495).

J.R.'s heart was broken, and he would never really get over her death. His love for Mary continued, even though later, he would marry again. His devoted love to Mary was demonstrated in his last will and testament in the words: "I request to be buried at Fayetteville, Tenn., beside my first wife; Mary E. Bradley" (Will Book 7, p. 67, Fayetteville, Tennessee). Throughout the summer, J.R. was very sad and lonely. He did not report any more work until fall of that year, leaving this writer to wonder if he just stopped preaching for a while.

The first report to come from his pen after Mary's death was written in September. The report was written from Hattieville, Arkansas as follows:

> Our meeting at Economy began on the first Sunday night in August and closed on Wednesday night after the fourth Sunday, with two baptisms. We could have preaching only at night, except the two Sundays, on account of the school. The greatest hindrance was the rain. It rained nearly all the time. The two confessions were right at the close. We closed at the water. People of the denominations, who are not in the habit of attending the meetings of those who claim to be Christians only, attended all the time, helped sing, and were attentive. We feel sure that much good was done in the meeting just closed. I will teach a class in music in Hattieville, beginning next Monday night. Our meeting at Hattieville will begin on the third or fourth Sunday in this month; the one at Atkins, about the second Sunday in October (*G.A.*, Sept. 21, 1911, p. 1078).

This trip to Arkansas kept J.R. so busy that it helped him to recover, at least a little, from Mary's death. It was good that he had made the trip to Arkansas the previous year. It kept him so busy doing the Lord's work that he did not have much time for grief. Mary's death, however, must have affected his preaching to some degree. That would only be human. It was good that he had family in Arkansas. This also comforted him. They had prevailed upon him to make this second trip to Arkansas and preach. It could not have come at a better time. Perhaps that was God's way of looking out for J.R.

His next letter reported on his meeting at Hattieville, Arkansas. He wrote:

> Our meeting here closed last night with a fine crowd and a fine interest. We had only two baptisms. I feel sure, as do the brethren here that a better feeling exists between the church of Christ and the Baptists. The Baptists are our most bitter enemies at this place. The preacher and most of his flock were out last night. Our brethren here are getting up money to build. I have baptized seventeen persons so far. I shall begin at Atkins next Sunday (*G.A.*, Oct. 12, 1911, p. 1174).

To J.R., his trip to Arkansas was worthwhile. Up to that point his preaching had helped bring about seventeen baptisms. To him that was success.

His final report from Arkansas was written from Atkins on October 12th. It was rather a short report and to the point. It read:

> Our meeting at this place closed with one baptism, which makes five of the Atkins' people I have baptized since I have been in the State, four others having made confessions at the water some time before the meeting. I have baptized eighteen in all since I have been in the State. I will remain here till October 23rd, and then go to Tennessee (*G.A.*, Oct.19, 1911, p. 1204).

From Atkins, he boarded the train for Fayetteville, Tennessee. No doubt he dreaded arriving there. This had been his first protracted meeting since Mary had died. The last time he had returned from Arkansas Mary met him at the station with the buggy. This time there was just loneliness to greet him. The gate in front of his house was not so inviting and the house was silent and cold. There was no fire burning in the fireplace and no warm food waiting on the table. The scene must have been one of greatest sadness. The saddest scene was the absence of a warm kiss and a gentle hug from the woman of his life, who had prayed so many prayers for his success and safe return. No doubt as J.R. walked the three miles homeward from the train station, he must have dwelled upon these things. His love and trust in God would give him the strength to survive the rapidly approaching winter.

It should be noted here that the plans that J.R. had made the year before for his work in Arkansas did not turn out the way he had intended. He was counting on his friend, Dr. J.J. Horton of Elora, Tennessee, to travel to Arkansas and work with him in his meeting (*G.A.*, Nov.3, 1910, p. 1221). Horton had "conditionally agreed" to go with him on his second trip to Arkansas. This did not happen. Dr. Horton, like Bradley, suffered with some serious ailments from time to time. He may have been in bad health at the time. J.R. never mentions Horton on his second trip. Horton's wife, also like Mary, was seriously ill most of the time. She may have been ill at that time. Horton, later, would have to terminate his work with S.H. Hall in Atlanta because of his wife's illness (*G.A.*, April 24, 1912, p. 396). Whether he or his wife was sick or not, something hindered him travelling with J.R. No doubt J.R. felt the weight of the years closing in on him and his friends. He was sick more often and longer. His friends were getting older and sicklier, just like himself. J.R. did, however, take this as a positive thought. It would not be many years from now that they would have a heavenly home where there was no pain nor illness. That was what drove him and his Christian friends onward. They longed for that time to come. This hopefulness was expressed time and time again in J.R.'s letters in expressions such as "May God Bless Us."

The year's work was not over just yet. He still had weekly and monthly duties to perform, old friends to encourage and maybe a wedding to perform. Then there was that duty that no preacher liked – funerals to perform. Whether a friend or a total stranger, a funeral was never an easy thing to do. J.R. ended his year with the funerals of two of his dear friends.

His first funeral after returning from Arkansas was that of Aunt Docia Gammil. Her obituary did not appear in the *Advocate* until February of 1912. J.R. had sent the report of her death. He had known sister Gammil and her husband T.E. for many years. She was known as "Aunt Docia" to the people at the Chestnut Ridge Church of Christ. She had lived there nearly all of her life. She had been baptized by W.H. Dixon many years before. Bradley wrote: "It was my privilege to enjoy her hospitality in her home, having preached for many years at Chestnut Ridge, her home congregation" (*G.A.*, Feb.15, 1912, p. 216).

J.R. counted the Gammil family among his best friends and sympathized with her family and friends. She was a woman whose faith could be seen in her kind everyday Christian living. It was said by someone in her community, "Aunt Docia is too strong in the faith" (*G.A.*, Feb.15, 1912, p. 216). J.R. explained that expression was meant as a compliment to Sister Gammil. He preached her funeral on November 15th, 1911. He preached the funeral of another sister in Christ in December. She was Fannie Bledsoe, the wife of T.N. Bledsoe. She had been baptized by T.J. Shaw many years before. She died on the morning of December 8, 1911. J.R. wrote the following concerning the details of her death:

> Mr. Bledsoe and his loving wife had just had breakfast on that fatal morning. He had just gone a short distance to his barn to feed his stock, when he heard her screaming, and while running back to their house he saw his wife come to the door all enveloped in flames. Just as he reached her, she fell out at the door. Mr. Bledsoe threw a bucket of water upon her, thus extinguishing the flames, but she was unable to speak. O how sad (*G.A.*, April 4, 1912, p. 433).

It seems they never knew how she caught fire. With open fire-places and old wood stoves there was always a danger for accidents such as this. That kind of death was common in those days. It was a cold December day and there would have been fire in the fireplace. She may have been standing too close to the open fire and ignited. J.R. stated as much in his report. He informed the readers of the *Advocate* that she had lived all of her in the Chestnut Ridge community, near the Church of Christ. She had been neighbor to Sister Gammil, who had died a few weeks before. J.R. said that he had enjoyed the hospitality of Sister Bledsoe's home, also. One of the blessings of a minister is to make many friends and enjoy good Christian hospitality. J.R.'s work was no exception to these rewards of the ministry.

With the two above obituaries, J.R. closed his reports on his labors for 1911, even though these last two reports were published in the early months of 1912. It appears that his usual wintertime maladies were more kind to him during that winter than in past winters had been. He would keep his regular appointments, read the *Gospel Advocate*, study his Bible, and perform his farm chores of feeding the stock and cutting wood for the fireplace and cook stove. He was still tough and strong to do these kinds of chores at his age. What would the coming year bring?

1911 had been a bittersweet year for him. His loss of Mary and his success in Arkansas was quite a mix for J.R. One thing J.R. had learned through the years was that no matter how alone he might feel without Mary, God had promised to be with him wherever he might lay his head. That kept him going and looking forward to the approaching New Year and more opportunities to preach to the lost.

21

Work Along the State Line

J.R., apparently, had many studies during the winter, as is evident in the following writing:

> Brother Sewell: What "Sabbath" is referred to in John19: 31 that is called "a high day?" (2) Why is it called "a high day?" (3) What "Sabbath" is mentioned in Lev. 23: 11? (4) Does the expression, "three days and three nights" (Matt. 12: 40), mean full days and nights? Fayetteville, Tenn. J.R. Bradley. (*G.A.,* January 18, 1912, p. 70)

The New Year did not begin the way J.R. had wished. The one and only report on his work for that year was published in the *Advocate,* for October. He reported the following:

> My first meeting began on the first Sunday in August at Friendship, Lincoln County, Tenn. Brother B.F. Hart, of Petersburg, assisted us for almost a week. We closed on Wednesday night after the second Sunday at the water, with only one confession and baptism. We were hindered much on account of rain and wheat thrashing (*G.A.,* Oct. 24, 1912, p. 1173).

Friendship had never been mentioned before by J.R. as one of his preaching points. He described B.F. Hart (he was a Mars Hill College boy, also) as the circuit preacher for Friendship. He wrote that "Brother Hart preaches monthly for these dear people. He is held in high esteem there, and much good must surely grow out of their united efforts (*G.A.*, Oct. 24, 1912, p. 1173). J.R. may have known Hart from their Mars Hill days, even though they were not there at the same time. He never says if they had met before.

He held his second meeting of the season at an undisclosed location in Madison County, Alabama. His report stated:

> My second meeting began on the third Sunday in August under a brush arbor in Madison County, Ala, and closed on the fourth Sunday, only one from the Cumberland Presbyterians, who claimed that he had been "baptized" for all there is in baptism. Did we do right in receiving him? Rain hindered much in this meeting (*G.A.*, Oct. 24, 1912, p. 1173).

We do not know what became of that effort at planting a church in this Madison County community. Nor do we know who invited him to come and hold this meeting. There may be some church there today (2019) because of this effort, but we have no documents to say one way or the other.

His third meeting was held at Taft, Tennessee. This work was begun by J.R. a few years before. It was only about three miles up the railroad from Elkwood and about four miles from Toney or Madison Cross Roads. These two works had also been begun by J.R. The Taft meeting had begun on the first Sunday in September and continued eight days. This resulted in three baptisms. J.R. described the meeting as follows: "Brother G. Dallas Smith, of Fayetteville, came down and preached one fine sermon for us in the beginning of the meeting. The writer has done much preaching at Taft, but we had the largest attendance all through this meeting we have ever had there (*G.A.*, Oct. 24, 1912, p. 1173). You may recall that J.R. had planted the church at Taft as a brush arbor meeting some years before. Taft was one of his favorite places to preach.

From Taft he travelled almost due west into Limestone County, Alabama, to Reunion. This congregation had been planted by J.H. Dunn many years before. The meeting was described as follows:

> Our fourth meeting began on the third Sunday in September at Reunion, Ala., and closed on the fourth Sunday, with one baptism, one from the Baptists, and four restored. We held a meeting at Reunion sixteen years ago and baptized twenty-one. At our recent meeting there we had large crowds all the time (*G.A.*, Oct. 24, 1912, p. 1173).

The good old days had come and gone. It had become more difficult to convert people in meetings at that period. This, however, perplexed J.R. to think that some people would not be moved to conversion by the preaching of the pure simple gospel of Christ

His fifth and final protracted meeting for the year was at Elkwood, Alabama, just below Taft, Tennessee. This meeting began on the first Sunday in October and closed eight days later. J.R. reported nine baptisms and one restoration at that place. He said: "None of our preachers of the church of Christ had ever preached there" (*G.A.*, Oct. 24, 1912, p. 1173). Good audiences attended every night of the meeting. He further stated that "this is a fine opening for evangelistic work," He promised to return for monthly appointments in the coming year. In passing he stated that his health was fine and was thankful to God for it. His closing line in his letter was: "May the Lord bless us all. Success to the dear old *Gospel Advocate*" (*G.A.*, Oct. 24, 1912, p. 1173). With this report J.R. bid goodbye to 1912. His hope was that he could be more productive in his work for the Lord in the New Year.

The year of 1913 turned out to be a good year for J.R. It began in a typical way. He had been ill "off and on" during the cold damp winter months, but spring revealed better times ahead for him. His hoping and praying had brought forth fruits of joy. J.R.'s son-in-the gospel and friend, A.H. Rozar of Lincoln County,

269

Tennessee, worked with J.R. much of that year. It was always good to be able to work with someone whom you had helped grow to the point that Rozar had reached. There were others whom J.R. had converted and helped train. One of these young men was converted early in the New Year and J.R.'s hopes were that he would be an able worker in the Lord's vineyard.

His conversion appears in J.R.'s first report of 1913. The first report was a full-length letter to the Advocate, and was as follows:

> We had Brother A.B. Lipscomb with us on the night of March 20. It was the first sight of him the writer had ever had. Come again Brother Lipscomb. We baptized Brother Earl Dixon, son of Brother J.A. Dixon, who is one of our Molino elders. J.A. Dixon is a brother of the lamented W.H. Dixon, who lived near Petersburg, Tenn., and died a few years ago. We are counting on Brother Earl to be of great help to the Molino congregation in many ways. He is a bright young man and seems to want to do his duty as he learns what it is. Our Taft and Elkwood work seem to promise much growth and good for the future. I visited Booneville, Tenn., and preached last Sunday night. We have several brethren and sisters in Christ there. They have no house of worship in Booneville, but a splendid schoolhouse. A few years ago, they met regularly upon the Lord's day, but for some reason have quit. Our home was with these dear people several years ago, and we learned to love them very much. May the dear old *Gospel Advocate* continue to send out the blessed word as it was taught in Christ our Lord, and may its editors, Publishers, and contributors all remain faithful to the "old paths" (*G.A.*, April 10, 1913, p. 349).

This report gave quite a bit of useful information about J.R.'s first part of the year. First, we learn of A.B. Lipscomb's visit to Fayetteville. It was the first time Bradley and Lipscomb had ever met. Lipscomb wrote of meeting J.R. in Fayetteville. He describes the meeting in the following way:

I also met Brother J.R. Bradley, an old-time friend of the Advocate and a faithful preacher of the gospel, who is known to hundreds of Advocate readers. (*G.A.*, March 27, 1913, p. 300).

We also learn that Taft and Elkwood seem to be his main preaching points for the year, as well as Molino. These three works had been established by J.R. Booneville, which was seemingly not a regular point for J.R. in 1913, had also been established by him. Now that he was older and ill more often, his labors seemed to be confined to keeping established congregations strong, rather than trying to establish new ones. That was still a needed work and he could do that well. He would, however, continue to do protracted meetings.

July found J.R. very much engaged in protracted meetings. The Advocate published J.R.'s itinerary for his meetings for the year. The schedule was as Follows:

Kelso, Tenn., July 28.-I will begin a meeting at Elkwood, Ala., on the third Sunday In August; at old Sharon, Ala., the first Sunday in September; at Reunion, Ala., the third Sunday in September; at Holland's Gin, the first Sunday in October; and at the Elk Cotton Mills, Fayetteville, Tenn., the fourth Sunday In October. These are all the meetings I have promised. Pray for us.

J.R. Bradley. (*G.A.*, August 7, 1913, p. 756).

Sometime before August 7th, Bradley and Rozar held a meeting at Corder's Cross Roads in Tennessee (G.A, August 14, 1913, p. 780). He and A.H. Rozar, his "son in the gospel," were together in several meetings that season. They held a meeting at Taft, Tennessee, where four were baptized. This meeting began on the third Sunday of July. Taft was located on the Nashville, Chattanooga, and St. Louis Railroad and on the Fayetteville, Tennessee and Jeff, Alabama spur. The road from Ardmore, Alabama, to Fayetteville, Tennessee, crosses the railroad at Taft. This congregation had been established by Bradley a few years before and is still an active congregation in 2019. They began plans to build a new house of worship in 2011. Their original house, which was built with the funds raised by J.R., still stands. It has only been slightly modified since it was built. From Taft, J.R. and Rozar went northeast to the church at Molino to hold their second meeting. It began on the fourth Sunday of July and lasted one week. Three precious souls were baptized at Molino (*G.A.*, Aug. 7, 1913, p. 757).

From Molino they traveled to Roland Hill and began a meeting on the first Sunday in August. The *Advocate* reported that the meeting at Roland Hill had good prospects (*G.A.*, Aug. 7, 1913, p. 757).

That meeting ran through the second Sunday night of August. J.R. reported only one baptism, which was not the result anticipated by J.R. and Rozar. The *Advocate* had published that the prospects for the meeting looked good; but that is not the way the meeting ended (*G.A.*, Sept.11, 1913, p. 877). This was a new work begun by Bradley and Rozar. Roland Hill was just off Prospect Road and about four miles southeast of Wells Hill Church of Christ, Lincoln County, Tennessee.

From Roland Hill they traveled about ten or twelve miles to the State Line community. The Huntsville-Fayetteville Road ran north and south through that community. They began the meeting on the third Sunday night of August, and it was to last an entire week. "Sickness," as J.R. put it, ended the meeting after four sermons. Some unnamed disease was rampant in that community. Rozar left J.R. after the first day (*G.A.*, Sept.11, 1913, p. 877). The August 14th issue of the *Advocate* reported under the heading: "When Last Heard From," that J.R. was at State Line church. It also said that the brethren had a new building at that place (*G.A.*, Aug.14, 1913, p. 781). Rozar went back there during the middle of the month of September and held a twelve-day meeting and had twenty-seven additions (*G.A.*, Oct. 11, 1913, p. 997).

J.R.'s next stop was about ten miles westward to the community of Elkwood. Elkwood was situated on the same railroad as Taft,

Tennessee, and a couple of miles from Madison Cross Roads. Elk-wood seems to be the result of all the work that J.R. had done in the Toney-Madison Cross Roads community of Madison County, Alabama, which in 2019 are the same community. The work at Elkwood seems to be the fruits of his labor in that surrounding area. The road that ran east and west through Elkwood (the State Line Road) and the north-south railroad made Elkwood an important country community and a growing one also. It was a prime place to begin a work. J.R.'s meeting began on the third Sunday and continued through August 26th, which was a ten-day meeting. He baptized seven people during that meeting (*G.A.*, Sept.11, 1913, p. 877).

He left Elkwood for home, which was about twenty-five miles away. He arrived home on the 28th. He planned to rest a few days before his next appointment, which was on August 31st at Elora, Tennessee. On Sunday he preached both Sunday morning and Sunday evening. Elora was in the southeastern corner of Lincoln County, Tennessee, and near the Alabama-Tennessee state line. That was one of his regular preaching points for 1913. He would live out his final days at Elora. He gave no report from Elora, on that occasion. From there he traveled back home to a much-needed rest.

His rest was interrupted by the death of a dear old friend of the State Line congregation. Early on the morning of September 3rd, J.R. and his friend A.H. Rozar left for the State Line community. The two men conducted the funeral of Brother Jesse A. Rogers late that afternoon. Brother Rogers had been the key figure in getting J.R. to come to his community and preach. That is how J.R. became affiliated with the State Line work. He did the first preaching ever done there by a gospel preacher. The result was the establishment of the Church of Christ at State Line. Rogers had been J.R.'s number one encourager in this work. J.R. wrote the following statement:

In his efforts to have the gospel preached to his neighbors, he
in years gone by and of recent years sacrificed much of his
hard-earned means and labor. Tent meetings have been held
near him, largely at his own expense. In the erection of our
new house of worship there (now called State Line), Brother
Rogers did more than any two others. The cause there would
long have gone down had it not been for the energy and untir-
ing zeal of Brother Rogers (*G.A.*, Jan. 1, 1914, p. 30).

To illustrate the love and respect held by the people of the State
Line community, J.R. attributes the death of Rogers to the reason
for so many of that community having been baptized within two
weeks of the funeral. He reported that Rozar conducted a meeting, almost immediately after Rogers' death, in which he baptized
twenty-seven persons (*G.A.*, Jan. 1, 1914, p. 30).

After the funeral, instead of returning home, J.R. headed westward about forty miles into Limestone County, Alabama to the
home of his dear deceased friend, Thomas L. Weatherford.
Weatherford and J.R. had been classmates and preaching "bud-
dies" at Mars Hill College and continued to work together until
Weatherford's death. Most of his remaining meetings for the season were in Limestone County. His schedule was published twice
in the *Advocate* (*G.A.*, Aug. 7, 1913, p. 756; Sept. 11, 1913, p. 877).
The remaining part of his schedule was as follows: "... at Old Sharon, Ala., the first Sunday in September; at Reunion, Ala., the third
Sunday in September; at Holland's Gin, the first Sunday in October; and at Elk Cotton Mills, Fayetteville, Tenn., the fourth Sunday
in October. These are all the meetings I have promised. Pray for
us" (*G.A.*, Sept. 11, 1913, p. 877). For some reason J.R. included
his schedule in two reports. As with most preachers, he may have
been hoping for more appointments before bad weather set in for
the winter.

His first appointment was at Old Sharon in Limestone County,
Alabama. Several efforts had been made by J.R. and others to establish a permanent work at that community but had failed. J.R.
was not the kind to give up easily. This time he hoped that the

work would be established permanently. The following is his account of that effort:

> Our meeting, beginning the first Sunday in this month [September], which was announced to be held at "Old Sharon," had to be moved two miles below Sharon, near a Baptist church called 'Charity," We preached fourteen times in a nice grove, once in the Charity Baptist Church, twice in the Kellogg Schoolhouse, and once in the "Light" Schoolhouse, and closed with ten baptisms eight from the Baptist, and two from the Methodists. All claiming their baptism were to obey God and was to get into Christ. I am at Reunion now. Pray for us (*G.A.*, Oct. 16, 1913, p. 997).

From the above report, twenty people were added to the core group at Sharon and would become the church at that place. One cannot help but notice the many times they had to relocate during this meeting. We do not know the reasons for these relocations, since he never reveals the reasons in his reports.

He also ended his report by saying that he had gone to Reunion, which had been one of Old Brother J.H. Dunn's regular preaching points for more than thirty years. Dunn had worked in Limestone County from 1848 until his death in 1877. The meeting at Reunion began on the third Sunday in September and continued for two weeks. The result from that meeting was ten baptisms, two restorations, and one from the Methodists (*G.A.*, Oct. 16, 1913, p. 877). From Reunion he traveled to Holland's Gin and conducted a brush arbor meeting. The meeting began on the first Sunday in October (*G.A.*, Oct. 9, 1913, p. 973; Aug. 7, 1913, p. 756; Sept.11, 1913, p. 877). He never reported the results from Holland's Gin.

We have no reports, directly, on any more work by J.R. for the remaining part of 1913. We do know, however, that he kept his weekly appointments. At one of these appointments at Taft, he challenged a "Holiness" preacher to a debate. The debate would be held at Taft and it would last for two days. The date was set for January 8-9, 1914 (*G.A.*, Jan. 1, 1914, p. 16). The "Holiness" preacher was Samuel Ford. Their subject for discussion was "Holiness" and "Sanctification." J.R. had written the letter on December 23, 1913, but it had not been published until January 1, 1914. With that letter J.R.'s work for 1913 was finished. That year had been one of his better years in many years.

22

FORD, ELORA, AND EMMA

By the end of 1913, J.R. was lonely for companionship. More than two years had passed since his beloved Mary had died. The winter evenings had grown very lonely and dreary. Sometime during 1913, J.R. had met Loula Emma Sloan of Madison County, Alabama and they were married in Madison County on January 5, 1914. At that time J.R. was 67 years of age and Loula Emma was 40 (*Alabama Marriages 1816-1957*, Huntsville, Madison County, Alabama). At that time Loula Emma was living at New Market, Madison County, a few miles south of Elora, Tennessee where J.R. lived. Elora was only two miles north of the Alabama-Tennessee Stateline, which was also the northern boundary of Madison County, Alabama. It is interesting to note that nothing was ever published in the *Gospel Advocate* about the marriage; especially since J.R. had reported so many marriages through the pages of the *Advocate*.

J.R.'s labors for the New Year began with the much-advertised debate between himself and Samuel Ford at Taft, Tennessee. W.J. McAllister reported the debate in the *Advocate* of January 22, as follows: "I attended the debate between J.R. Bradley and Samuel Ford. The debate passed off very well. We were highly pleased with the way it was conducted. The church was well taken care of by Brother Bradley" (*G.A.*, Jan. 22, 1914, p. 112).

It is interesting that J.R. never commented on this debate, which, for him, is not unusual.

Another preaching friend, A.H. Rozar, gave a full report on the debate. We include the entire report, as follows, to give a sense of what this public discussion was like:

> The debate between Brother Bradley J.R. Bradley of the Church of Christ, and Samuel Ford of the modern "holiness faith," is a thing of the past. This discussion was held in the Christian house of worship at Taft, Tenn., on January 8th, 9th. Brother Bradley affirmed the first day: "That all men and women who are converted, or sins pardoned, are at that time sanctified." Mr. Ford affirmed the second day: "That men and women are sanctified according to regeneration, or conversion, or sins pardoned and that all saved people or Christians, live lives of sinless perfection."
>
> Brother Bradley argued that in every instance where "sanctification" is used either in the Old Testament or New Testament, it is synonymous with "set apart," He read a great many passages from both Testaments to prove it, and also read from Thayer's Greek-English lexicon of the New Testament the use of the word "hagia" as agreeing with that idea. He also read Webster's definition of "holy," "sanctify" and "set apart" etc. as meaning the same. Mr. Ford agreed to this as applied to the use of those words in the Old Testament, but not in the New Testament. Brother Bradley certainly maintained the idea that all the church is sanctified and often spoken of as "a holy people" and "a holy nation," He certainly sustained his affirmation, if I am any judge at all.
>
> Mr. Ford did not define his affirmation, as did Brother Bradley. He tried to claim the measure of the Holy Spirit that the apostles received on Pentecost as proof of his "subsequent sanctification." But Brother Bradley brought down with telling effect the fact that the apostles were enabled to raise the dead, unstop the deaf nears, cast out devils, etc., but that power or measure of the Holy Spirit, and that Brother Ford and his "holy crowd" must do the same or give up the claim. Ford's moderator tried to stop Brother Bradley from making that

argument, but the presiding moderator ruled that Brother Bradley was correct. This certainly made them rustle.

We are well satisfied with Brother Bradley's defense of the truth and believe the debate will do good. Large crowds attended. Brother Bradley challenged Ford to meet him again on the same propositions or others. Elder J.V. Kirkland, Baptist, acted as chief moderator; Mr. Beddingfield, a "Holiness" preacher, as Ford's moderator: and the writer, acted in that capacity for Brother Bradley. Two Christian preachers (myself and Brother A.D. Rogers, of Elkwood, Ala.), were present, besides Brother Bradley. Two Holiness preachers were there besides Mr. Ford. The rules laid down in "Hedges' Logic" governed the debate. Everything passed off nicely and with all feeling good; so far as we could see. Ford just would have hour speeches. This wearied the congregation some. We believe that in all discussions the speeches should not be over thirty minutes. We pray God's blessing upon the efforts made: (*G.A.,* March 5, 1914, pp. 293-294).

One can tell that Rozar was highly in favor of J.R.'s work, and why not? It was J.R. who had converted Rozar from the Baptist and baptized him. J.R. was his "father in the gospel," Rozar understood J.R. better than his own family ever understood him. This writer grew up in the Bradley family and had never heard of J.R. Bradley until reading the small sketch by F.D. Srygley in his *Larimore and His Boys,* (p. 159). Then through curiosity he inquired of a great-aunt, who was one of J.R.'s nieces, and she told him a little about J.R.'s work as a preacher. We learn more about the man, James R. Bradley, through his friends than through his own family. What Rozar saw in this debate is very revealing about Bradley.

Let us take an inquiring look into this debate and learn about J.R. First: we learn that the challenge came while J.R. was on one of his appointments at Taft. This congregation was dear to J.R. because he had established it from brush arbor meetings and had even raised the money to build their meeting house. No wonder that he would want to conduct the debate at that place.

Second: We see his use of logic becoming more and more apparent as the debate developed. Srygley had remarked in his book that J.R. "attained a fair degree of proficiency in English grammar, logic, rhetoric, and a general outline of history" (F.B. Srygley, *Larimore and His Boys,* p. 159). As one reads through Bradley's reports, he can see the truth in Srygley's statement. Third: We see a new method of teaching that Srygley was not familiar with; at least on J.R.'s part. J.R. was using a Greek lexicon. Where did he learn enough Greek to use the lexicon? It must have come through hours of hard study on J.R.'s part. Not only was he using the lexicon, but he was using it correctly. His opponent had no real comeback for Joseph Henry Thayer's *Greek-English Lexicon.* J.R. had referred to the Greek in other places through his career, but never as devastatingly as with Mr. Ford. You may notice that J.R.'s challenge for a second debate went unanswered by Mr. Ford. As a matter of fact, Ford never responded in any way. This report from Rozar gives an insight into the man, J.R. Bradley.

It seems that not long after the debate J.R.'s health began to decline. He had to scale his preaching appointments back. He had no gospel meetings reported, which usually was the case when he had another period of illness. Another event that demonstrates the seriousness of his failing health is the writing of his will. By May 5, 1914 he had made out a will to help get his affairs in order. J.R. was always thoughtful of others and he demonstrated that fact by preparing his will to help his second wife. Our first knowledge of Loula Emma is in the "Will of May 5, 1914,"

J.R.'s concerns for Loula Emma's welfare are demonstrated in the following documented will, which is recorded in the Lincoln County Courthouse, Fayetteville, Tennessee. The will reads as follows:

This is to certify that I, this day, will to my wife, Loula Emma Bradley (Nee Sloan) all my real and personal property, everything I own, except enough to give me a decent burial, I request to be buried at Fayetteville, Tenn., beside my first

280

wife: Mary E. Bradley, my casket to be same in value as hers."
The casket (is) to be covered with a good flat stone, such as
that of my first wife.

I also request the tombstone be such as hers.

J.R. Bradley
Witnesses:
Oscar Parks
J.S. Robertson
(Lincoln County Tennessee Will Book 7 p. 67)

The will sounds so ominous, as though J.R. was expecting to die
at anytime. He would however, live another nine years. This tes-
tifies to the rapid deterioration of his health since his debate at
Taft in mid-January.

His final report for 1914, in the *Advocate*, supports the fact this
health was on the decline. He wrote:

> The fact that I have written nothing for the "cheerful page"
> does not indicate that I have nothing "cheerful" these days.
> No! No! Our little band here is doing well we think. I am
> preaching monthly at Lexie and here – only two regular ap-
> pointments. In the absence for the Baptist preacher, I was
> asked to preach for them here last Sunday. I had a large audi-
> ence. Dr. J.J. Horton also preached last Sunday to a good-sized
> audience at the church of Christ here. Pray for us – J.R. Brad-
> ley (*G.A.*, June 19, 1914, p. 676).

By his schedule reduced to two regular appointments per month,
one would conclude that something was hindering his work
schedule. Sickness is the most likely cause, as J.R. had been sick a
lot before this time. This would explain his "will" and J.S. Robertson's letter. They both indicate that, at least for this period of time
in 1914, J.R. was not his old self. The letter just mentioned was his
last correspondence for 1914. He held no meetings that year.

What had started off as another good year seemingly ended on
a sour note for J.R. The year that seemed to burst forth as a year
of hope and promise for him ended basically in June, for him, as

far as much work for the churches. Little is known for the last part of the year, except that poverty was a way of life for him during that entire year.

From the time of the debate in January of 1914, J.R.'s health had declined more and more. It was to the point that the brethren at Elora, his home, were becoming concerned for him. A.B. Lipscomb wrote under the heading "Plan to Help Brother Bradley":

> The brethren at Elora, Tenn., are planning to help our venerable brother, J.R. Bradley in a very practical way –that is, they put him in a position where he may help himself. There are hundreds to whom Brother Bradley has preached and many whom he has baptized who will doubtless be glad to have fellowship in this matter when it is presented to them in the letter that follows. The worthiness of this appeal cannot be questioned. Brother Bradley has labored faithfully, and many times at a great sacrifice, and those who have been the chief beneficiaries of his labors should heartily respond (*G.A.*, March 11. 1915, p. 244).

Lipscomb felt sure that the people to whom Bradley had ministered for so many years, and many times at great sacrifice to himself, would want to help him in his declining years. Lipscomb included a letter in its entirety, from J.S. Richardson, an elder in the church at Elora.

The following letter is a statement by an elder in the church at Elora, Tennessee. It reads:

> Dear Brethren: I take this method of making known the condition and wants – indeed, the real needs—of our venerable old brother J.R. Bradley, who lives here with us. Brother Bradley is now in his sixty-ninth year. He has been actively and constantly engaged in the gospel field since 1878 [since 1873], except a period of about three years' disability, caused by "gravel" or stone in the bladder. He was operated on by Dr. C.N. Cowden, then of Fayetteville, now of Nashville, Tenn. This was about eleven years ago. While he has been constantly

engaged since the operation, he has never fully recovered his former vitality and strength, though he is now strong in mind and memory and is doing all he can. He is preaching once per month for our little congregation, and we think his sermons are splendid. I am certainly acquainted with him and know his condition and all his needs and ask to place him before you. Just two, Brother Bradley and his wife, in their family (sic). Brother Bradley realizes the fact that he cannot now depend upon preaching for support or financial aid, as in days gone by. We are wanting (sic) to get him into a small business like a small stock of groceries or a little gasoline mill, or anything that would make bread for him and his wife – a business that is just and honorable. Now, then, let me say that our little congregation here is contributing to our aged brother practically everything that he gets, and that amount will not exceed five dollars per month. Our congregation is young and poor, and very small. We are appealing, not to those who are strangers and who do not know our old brother, but to those who know him, to those for whom he has labored, and to those who are now enjoying the fruits of his labor. Will you help us, dear brethren and sisters, to start our old brother in just a small business, so he can be at home, and also not dependent upon the evangelistic field and work? His wife is a splendid financier and a good woman. She and Brother Bradley own a nice little cottage here, with not a dollar's indebtedness on it. They are both willing to work at anything that is just and right. Can you help, and do so now? Brother Bradley thinks of work he has done in younger days in Lawrence, Wayne, Giles, Lincoln Marshall, Franklin, Moore, and Bedford Counties, Tenn.; also, Lauderdale, Madison, Jackson, and Limestone counties, Ala. He has done some preaching in Arkansas and Mississippi. Brother Bradley speaks of Brethren often and sisters, too, at all the places where he has labored. It is to you who know him we make this appeal especially but will gladly and thankfully receive help from others. Post-office address: Elora, Tenn.

Your Brother in Christ,
J.S. Robertson, Elder
(*G.A.*, March 11, 1915, p 244)

This appeal by Robertson just accents the love and respect the church at Elora, and other places, had for J.R. Apparently the brethren at Elora could see J.R.'s health deteriorating to the point that he needed permanent help. To his friends this was very clear. J.R. showed a degree of concern, himself, by having made out his will the previous spring.

The grave concern for J.R.'s well-being was further shown in a second appeal to the *Advocate*, by Robertson. One of the editors at the *Advocate* wrote a brief introduction to Robertson's second appeal:

> "Brother J.S. Robertson, an elder in the church at Elora, Tenn., writing in behalf of a faithful preacher of the gospel, makes a suggestion which is worth of consideration by the churches" (*G.A.*, May 6, 1915, p. 450).

The letter is as follows:

> Please allow us here at Elora to make an additional proposition to you regarding our old brother J.R. Bradley. You have, doubtless, read the letter which appeared in the *Gospel Advocate* of March 11, p. 244, regarding Brother Bradley. Our suggestion is this. Write Brother Bradley and have him visit your congregation and preach for you at least one or two sermons. He can give you any Sunday, except the first and second Sundays in May, which time he has promised Greenwood Church, near Etheridge, Tenn. While the fourth Sunday is his regular tie here with us, we will yield that time if any congregation should desire it. Brother Bradley has just returned from Liberty, near Belfast, Tenn., where he preached two sermons. They gave him thirteen dollars. Other parties up to that time had sent us ten dollars. This is all we have received so far. The brethren at Liberty, through Brother R. B. Cummings, one of their leading members suggest the publication of this letter, and ask me, as an elder in the Elora congregation, to make you this proposition. The Greenwood and Liberty brethren have accepted a visit each from Brother Bradley, and we think

possibly it will suit may other congregations to do the same. Springtime is now here, and Brother Bradley says he would be delighted to make a trip to many of our congregations. I saw our old brother this morning, and he is in good shape for preaching now, and agrees to visit you if you will call him (*G.A.*, May 6, 1915, p. 450).

With this appeal it appears Robertson had given up on the idea of getting a small business for Bradley. Only ten dollars had come because of the first appeal. This must have been disheartening to Robertson and the brethren at Elora, as well as to J.R. himself.

J.R.'s poverty was further highlighted by a lengthy letter he wrote to Elam at the *Advocate* in February. Elam published the letter in the *Advocate* in its entirety, as follows, in May:

Elora, Tenn. February 5, 1915, To the Editors and Publishers of the *Gospel Advocate*, Dear Brothers: I do certainly note with special care and interest your proposition to send the paper fifteen months, with a fountain pen, for one dollar and seventy-five cent. Please allow me to thank you heartily for giving me the paper so long. Yes, I wish I could take advantage of your liberal offer, but I just cannot do so. I have lost my fountain pen, and in accepting your proposition would not only get the best paper published and the pen, but also the twelve special numbers, which I want to enjoy so much. Please be patient a little while and let me give my reasons. (1) I am sixty-eight years of age, and past; (2) I have only one preaching appointment per month, which does not average five dollars to me per month; (3) I did not hold a single meeting last year; (4) I am in debt about fifty dollars for groceries and other things much needed; (5) I cannot pay the debts already contracted, and therefore cannot take the paper, not withstanding your liberal offer. Ask Molino brethren who worked for them at his own charges until they became a congregation, and begged money to build their house, and for twenty-five years continued to preach for them furnishing his own horse and buggy and "raised his own salary" on the farm: ask Taft brethren who held meetings in their community under brush arbors at his own charges, and then begged money for their splendid house and none for himself; ask Stoney Point brethren the same thing; ask Stateline (Lincoln County) brethren the same. Ask the elders of all these congregations who for thirty years has gone into these rural districts at his own charges, almost, all over Lincoln County, and some in other counties, and a lot in Alabama, and did not get enough to buy medicine for a sick wife. Brother Elam, will you please write the elders of especially the six congregations I have named, and see if I am telling the truth, even if it is on myself? No, no Fayetteville does not know what I have done, nor what I need. Yes, Fayetteville is a large congregation and did a good part by me some years ago when I had to undergo a serious operation for stone in the bladder, and I certainly am thankful to them for it; but I am sure they do not know of my work in the county like the elders of those churches. Ask Brother B. F Hart, of Petersburg (he knows it all); ask the elders at Elora; ask the elders at Chestnut Ridge – all in Lincoln County.

No. I cannot take the *Advocate*. I am completely "knocked out of the ring" by our younger brethren, who beg for themselves and "foreign missions" and never a word for poor old worn out and "knocked out" preachers.

Brother Elam, in your recent articles you certainly hit the "professional preachers" some good hard licks. Each one, no doubt, this he can justify himself, or "make believe" that he can.

Brother Elam, I will soon be behind a whole year on the good old *Advocate*. I can pay for this past year much easier than I could to let it run on. Please allow me to ask you to have the manager of the paper to stop it for me. I had rather have it than all the others, but I must have it discontinued. I have delayed this, trusting something in my favor might turn up, so I could pay for it. May God bless you all. Pray for your old brother.

J.R. Bradley.

(*G.A.*, May 20, 1915, p. 484).

The foregoing correspondence reveals the heart of a broken spirited J.R. Bradley. He had become almost bitter toward some of the older congregations, which were the fruits of his labors. Unlike Paul's plan for a laborer in the vineyard to eat fruit of the vineyard, J.R. had gleaned very little fruit from his fields of labor. He was in poverty and the churches who owed so much to J.R. for their existence had forgotten him in his old age. To J.R. that was totally unacceptable. He had hoped that maybe Elam's influence might convince these churches to help him in his time of need.

Elam wasted no time in defending Bradley and other preachers in the same kind of situation as J.R. He wrote an answer to a question concerning the "pay and hiring" of preachers. He wrote that a church was cursed that would not be fair in paying preachers a fair wage for their labor (James 5: 1-6). He pointed out that godly preachers would never set a price for their work. This placed them at the mercy of the churches. They did, however, hope for fair wages. He further wrote:

> If Christians were as much interested in the salvation for their own souls and the souls of others as in preserving the lives of their stock and saving money, they would do all in their power to preserve the health and lives of good and faithful preachers to sustain them and to prolong their days of usefulness. Certainly, they would never turn such old preachers out, like old horses, to die. Good and true preachers, loving God and truth and seeking the Salvation of souls, will preach and work on until death; but woe to the congregations and individuals who neglect them and fail in their duty to support the gospel (*G.A.*, May 20, 1915, pp. 487-489).

Elam explains that this answer also answers J.R.'s dilemma. Elam may have saved J.R.'s letter, which was written in February, until May 20th for the reason of getting the letter from J.R. and his answer to another person's (Ed C. Gregory) question in the same issue of the *Advocate* (*G.A.*, May 20, 1915, pp. 487-489).

Elam also added "Brother Bradley will receive the *Gospel Advocate*" (*G.A.*, May 20, 1915, pp. 487-489). Elam had a soft spot in his heart for J.R. and men like him, who had sacrificed so much to help the small country churches. No doubt, their Mars Hill days together helped in this relationship of love and respect toward one another. Elam's answer seemed to help J.R. to a degree; then maybe it was Robertson's letters, or maybe both.

23

NEWFOUND VITALITY

In J.R.'s next letter, he seems to reveal the facts that showed something had changed somewhat in his favor. He had written his next letter or had at least begun it on May 18. There is a possibility that he had finished it later, or maybe he wrote it all in one sitting. Either way he reveals that the Etheridge congregation had invited him to speak on the second Sunday, which traditionally had been a standing appointment with the Greenwood brethren (*G.A.*, May 6, 1915, p. 450). His first Sunday appointment had been kept at Greenwood. It seems that Greenwood had relinquished their second Sunday to Etheridge. There was always a close affinity between Greenwood and Etheridge. His visit to Greenwood caused Bradley to reminisce about his early childhood in that community. He reveals so much about his life that it is fitting to include his letter in its entirety, as follows:

> I spent the first and second Sundays in this month with the Greenwood and Etheridge congregations. Greenwood is in Giles County and Etheridge in Lawrence County. I think it was in 1883 – Thirty-two years ago – that Brother W.B. McQuiddy and I held a meeting in a little schoolhouse about two miles north of Greenwood, near the home of Brother J.R. Ball. The schoolhouse was called "Center Point." O, what a splendid

meeting that was! Old Brother and Sister Clifton, about seventy-five years of age, and many of their children, all married and with large families, except Miss Sarah, and many others outside of the Clifton family were added to the faithful. I remember that some of Brother Ball's children obeyed the gospel during that meeting. I also remember some of the Richardson family. There were only a very few members in that immediate community when that meeting began. Someone told me while on this trip that we baptized twenty-five in that meeting. Out of that meeting Greenwood was established. I think it was in 1890 that the new house was opened and named "Greenwood" because of the beautiful trees composing the grove in which the house was built. I certainly enjoyed a visit over there after an absence of twenty-three years. Many pleasant faces which I saw there in former days failed to greet me. They are gone to "the other side," Little boys and girls of twenty-five years ago now have families of their own and are beginning to show that the "corroding tooth of time" is doing its work with them. They all knew me. My father, John C. Bradley, lived in the Greenwood community from 1847 to1850, and ran a wagon shop. In 1846 I was born, on Aggnew's [Agnew's] creek, near Pulaski. I was, therefore, about one year old when we moved to "Dry Weakly" in 1847. There are some old people there now who remember my father and an uncle of mine, by the name of "Shade East," and their shop on the road. These are all happy reminiscences with me, and yet they are sad. Sad, indeed, to see the old house, the place of childhood. Now I wish to remind my old "yokefellow" and brother, W.B. McQuiddy, that he, too, is due them a visit. Go down there, "Brother Willie" (that's the way they speak of you) and have "a dinner-on-the ground meeting," and preach two sermons at least, and catch some the inspiration as in days of yore. You need a rekindling, I guess, of that inspiration (which such a visit would certainly give) of days gone by.

J.R. Bradley
(*G.A.*, May 27, 1915, pp. 531-532).

One can sense the joy and excitement of the "Old J.R." in this report. It always does one good to revisit old home-places and old friends. Even though a note of sadness may be found over loved ones and friends who have died, there is joy in rekindling old acquaintances and making new ones. To J.R. this trip proved that he was still loved and still useful to the "Lord's Kingdom," There is quite a difference between his letter of February 5, 1915 and this letter. It was as though two different people had written them; and in a certain kind of way two different people had. The first letter had been written by a man who felt neglected, rejected, and dejected. The second letter was written by a very happy man who still felt useful and loved by the brethren. If we of later times had to be subjected to the conditions in which J.R. had to live, we would probably react the same way he reacted. The Greenwood – Etheridge trip gave J.R. a new vitality which recharged him for the rest of his life.

The new vitality showed through in Bradley's next report. He reported of having preached for the congregation in Lawrenceburg on the fifth Sunday. He preached at eleven in the morning and in the evening. He stayed over in Lawrenceburg and worshipped with them on Wednesday night. Here he met J.E. Thornberry for the first time. He also met T.C. King. Both men labored with the Lawrenceburg congregation as well as surrounding congregations, some of which J.R. had helped establish. On the first Saturday night and Sunday morning of June, he preached at Appleton. This appointment was advertised in the *Florence Times* in Florence, Alabama on June 4, 1915, on page 3. This was a rare appearance of J.R.'s name in an Alabama paper. The advertisement read as follows:

> Rev. J.R. Bradley, of Elara (sic), Tennessee, will preach at the Appleton Church of Christ on Saturday night, June 5th, and at 11 a.m. and 2 p. m., on Sunday, June 6th. Dinner will be served on the grounds, and a cordial invitation is extended to everybody.
>
> (*Florence Times*, June 4, 1915, p. 3)

You can imagine that J.R. was not very happy over the title "Reverend" attached to his name in the paper.

In the evening, following J.R.'s appointment at Appleton, he traveled back to Leoma, which was a struggling congregation and preached for them. He wrote of them: "The Leoma congregation has a splendid new house of worship. I feel sure that a good congregation can be built up there, with proper effort" (*G.A.*, June 17, 1915, p. 601). He promised to return and preached to them on June 19-20 of that year. He also promised the Long Branch congregation to come and preach for them on June 26-27. This trip developed exactly like Brother J.S. Robertson of Elora, Tennessee, had suggested. The churches seemed to finally have felt the need to help J.R. They were letting him come and speak one or two days at a time, which was better for J.R. than holding one- and two-weeks' meetings. His health would not permit that kind of preaching at this time. This trip further strengthened J.R.'s faith that the brethren would try to help him.

He wrote the following about the brethren he had revisited, after so many years:

> On our trip to Lawrenceburg, Appleton, and Leoma, I met a great many old friends of the "long ago." I have done quite a lot of preaching over that county in schoolhouses and private residences. Tears flowed freely at the meeting of so many old friends of twenty-five and thirty years ago. I thank and praise God that he has permitted me to live to meet them again and pray that all may live so as to meet where there is no separation (*G.A.*, June 17, 1915, p. 601).

J.R. traveled around Lawrence County, while on this trip. He says nothing about preaching at Iron City or St. Joseph, but we are left to wonder if he also visited old friends and family members in the Iron City area. After keeping his appointments at Leoma (June 19-20) and at Long Branch (June 26-27), he returned home to Elora. His preaching at Long Branch must have rekindled an old spark at that place. They invited him to come back in July and preach in a nine-day meeting.

J.R. returned on Saturday, before the third Sunday of July, as was his custom. He spent the night with old friends and rested. Excitement must have been at a high pitch for J.R. It had been more than two years since J.R. had held a meeting and just a few monthly appointments at Lexie and Elora; and of late, some two-day appointments. To be back in the pulpit and to preach in a full-length meeting must have excited him greatly.

His last report for that year reveals some of his excitement. On August 24, 1915 he wrote the following letter from home in Elora:

> Our meeting with the Long Branch congregation, which began on the third Sunday in July, closed on Monday night after the fourth Sunday, with four confessions and baptisms, one restored, and one by membership. We preached fifteen times at the meeting house and two sermons at private houses for sick people. They have a nice little church building and a strong membership (though not very large) of loyal Christians. We are expecting to make a preaching trip into Mississippi during the latter part of the summer and early fall (*G.A.*, September 2, 1915, p. 890).

You can feel the joy in J.R.'s heart as he wrote this final report for the year. Unlike so many years before that had started out so well and ended so badly for him; this year began very badly and ended in a good way. Much of the change, no doubt, was due to Elam's article, the two letters from Robertson, and J.R.'s own pleadings. It appears the brethren had gotten the message about helping older preachers. At least, it seemed to have worked in J.R.'s favor. His last report even ended with expectations of a preaching tour to Mississippi.

The former report, however, was not the end of correspondence for J.R. in 1915. He wrote to E. A. Elam concerning some statements he had made upon the subject of David's throne and its connection to Christ's reign. He makes a lengthy comment and then asked some questions:

> "Brother Elam: Isaiah (9: 7), in speaking of Christ, says: 'Of the increase of this government and peace there shall be no end, upon the throne of David, and upon his kingdom, to order it, and to establish it with judgment and with justice from henceforth even forever. The zeal of the Lord of hosts will perform this.' The prophet in this utterance does not exactly say that Christ shall occupy the throne of David, but he very nearly does. In Acts 2: 30, Peter doubtless quotes, or has reference to. 2 Sam. 7: 12, 13, and to Ps. 132: 11, where we have God's oath and promise to David concerning his kingdom and throne. In Luke 1: 32, 33 we have the angel's announcement to Mary before Christ was born: 'He shall be great and shall be called the Son of the Highest: and the Lord God shall give unto him the throne of his father David: and he shall reign over the house of Jacob forever; and of his kingdom there shall be no end.' Paul says: 'For he must reign, till he hath put all enemies under his feet.' (1 Cor. 15: 26.)
>
> "Now, Brother Elam, I would like to ask some questions. (1) Is our Savior on 'David's throne' at this time? (2) Is he not on the throne of God at this time? (See Heb. 8: 1; 12: 3; Rev. 3: 21.) Please tell us about all these thrones. (3) He, it seems, will 'sit upon the throne of his glory' in the judgment. (Matt. 25: 31.) Is this not a different throne from the one he is now on? (4) We want to know, also, if the actual throne of David has been preserved through all these years, either in Jerusalem or anywhere else, so that Christ can come to it and sit upon it and reign as did David. J.R. Bradley.
>
> (G.A., December 23, 1915, p. 1290)

24

REVISITING FAMILIAR PEOPLE

We know nothing of whether J.R. got to make a third trip to Mississippi or not. His health, seemingly, had improved through the summer of 1915, but we do not know if it held out for him until autumn came. He had gotten to where he did not report this work as he had in "years gone by," We are left to wonder – Did he go to Mississippi or not? He never mentions the trip again, beyond the last letter of August 24th. We would like to think that his heart was cheered by making the trip, but once again we do not know. His hopes were that the coming year would be as good for him as 1915 had been.

The New Year found the Bradleys making the best of their situation. J.R. had only preached a few times at Lexie and Elora during that winter, with an occasional preaching appointment at other nearby congregations. His home congregation was becoming more prosperous with the cotton gins and saw mills expanding. Elora was growing in prosperity and in more citizens. That gave the Elora church opportunity to grow in the same way. J.R. and Dr. J.J. Horton continued to work together and preach monthly appointments at Elora. The prosperity had given the little church enough money to replace old worn out benches with badly needed new ones. E. Gaston Collins, a young preacher from the Huntland, Tennessee community, just a short distance north of

Elora, preached at Elora one Sunday and wrote: "The brethren at Elora are getting along fine. They are putting in new seats, which, when done, will give them a first-class house of worship" (*G.A.*, April 6, 1916, p. 340). That same building is still standing in 2019, and still houses the Elora Church of Christ. This congregation was Bradley's and Horton's pride and joy.

Apart from preaching monthly at Elora and Lexie during the winter months, J.R. had other ministerial duties. There was that occasional wedding and often a funeral for an old friend. His first recorded act for 1916 was the funeral of his old friend, John C. Hollingsworth of Huntland. Hollingsworth had been one of the prominent members in the Huntland congregation. He and J.R. had been friends for many years. In the afternoon of March 30th, J.R. received word that his old friend had died that morning and the family desired J.R. to conduct the funeral. The following day J.R. conducted the funeral and Hollingsworth was buried in the Huntland Cemetery (*G.A.*, April 6, 1916, p. 349). J.R.'s old friends and brothers-in-Christ were going home one by one. He knew his time was not long off in the future, but as long as he had breath in his body he would continue to work for the Lord.

His annual appointment at Greenwood came on the first Sunday in May. He wrote of this meeting:

> A large crowd gathered about 10:30 A.M and I am sure that for about thirty minutes we had as fine singing as I have heard in many a day, if not the best. Brother John Kincaid led that day, and he did it well. I think he is the principal leader in song at Greenwood. I tried to preach for about fifty minutes with the earnestness as in days of yore, and many old brethren and sisters remarked at the close: "Brother Bradley, we think you preach just as well as you did thirty years ago when you and W.B. McQuiddy were here, if not better." Of course, this made me feel good. We then had a bountiful dinner under the green trees, and rest for an hour, with handshaking and greeting. Many of the old-time friends who were there when Brother McQuiddy and I were there are gone. Then another service in

the afternoon closed my meeting at Greenwood for this year. They tell me that I have a standing appointment, for that time every year, as long as I am able to go (*G.A.*, July 20, 1916, p. 743).

It always thrilled J. R's heart to return to Greenwood. It was one of his special places, no doubt, because he had lived there as a child; but more especially because he and his dear friend and co-laborer, W.B. McQuiddy, had established that congregation back in 1883. It is of interest at this point to mention that neither Bradley, nor McQuiddy, nor did anyone else report the meeting that established Greenwood in the *Gospel Advocate*. We only learn the date of its establishment through later comments by Bradley upon other visits to Greenwood.

From Greenwood J.R. seems to have returned to Elora, since he mentions nothing of an extended visit with old friends. He, however, returned the following Sunday to Ethridge and preached in their morning and night services. He commented on the work at Etheridge: "We have a loyal congregation at Ethridge, and I heard no dissensions among them. They furnished me two good-sized audiences" (*G.A.*, July 20, 1916, p. 743).

The Ethridge congregation had originally been the Wayne Station Church of Christ. They had relocated less than a half mile northward and became known as Ethridge, due to the post office near it being the Ethridge Post Office. For some reason, Ethridge had a close attachment to J.R., and he had not had a part in the establishment of their congregation. He probably had preached for them several times while he lived near Lawrenceburg. Back in the early 1880's, J.R. had preached in that vicinity.

His next appointment for that summer was at another congregation with which he had labored from 1882 until 1885. J.R. wrote:

"I visited old Robertson Fork on the second Sunday in June. We lived and labored with these dear people many years ago. This was my first visit after an absence of twenty-nine years.

They have a nice new house of worship" (*G.A.*, July 20, 1916, p. 743).

From Robertson Fork he intended to preach a few nights at the "Blue Creek Schoolhouse," which was near Robertson Fork. Incessant rain prevented him from preaching a single sermon at that place. The work at Blue Creek may have been sponsored by the church at Robertson Fork, since J.R. mentions them along with the Robertson Fork congregation. In the past, Robertson Fork had sponsored some new congregations in their area, even when J.R. labored with them.

After Robertson Fork and the failed attempt at Blue Creek Schoolhouse, J.R. traveled to Wilson Hill in Marshall County, Tennessee, and preached twice. He commented about this visit:

> On the third Sunday in June I was at Wilson Hill. They had two sermons and dinner. This is in Marshall County. I preached there many years ago a great deal. Pleasant faces that used to greet us here are seen no more. We had splendid audiences at both services, and dinner enough for as many more people. Old Brother Ben Phillips was buried there just a few days before our visit (*G.A.*, July 20, 1916, p. 743).

That summer was very good to J.R. It turned out to be his busiest summer in three or four years. On the fourth Sunday in June he preached at Cornersville two times and once the following Thursday night. He wrote that "these brethren seem to be at peace with one another, no troubles that I heard of" (*G.A.*, July 20, 1916, p. 743). The reader may wonder why in this latest report of J. R's that he twice mentioned churches being "at peace with one another" or "I heard no dissension among them." The reason for these kinds of comments were that at that time there were men in the church, especially under the influence of O.P. Spiegel of Alabama, who were trying to introduce the instrument of music into the worship in churches of Christ. The church in Florence had divided in 1914 when J.R. Jolly led a group of fifteen out of the

Poplar Street Church of Christ and started a new congregation with the use of instrumental music in worship. Our brethren in Middle Tennessee and North Alabama were genuinely concerned and so was J.R. He simply let the brethren know that none of these problems were among the brethren at Cornersville.

From there he traveled to Beech Grove and preached once on the fourth Sunday in June. He had preached for that congregation through the years. Again J.R. mentions that "Quite a lot of the old ones are there no more" (*G.A.*, July 20, 1916, p. 743). It is apparent that J.R. is thinking more about his own demise. With all his older friends dying, and many of them the same age as he; how could he not think about such things? It was not a lack of faith or fear of dying on his part; but, rather a looking forward to going to be with the Lord. That, in his way of thinking, would mean seeing Mary and those old friends in heaven. His next appointment (at the time of his writing the report) was to be at Ostella, near Cornersville, on the third Sunday in July (*G.A.*, July 20, 1916, p. 743).

From the third Sunday in July to the fourth Sunday of September, we know nothing of J.R.'s work. We next hear of him in a letter dated October 17, 1916. In that letter, he included a lot of material about his family and early childhood acquaintances. He visited his brother, Andrew Jackson Bradley, who lived about five miles west of Iron City, Tennessee. He preached six sermons in a schoolhouse, which was near A.J.'s home. The meeting began on the fourth Sunday in September. J.R. wrote:

> "I do not think I did any good at all. My brother is trying to keep up the Lord's –day service there but is having a hard time. We intended, in our recent effort, to hold over the next Sunday, but because of "wild cat" or some other kind of liquor we had to close" (*G.A.*, Oct. 26, 1916, p. 1077).

The above-mentioned schoolhouse was known as the "Jack Bradley School" and was in Wayne County in the Fairview community. Andrew Jackson (Jack as he was known in the family) and much of his family are buried in the Old Railroad Church Cemetery in that community.

From Jack's house J.R. travelled to John D. Wade's old home and persuaded the people of that community help him clean the old Wade Cemetery once more, which was on September 30, 1916. He wrote as follows:

> A few of us met at the Wade graveyard on Saturday, September 30, to remound and otherwise beautify and identify the graves of fathers and mothers, and other loved ones, and expected a service there, but business and other things, which seemed to control most of our Iron City people, brought out a very small number, and the service was declined. The writer holds the Wade graveyard in sacred remembrance because of the sleeping remains of loved ones there (G.A., Oct. 26, 1916, p. 1077).

J.R. had more success back in 1902, when he succeeded in getting the brethren and other people of the community to work one day in the cemetery and make it look respectable. On that occasion they had a service and dinner on the ground. Prosperity had interfered on this last occasion. J.R. felt let down by the small number to show interest in something that was so important to him.

On Sunday morning he forded Shoal Creek, near the Wade place, and travelled about a mile east to the Wolf Creek Schoolhouse, near John D. Wade's old mill, and preached two sermons. They had dinner on the ground (G.A., Oct. 26, 1916, p. 1077). This was typical when they had a visiting preacher. It had been just three years before (1913) that Nellie Hill (later to marry J.R.'s nephew, Johnnie Bradley) was baptized by Will Behel in Wolf Creek near the schoolhouse. She heard J.R. preach for the only time in her life on this day at Wolf Creek. She has related this information to the writer (who is her grandson) not long before she died at the age 101. She also said that this was the only time she ever met J.R., as he lived so far away.

The Wolf Creek School and meeting house was sitting in a narrow valley that lay along the cold waters of Wolf Creek on either bank. An old cemetery is located on the hill just south of the building, where many of the old pioneers to this valley are buried, including the grave of John Boron, who was murdered by Tom Clark's gang. J.R. was well acquainted with the facts surrounding Boron's death. J.R. had preached there many times in his early days. One of the first sermons he ever preached was preached in the old schoolhouse there.

Even with some disappointments, the trip to his old home place was not a loss to J.R. He was able to visit family and old friends, and like Paul with the Ephesian elders, he knew that this trip might well be his last visit to see them. He told of his visit with A.J. and his family, perhaps because of the church connection in his neighborhood. He does not tell of other visits with family, but it can safely be assumed that he visited Lafayette's family. They only lived about two miles from Wolf Creek School. Lafayette and his wife are buried in the Cauhorn Cemetery which is only about three miles from Wolf Creek.

It seems only logical that J.R. would visit this family. It could have been on this trip that J.R. asked Lafayette to settle his affairs when J.R. died. It was Lafayette who had to travel to Lincoln County, Tennessee and settle J.R.'s affairs at the time of his death (Carrie Bradley Danley interview).

From Wolf Creek J.R. travelled back to Marshall County, Tennessee to the Gnat Grove Church on Gnat Branch. He reported as follows:

> On the second Sunday in October we began at Gnat Grove, in Marshall County, and closed on the third Sunday morning, preaching fourteen times. Two were baptized and one was restored. I have done quite a lot of preaching there for about twenty-five years. We certainly have quite a lot of good people there, and at the close of the recent meeting they remembered their old brother in a very acceptable and substantial way. Our audiences there increased till our crowds

could not be seated. They had me to promise to be with them again next October, should I be spared and able to attend (*G.A.*, Oct. 26, 1916, p. 1077).

J.R. had helped establish the Gnat Grove congregation during his labors with the Robertson Fork church.

His next appointment was at Diana in Giles County, where he had preached many times in years gone by. Old Sister Trigg was responsible for persuading J.R. to come and preach at her house, thus laying the foundation for the church at Diana in the latter part of the year of 1886. He preached on the second Sunday night only. He never spoke of any results of his preaching at Diana on this trip, but he did report that the brethren there were trying to raise money to build a house for worship. From Diana he made the thirty-mile trek home for a few days of rest.

His final preaching trip for 1916 was to Mars Hill where he had attended college under T.B Larimore. He arrived some time on Saturday, November 4th. That was his first visit back to the old college site since he finished his studies in the 1880's. That had been more than thirty-six years since he had seen his dear old teachers and some of his old classmates on this site. He had mixed emotions over the changes he saw. He described what he saw in detail:

O how much changed is everything! Some changes, I hope, are for the better, but other changes, if not for the worse, are such as to make me feel so sad! Brother Larimore's residence looks somewhat the same, though very lonely. No one occupies the building now. No large eighteen-hundred-pound bell, nor even the belfry, can be seen there now, from which at one time peals, almost as of thunder, would awaken a happy band of young preachers and other students to the duties of a new-born day. I preached (or tried) three times- Saturday night, Sunday and Sunday night- to fair audiences in a splendid house of worship which stands on the very spot where the Bible Hall stood, in which we "boys" read, studied, and debated the things pertaining to the kingdom of God and the name of Jesus Christ. I certainly felt, very sensibly, that schoolboy embarrassment which I used to have to suffer in making speeches and in trying to preach in the presence of Brother Larimore. I did certainly wish for him there to take my place, if he would, but glad that he was not present, if I had to try to preach. I could not help, even while in the pulpit, thinking of not only Brother Larimore, but Sister Larimore also, and her sweet and melodious voice in singing the praises of God. Precious to us all was the "Mother of Mars Hill." (*G.A.*, Nov.16, 1916, p. 1149).

Imagine the excitement that raced through J.R.'s mind when he arrived at his old school grounds. You can feel the emotional rush he must have felt on that occasion.

J.R. revealed a few things about life as a student at Mars Hill that perhaps have gone unnoticed before he wrote this letter to the *Advocate*. He revealed just how big the bell at Mars Hill really was. J.R. said that the bell was eighteen hundred pounds in weight. That was crowding one ton. The bell could have been heard all the way to downtown Florence on a quiet morning, no doubt. He also said that the new church building, which he saw for the first time, was standing on the site of the old Bible Hall. He further stated that the students debated "the things pertaining to the kingdom of God and the name of Jesus Christ." Many people are under the conviction that Larimore did not tolerate debating. J.R. revealed otherwise. He reminisced about the embarrassment and ineptness he and others felt when trying to preach in Larimore's presence. He even felt it in the new building at Mars Hill, just knowing that that had been Larimore's pulpit. He also remembered Sister Larimore's "sweet and melodious voice in singing" and her influence upon the "boys" at Mars Hill, so much so that she was known as "the Mother of Mars Hill." This last visit to Mars Hill was so precious to J.R.'s memory, even though he said he felt sad over some memories, or at least over some changes he saw there.

While J.R. was at Mars Hill, Herchel and Virgil Larimore and their wives came out from Florence to hear him preach. Brother W.H. Gresham opened his home to J.R. He spent Saturday night and Sunday with the Gresham family. J.R. said that he was "royally entertained." He also said that Brother Gresham's daughter, Esther, was the only Gresham child left at home. W.H. Gresham's sister was living with them at the time. Sunday night, after the evening service, he was taken into town to Brother E.G. Prosser's house, where he spent Sunday night.

E.G. Prosser was part of the Richardson Lumber Company. W.M. Richardson, who was owner of the lumber company, and his wife, were living with the Prossers, due to a fire in the Richardson house. The Prossers and the Richardsons were old friends of J.R.'s from his Mars Hill days. The following day, which was Monday, J.R. may have taken his very first automobile ride. Sisters Prosser and Richardson drove him over Florence in their car. He remarked that Florence had grown maybe three times larger than when he was in school at Mars Hill (G.A., Nov.16, 1916, p. 1149). One can almost sense the feeling in J.R.'s mind that this would be the last time he would ever see Florence or Mars Hill again. This trip to Mars Hill was the last preaching tour for the year of 1916 for J.R. That year had been a good and busy one for him. What would the New Year bring his way?

25

CHALLENGES AT HOME AND ABROAD

The year 1917 was difficult for the entire country. The First World War had escalated from an obscure skirmish in Bosnia in August 1914, to a full-blown war which demanded that American soldiers be sent to the European war front. Even though that would happen much later in the year, it was the topic of discussion in every community throughout the United States. Elora was no different. No doubt this plagued J.R. and his friends. He had lived through two wars- the Civil War and the Spanish- American War. He remembered how terrible they were and how draining they were on the country and the people. The half had not begun to be told about the latest war. It would be the cruelest of all wars up to that time. Everyone was filled with anxiousness, not knowing whether a father or a brother or even themselves might be sent to war. J.R. was too old to worry about being sent to war; but he had friends and brethren who just might have to go and fight. He remained concerned for others during the entire conflict.

His first appointment for 1917, other than a few regular appointments, was at New Hermon in Bedford County, Tennessee. It was situated at the southernmost tip of Bedford County, about twelve miles south of Shelbyville, the county seat. It was in a beautiful little valley which ran southwest of Flat Creek. A cool, clear stream of water ran within twenty or thirty yards of the beautiful little white meetinghouse that J.R. had helped raise the money to build in the spring and summer of 1893 (*G.A.*, June 22, 1893, p. 392). One of the earliest located minister, at New Hermon lies buried in the little cemetery on the hill just south of the building. He was Joshua K. Speer, a former Baptist minister, who by 1830 had studied himself out of the Baptist Church. Speer had established many churches throughout southern Middle Tennessee and had preached some in North Alabama. It is interesting to note that J.R.'s preaching field was much the same as Speer's field of labor had been.

J.R. described this appointment and the reminiscences he had, concerning that visit. He wrote:

> On the fourth Sunday in May I was with the faithful at New Hermon. We had two services that day, with fair audiences. I will be with them again the first Sunday in July. Brother R. A. Largen is preaching for them monthly when not engaged in protracted meetings. He is held in high esteem by them all. We learned that Brother F. B. Srygley is to hold a meeting there sometime this year. We have done quite a lot of preaching at New Hermon in years gone by. Many faithful ones have crossed over to the other side, and there are yet many more there who will have nothing but the will and way of the Lord. We are always glad of an opportunity to visit them (*G.A.*, June 28, 1917, p. 633).

J.R. had so many special places so dear to his heart, but New Hermon was very special to him and him to them. He had helped them through some very difficult times (see page 112 of this work). He had helped them build their new house of worship. He truly had expended much labor with the New Hermon congregation, and he loved the memories of it.

His next appointment was on the second Sunday in June, at Wilson Hill, in the northwestern corner of Marshall County, Tennessee. Here he had preached many times in the past. During the "80's and 90's," he was one of their monthly preachers. This congregation had been originally known as the Globe Creek Christian Church or Church of Christ. It may very well be the only church south of Nashville to have been founded by the venerable Barton Warren Stone of Cane Ridge, Kentucky. J.R. reported his visit to this historical place:

> On the second Sunday in June I was at Wilson Hill and had two services that day. They furnished two good-sized audiences. This is another one of the old congregations with which I did much work in the past. Many of the old soldiers there, too, have laid aside their armor and gone home. There is some of the old guard yet there, and many of their children, both, of those gone and those remaining, have enlisted in the Lord's army. They seem to be determined that the warfare shall be waged (*G.A.*, June 28, 1917, p. 633).

Wilson Hill, in 2019, continues to worship in the very same building in which J.R. did all his preaching to them throughout his labors there. The building sits on a little knoll in a beautiful valley near Globe Creek, a small clear stream of cool water that courses the length of the valley. The site of the church house is in an all but deserted location. There is a mysterious beauty to this scene. It always looked inviting to J.R. and maybe just a little reminiscent of his old home near Shoal Creek in Lawrence County. A good-sized congregation still worships there at that place, as is the case with most of the Tennessee churches with which J.R. had labored. Wilson Hill is representative of most of the rural congregations of Middle Tennessee.

From Wilson Hill, J.R. travelled southward a few miles to Robertson Fork, where he had labored in times past. He gave the following report on his trip there: "On the third Sunday [June], I was at Robertson Fork, where I met a very large crowd. We lived and labored with them for many years in days of yore. Brother Rutherford, at Lynnville, is preaching for them on the first Sunday in each month. They like him very much" (*G.A.*, June 28, 1917, p. 633)

He did not preach that night at Roberson Fork. A new work, which Robertson Fork was helping to sponsor, needed J.R. to come and preach for them that Sunday night. Robertson Fork had been involved in this kind of work for many years. They had even helped J.R. establish some new works when he labored with them. The new work was called Bluff Spring.

At Bluff Spring, which was situated between Robertson Fork and Lewisburg, he found some old friends who had formerly worshipped with other congregations with which he had labored in the past. He wrote: "Some of those at Bluff Spring used to worship at Wilson Hill. I certainly enjoyed meeting with all these old-time friends, and they made the impression on my mind that they enjoyed my presence and preaching. May the Lord bless them all" (*G.A.*, June 28, 1917, p. 633). This was the first "new work" J.R. had been involved in for some years, due to his failing health. He was very happy to sense that old feeling that he had experienced so many times in his prime.

From Bluff Spring he travelled back to Elora. At home he got much needed rest and relaxation. He looked cheerfully to the future. He had appointments lined up for the rest of the year. He would travel back to New Hermon for the first Sunday in July, to Stoney Point on the second Sunday, and to Lois on the fourth Sunday. The third Sunday was his regular appointment at Corder's Cross Roads. He wrote the following summary of the work at Corder's Cross Roads and Elora: "Brother J. D. Luna, one of the elders at Elora, preached in my place at Corder's Cross Roads last Sunday to allow me to visit Robertson Fork. Brother Luna is certainly a fine talker. He has a very pleasant and happy manner of address. I think he ought to make preaching of the gospel his work" (*G.A.*, June 28, 1917, p. 633).

It seems that Elora was blest with a lot of talent at this time. J.R. called Elora his home. Dr. J.J. Horton also called that congregation his home. With elders like Luna, who could rise to the occasion, the talent was abundant at Elora.

While upon his ten-day preaching tour, an old friend died at Elora. Brother L.E. Hamilton, who had worked on the railroad for twenty-one years, crossed over the river of death. Illness had forced him to retire in April. He gradually grew worse and died on June 17, 1917 (*G.A.*, Dec. 13, 1917, p. 1219). Brother J.J. Horton conducted the funeral. J.R., upon his return home, wrote the following: "While on my trip of ten days preaching tour, L.E. Hamilton of the Elora congregation, crossed over the dark river to be more fully in the sunlight of God's love. May our Father bless and comfort his sorrowing family. He died of Bright's disease and heart trouble" (*G.A.*, Dec.13, 1917, p. 1219).

This was a chilling reminder to J.R. of what, perhaps, lay ahead for him. He too had suffered for years with the same kidney problem and would eventually die because of that dreaded disease. At some point, perhaps while on his preaching tour, J.R. wrote the following note to the editors of the *Gospel Advocate*:

> Please allow me to speak of my appreciation of some good things of late in the dear old *Advocate*. Brother Kurfees does certainly 'lay up the gap' left down by Brother Briney [J.R. used a farm term of closing the gate or gap in a fence which allows passage through the fence]. What can Brother Slater say in answer to Brother Larimore? Brother Elam has certainly been giving us some good things on 'caring for old preachers.' He ought to do something old worn-out preachers, now 'laid on a shelf' or 'turned out on bare ground to survive or perish.' Why not put them on a little pension? It does look like those who built up the congregations by preaching in schoolhouses, under arbors, and under the shade trees, while doing so, raised their own salaries by plowing in the hot sun, should share with our young brethren, who now are called for all of the time, a little of what the congregations can give now, especially since the old preachers brought them to an appreciation of giving. Brother Elam must dispose of these thoughts before he is done. He has certainly 'hit the nail on the head' so far. How many of our young brethren, now advertise to hold meetings for congregations made ready to their hands by seventy-year-

old 'kids,' are starting up new con-gregations at new places without first appealing to these old congregations to send in the checks? May the Lord bless the honest efforts of all, both old and young (*G.A.*, June 28, 1917, p. 624).

J.R. was still very much concerned over the neglect by the older congregations seemingly ignoring older preachers who established them and help get them to maturity. He knew; he was one of those who had suffered greatly because of that neglect. To him that just was not fair. If J.R. could be accused of having a hobby, that was it.

We earlier mentioned how Elora was blessed with a lot of preaching talent. After holding a gospel meeting in Elora during the month of August, J.D. Northcut of McMinnville wrote concerning the talent at that place:

> Elora is blessed with three preaching brethren. Brother J.R. Bradley, who has done a wonderful work in this country in establishing churches in new fields, lives here. His life has been spent on the firing line, and now he has purchased a home in Elora, in the foothills of the Cumberland Mountains, to spend the remaining years of a well-filled life of good service to Christ and his Church. Dr. J.J. Horton also makes this his home and spends most of his time evangelizing. Dr. Horton dropped out of a very fine practice to preach the gospel of the risen Lord. He is a strong man and is doing a great work. Elora is also the home of Brother J.D. Luna, who is a leading stockman in Tennessee. He was a teacher in Texas for a time and has developed a great literary talent and will be ere long one of the leading writers of Tennessee. Brother Luna preaches occasionally for his home congregation and surrounding country. He is loved by all (J.D. Northcut, *G.A.*, August 16, 1917, p. 804).

From this report you can see that Elora was truly blessed to have so much preaching talent. Northcut, also, seemed to know a lot about Bradley. Everyone seemed to recognize the value of J.R.'s service to the Lord and his Church.

J.R. kept his appointments for July, but he reported nothing about his work at these places. We know nothing of his work in August; however, he did have appointments at Corder's Cross Roads and Elora. We can only assume those appointments were promptly kept, as there was no report of any illness on his part. His next reported meeting came not from J.R., but from one of the members at Gnat Grove. The report was written by Brother Tom Sanders and reads as follows:

> Brother J.R. Bradley, of Elora, closed an eight day's meeting at Gnat Grove Schoolhouse; five or six miles south of Corners-ville, last Sunday night [began on September 30th and ended on October 7th]. There were two additions by primary obedi-ence—George K. Love (brother of Jesse F. Love, evangelist of the church of Christ, of Pensacola, Fla.) and wife. There are a few of us who meet at the schoolhouse to worship because it is more convenient than to go elsewhere.
>
> (*G.A.*, Oct. 25, 1917, p. 1038).

This was one of the longest meetings that J.R. was able to conduct in several months. We do not know why J.R. did not report the meeting himself. As a matter of fact, this report was the last one made on behalf of J.R. for the rest of 1917.

26

A Good Year

J.R. and Loula fared well during the winter months. From his early work schedule for the year, it appears that his health was good and that he had no real problems during the wintery weather. He had traveled to Lawrenceburg and preached two sermons to the brethren there on the fifth Sunday in March. He continued to preach once a month at Corder's Cross Roads and at Elora. He wrote a valuable insight into his relationship with the Lawrenceburg church and into the church itself:

> ...Almost in the very beginning of my preaching I did much work in the vicinity of Lawrenceburg. There are many there who attended services and heard me and were baptized into Christ thirty and forty years ago, at places near the city. They have now Brethren Thornberry, Coffman, King, Kelley, and Possibly others, who are "declaring the glad tidings of salvation" to the people of that town and surrounding country. These are loyal and faithful soldiers of whom these people are proud. I enjoyed the time spent with them very much indeed. They invited me to visit them again at any time I can. I think I shall try to arrange another trip over there before winter (*G.A.*, May 9, 1918, p. 452).

J.R. was happy over his visit to Lawrenceburg. That was the first time in that place for many years. It always helped him to visit congregations and see old friends once again.

The last week of March, J.R. read an article written by E. G. Rockliff, entitled "Noah, A Just Man." It was published March 28, 1918, on page 302 in the *Gospel Advocate*. In the article Rockliff made the statement that Noah worked for one hundred and twenty years on the Ark. J.R. challenged him in an article published April 28, 1918, in the *Advocate*. He argued that from the birth of Shem, Ham, and Japheth until the flood, was only one hundred years (Gen. 5:32: Gen. 7:6-7). J.R. wrote: "I know those wicked people had "probation" of "one hundred and twenty years" (Gen. 6:3). But I am not at all certain that he did not. Now, Brother Rockliff, I do not write this to get up a controversy. I certainly like your article that I mention and say "amen' to all but your statement in question" (*G.A.*, April 25, 1918, p. 401).

Rockliff wrote again in May and his article was published on (May16, 1918, p. 476) to answer J.R. His attempt was very weak and did not satisfy J.R. He wrote in the *Advocate* of May 23rd in his second article to end the discussion. His article stated:

> Of course, God gave a time of "respite' of "a hundred and twenty years" (Gen. 6:3), as Brother Rockliff says, and the time of "God's waiting while the ark was a preparing" is certainly embraced in the "one hundred and twenty years," As Peter says; but that is quite different from saying "all the one hundred and twenty years were consumed in the building of the ark." May the Lord help us to be so prepared that we may enter into the rest that remains for the people of God (*G.A.*, May 23, 1918, p. 498).

Nothing else was written on the question concerning how long Noah took to build the Ark. Apparently all parties were satisfied. J.R.'s second preaching appointment, apart from his regular monthly appointments, was at Stoney Point in Lincoln County, Tennessee. He did much work for them in "the long ago" He had many friends there. A.H. Rozar and his son Vernon Rozar lived at Stoney Point. Bradley had converted A.H. Rozar from the

Separate Baptists in July of 1893 (Sept. 21, 1893, p. 601). Rozar had labored with J.R. in many meetings. J.R. said of the Rozars... "both splendid preachers and loyal to the cause of Christ" (*G.A.,* May 9, 1918, p. 452). J.R. said that he would try to visit them again that year.

From Stoney Point he expected to go home for the week and then travel the following weekend to Greenwood. That would be his standing annual meeting appointment with those brethren. He never seems to refer to Greenwood without bringing up the subject of the meeting that he and W.B. McQuiddy held at the establishment of that work. J.R. wrote:

> We do certainly have many fine friends there. W.B., why not make the visit? You can preach yet, as much as the Dutchman rode the mule ("shust a little bit"), can you not? They would certainly enjoy it. Write them and go. On my trip to Greenwood I will remain over and will possibly preach at some night through the week at a new church, a little way from Greenwood, called "Pleasant Valley"; and Pleasant Valley on the Second Sunday; and possibly at Ethridge at night (*G.A.,* May 9, 1918, p. 452)

J.R. planned to have a very busy schedule, while in the Greenwood community. Those were the kind of times that he loved. From that region of Giles and Lawrence Counties in Tennessee, he would move eastward to the Robertson Fork community. He intended to preach there on the fourth Sunday of May. From there he would travel to Wilson Hill and preach at that place on the first Sunday in June. Then on the second Sunday of June he would preach at the State Line congregation. That was one he had established through his own labors. He would preach at Cornersville on the fourth Sunday of June, and at Ostella on the fifth Sunday. He planned to preach at Corder's Cross Roads every third Sunday that season. He looked forward to having more appointments for the rest of the year (*G.A.,* May 9, 1918, p. 452). He never sent another report of any kind related to the work for that summer.

He did however, write concerning a new 'Teachers Testament, which J. C. McQuiddy had sent out for critique from some of the ministers. J.R. just happened to receive a copy. J.R.'s comment was prefaced by an explanation from McQuiddy:

> I wrote a number of brethren for a statement of their views concerning the merits of the "Teachers' Testament," a copy of which are are furnishing to old subscribers who send us one new yearly subscriber to the Gospel Advocate, accompanied by two dollars. Brother J.R. Bradley was among the number. We are glad to publish his reply in full, which follows: Elora, Tenn., June 6, 1918. Brother McQuiddy: I am sure you will not want to publish what I think of the notes (rather a failure to note at all) in the Testament you send me. See Mark 16: 16, where baptism is certainly a part of the plan of salvation, is left out of the "notes." See, also, Acts 2: 38, that "baptism for the remission of sins" is wholly ignored. Acts 22: 16-"Arise, and be baptized, and wash away thy sins" -is entirely left out. Rom. 6: 17, 18, where Paul certainly emphasized the obedience to be" made free from sin," is ignored. See, again, 1 Pet. 3: 21. This note is very ambiguous: "It must be interpreted with other passages of scripture." How much light does that shed? I am going to say this: I believe the "commentator" intended and did dodge the force of these passages.
>
> J.R. Bradley. (*G.A.*, June 13, 1918, p. 564)

McQuiddy tried to downplay J.R.'s concerns as follows:

> In the light of this statement, the silence on the passages to which reference is made is golden. The passages are not difficult, and the meaning is so evident and clear as not to need any comment. "He that believeth and is baptized shall be saved" is not difficult of meaning, according to the commentators, and they were too honest as commentators to seek to obscure its meaning by comment. In the light of their purpose their silence is much more valuable than their comment could be. They do, however. regard 1 Pet. 3: 21 a difficult passage and on it make an extended comment., giving the different

views of different religionists... J.C. McQuiddy. (*G.A.*, June 13, 1918, p. 564)

In July J.R. wrote a lengthy question to E.A. Elam concerning "When and Where to Preach the Gospel." His question included a lot of material about his past labors. We, therefore, include his question in full. He wrote under the heading of "Fifty Years' Attitude toward the Denominations," as follows:

Dear Brother Elam: I sincerely believe you to be strictly loyal to the truth, and also believe you to be capable above many of passing a scriptural and just criticism upon the life work of anyone of your brethren. I therefore submit this sketch of "my attitude toward the denominations of fifty years" and ask you to kindly point out my mistakes through the *Gospel Advocate*.

I shall be as brief as possible, so as to give you my acts for fifty years, which I wish to pass under your scrutiny. I can do this, I think, better, and in a shorter way, by speaking of one of my regular preaching points for thirty years. My first sermon in that town was in a small schoolhouse. Then the Baptists tendered us to use of their splendid house, both for monthly visits and also for a meeting. In that meeting, I think, I baptized twenty-two, and had a few from the denominations. Within a year a nice new house was built. The cause prospered. Other preachers did some preaching, especially in the protracted meetings. One faithful old brother (now dead) preached alternately with me for two years, I think. Finally, the Methodists built a house. There are Presbyterians nearby, but they have no church in town. The people of all these denominations, more or less, attend the services of the church of Christ, both Sunday school and preaching. Especially do the Methodists do so, because the services at the church of Christ are in the morning and in the evening at the Methodist Church. For almost a year we allowed the Methodists to use our house monthly. During all these years I am sure these people have heard me preach more than one hundred times and upon as many subjects. Let me give the subjects just as I have them set down in a memorandum book for 1901 at this place:

"The First Day of the Week," "Hear Ye Him," "Justified of many Things," "Crown of Life," "Faith," "Repentance," "Confession," "Baptism," "The reason of the Hope," "The Heart," "Purification and Religion," "In Christ," "Seek and ye Shall Find," "Salvation and Loss of the Soul," "The Righteous, Ungodly, and Sinner," "The Race for the Crown," "Take Heed Unto Thyself," "Labor in the Vineyard," "Heartfelt Religion," "Does God Ever Repent?," "The Family of God," "Preach the Word," "What Must I Do to Be Saved?," "Forgiveness," "Christ, the Only Way," "etc. I think I can find among my papers other memorandums of an earlier date. I am certain I can produce a book of subjects I preached on at this place of a more recent date. The ones I have given show about what these people heard from me.

I have been invited by the Methodists there several times to preach in their house. One time I was urged by their preacher to preach in his place. I consented. My subject that time was "Doing the Commandments," At another time (my memorandum does not state what year) the subject was "Seek, and Ye Shall Find." Last fall these Methodists invited me repeatedly to visit them again. I had not been there for several years. I consented. My appointment at that church was at 2:30 P. M. and at night. I attended worship at the church of Christ at 10:00 A.M., when the elder asked me to make a talk for the church, instead of having their regular Sunday-school lesson. We had a right good-sized audience for only a regular Lord's Day service. They invited me to visit them at some other time, which I agreed to do. My two subjects at the Methodist Church were "True Worship" and "Temptation,"

I have been censured very sharply for not using subjects of a more radical nature upon that occasion, such as "Baptism for the Remission of Sins," "Infant Baptism," "Mourners Bench Religion," "Sprinkling and Pouring for Baptism," "Faith Only," etc. The same brother has assured me many times under like circumstances, and upon the same grounds, during the many years that I have been preaching in this country. These very Methodists for many years have heard me upon those very themes and well know our teaching upon these issues.

Did I show unfaithfulness because I did not "pitch into" these Methodists upon their errors? Do you think, Brother Elam that I should have asked them to let the organ remain silent, which they were using in their own Sunday-school service just preceding the time for my sermon? Should I have preached a sermon upon "The Instrument and its Sinfulness," right there in their house? They well know that I do not favor its use in the service of God.

I was invited to preach in another Methodist Church last fall where they use the organ. A sister there asked for the use of the house for a few sermons and asked me to carry song books. I asked those people not to use the organ in our part of the service, but we asked them to help sing, which they did.

This is (and has been for fifty years) my course in regard to the denominations. Where are my mistakes? (*G.A.*, July 25, 1918, p. 708).

There are several things to notice concerning J.R.'s letter. First: He had much confidence in E.A. Elam's biblical knowledge and believed that he truly would point out any errors. He knew Elam would be honest in a nice way, not harsh like some other preachers with whom J.R. had dealt. Second: We learn that the Methodists had invited J.R. to preach for them many times during his ministry, and that he had accepted the opportunity. You may remember that his first major head-on conflict with the denominations was with the Methodists on Brush Creek, near Killen, Alabama. This resulted in his establishing the Church of Christ in that community and it eventually became the Killen Church of Christ (see p. 30). Third: J.R. kept written records from year to year, because he referred to them in this question addressed to Elam. J.R. seemed to be much more organized than the Bradleys with whom this writer is related. This entire letter, written in the form of a question, showed J.R.'s sincerity in teaching the gospel and teaching and practicing it correctly. When he was criticized, he sought others' advice before he reacted. Good actions for the modern preacher or teacher to follow.

Elam began his lengthy reply to J.R.'s question by stating:

> Three things are essential to the true and faithful preacher whose work God accepts —(1) the right theme, (2) the true and right motive, (3) the right manner. Error and all kinds of false doctrine may be preached in an earnest and attractive way, but that does not turn error into truth; the truth may be preached in a partisan and bitter spirit, a pungent way, a holier – than – thou and a condemnatory manner, a self-important and "knowing" air, or a "smart – alecky (sic)" style, which are the very opposite of humility and faith, wisdom and love, and grace and the Spirit of Christ, and are very hurtful to the speaker and the audience; and either error or the gospel may be preached through love of money, popularity, and place, or through any motive, except the true one of pleasing and honoring God and saving souls (*G.A.*, July 25, 1918, p. 708).

Elam's answer is basically the same as J.R.'s actions had been throughout his preaching career. He concluded by saying: "Brother Bradley would have done wrong had he refused to preach the gospel to the denominations or to any persons; and we know he would have committed sin against them, and God had he compromised the truth to please them" (*G.A.*, July 25, 1918, p. 709).

Elam also pointed out in his answer that "The sin is not in where they preach but compromising the truth or failing to preach the whole truth" (*G.A.*, July 25, 1918, p. 708). Elam and Bradley were on the "same page," perhaps, because they had studied with the same teacher – T.B. Larimore. We find no further correspondence regarding this "question and answer session," Apparently J.R. and the other readers of the *Advocate* were satisfied with Elam's answer.

The foregoing question had arisen, apparently during an appointment that J.R. had filled earlier in the year. We do not know where the criticism was made, nor who made the criticism. That was perhaps by design on J.R.'s part. He still considered that person a brother and friend. That was all a part of J.R.'s character. Throughout July he kept a few appointments; but during their annual meeting at Elora, both he and his preaching friend – J.J. Horton— attended the meeting while Brothers J.D. Northcut and E. Gaston Collins did the preaching. They baptized precious souls during that meeting (*G.A.*, August 15, 1918, p. 781). Northcut gave the report.

J.R. sent his final report for the year sometime in September. He wrote:

> I am seventy – two years young today. I have just closed a meeting near Elkwood, Ala., with two added. I will begin at Riversburg, Giles County, Tenn.; next Sunday (which was Sept. 8, 1918). I am in a good shape as to health. Wife got her foot sprained on our Elkwood trip. I preached seventeen sermons during this meeting" (*G.A.*, Sept. 12, 1918, p. 873).

J.R. was winding the protracted meeting season down in a very strong way. His health must have been very good for him to have preached seventeen times during that meeting. As the year closed there were good times and pleasant memories for J.R., his hopes were that the coming year would harbor the same for him and Loula. There were, however, a few sad memories also. There was one sad event that impacted J.R. That was the death of his friend, J.D. Northcut, who had just a few months ago written about J.R.'s work and the work at Elora. During this period, the Spanish Influenza was raging. When Northcut returned to Tracy City he found many of his friends and family members afflicted with the dreaded disease. He contracted the flu while trying to aid others with the sickness. He died on November 2, 1918. One of his obituaries stated: "His illness, influenza, followed by pneumonia, was short and painful, caused by giving almost continual attention to sufferers near him" (*G.A.*, Nov. 28, 1918, p. 1131). Tennessee had lost a very promising young preacher and J.R. had lost a dear friend. Northcut and J.R. knew one another very well. Northcut had held several meetings at Elora and other churches near where Bradley called home.

27

LABORS WIND DOWN

For the year of 1919, the *Advocate* was totally silent concerning J.R. Not once did his name, nor a reference to him, appear in the *Gospel Advocate*. We are left to wonder as to what was going on in J. R's life. Was he sick? Did some other mishap befall him? We have no way of getting answers to these questions. We do, however, know that in the next year he only reports obituaries of friends whose funerals he conducted. Something was very different in J.R.'s life at this time and we do not know what it might have been. His only activity to be reported in any of the brotherhood journals, for 1919, was a report published in R.H. Boles' *Word and Work*. This was a report sent by J.M. McCaleb for donations sent to his work in Japan. J.R. had sent a dollar to the Japanese work.

The first thing from J.R.'s pen, concerning preaching, to appear in the *Advocate*, since September 12, 1918, was published on July 8, 1920. That was a silence of nearly two years on J.R.'s part. His friend, Dr. J.J. Horton, had written his report on his meetings for the summer of 1919, and even preached in many of Bradley's usual preaching points and never mentions him. That was strange because J.R. and J.J. Horton were both members at Elora, and they had worked together in many meetings and especially the ones mentioned in Horton's report (*G.A.*, Oct. 4, 1919, p. 1030).

Otherwise they were good friends and good friends usually keep informed about one another. Why did Horton not say something about his friend J.R.? This leads us to believe that his old problems had returned "for a season." He did not report any preaching for the year.

He did send a report on a funeral of two friends at Cornersville that he had helped conduct on December 26, 1919. The report served as a double obituary. It was another of J.R.'s life-long friends- brother R.N. Nix and his son D.W. Nix. The son died about five o'clock Christmas morning and the father died about twelve o'clock, the same day. The Spanish Influenza may have been the cause of their deaths. It was running rampant throughout the countryside at the time. J.R. stated the Nix men were both faithful men of God. He wrote of R.N. Nix: "The father and I were young men at the same time, and of the same neighborhood, though he was almost nine years older than I. We were always very intimate. While neither of us was in the Civil War, we passed the sad ordeal in the same neighborhood" (*G.A.*, April 20, 1920, p. 385).

J.R. informed us that he had baptized the son some thirty-seven years before. The Nix family had moved from Lawrence County, Tennessee to Cornersville some years prior to their deaths. He gave us another peek into his early childhood at Iron City. That was the first and only double funeral for him to ever conduct in all fifty some odd years of preaching. He described the pitiable scene in detail. One coffin was on his right and one was on the left in the church building. The sight of the families of his friends grieving over their losses must have been about as much as J.R. could stand. This funeral was his last activity reported for 1919.
1920 started out with his health not doing so well. He did not send a single report on any of his preaching appointments, which was just not typical of J.R. This suggests that something had certainly changed for him, in his work. The only information in the *Advocate* relating to him is found in obituaries.

His first report was an obituary on the death of an old friend of his at Lynnville, Tennessee. J.R. was asked to do his funeral but was unable to go. This may indicate an illness on J.R.'s part. Due to so much biographical material, we include the entire obituary, even though J.R. did not preach the funeral. It reads:

At the age of eighty-three years, five months, and twelve days, our dear brother J.T. Robbins, of near Lynnville, Giles County, Tenn., only a short time ago passed over to his eternal reward. I have known Brother Robbins since 1884. He obeyed the gospel at Robertson Fork in 1884, under Brother Frasier. Brother Robbins fell out of his barn loft on January 2, 1918, from which he sustained an injury, and was not able to walk but very little any more. He was a splendid student of the Bible. He also read the Gospel Advocate all his religious life, except for one year. Being confined more than two years previous to his death afforded an opportunity for him to read much. He studied the "world war" in connection with some predictions in the Bible and fully believed those prophecies were fulfilled in the war. I am sure that I never knew a more conscientious and sincere man. Brother Robbins was a very retired sort of a man – that is, he never put himself forward in anything, nor did he ever make himself conspicuous in anything, and hence but few of his friends really knew how well informed he was on most of the issues of the day. I am sure I never had a single brother in Christ who was at any, and all times, more ready (sic) to help me than was J.R. Robbins. He was right successful in making money on his farm and in other honest dealings with his fellow man and was liberal in helping the worthy poor and in giving to the cause of Christ. Brother Robbins was never married. At the time I became acquainted with him, his aged mother was living with him, but a few years afterwards she passed away. A sister also (Miss Puss) lived there, and who still survives him. She, too, was never married. Though he had not been able to walk for about a year previous to his death, he was very active in rolling himself around in his invalid chair. His general health was good all the time. He kept up remarkably well with the war news. The Gospel Advocate was his choice of paper. His nephew, Brother G.M. Knox, a fine man, spent about two years with him before his death. He is still there with "Aunt Puss," Over a year ago I spent a day and night with Brother Robbins and Sister Puss after I had preached at Robinson Fork on Sunday before, and, with tears in his eyes, he expressed his sorrow to me over the loss of Brother David Lipscomb from the editorial staff of the Gospel Advocate. Though I was called to attend his funeral, I was unable at the time to go, and Brother H.N. Rutherford, of Lynnville, conducted the funeral services. May the Lord help us all to be "faithful till death" and to meet him in the "glory land" (*G.A.*, July 8, 1920, p. 677).

From the way J.R. described Brother Robbins' life, we learn that J.R. had a very close personal association with him. He had probably helped J.R. financially at times by the way Bradley says that Robbins "was liberal in helping the worthy poor and in giving to the cause of Christ." From that statement it seems that J.R. implied just that to the reader. It was in Robbins' household that J.R. always lodged whenever he preached in the Lynnville – Robertson Fork Community. J.R. also said that he was unable to be at Robbins' funeral, which was not typical for J.R., unless he was sick. This leads us to speculate that J.R. was having health problems at that time.

By July 8, 1920, he was able to travel back to Cornersville to conduct the funeral of his departed friend – R.N. Nix's wife. She was Mary E. Nix and had been married to R.N. Nix for fifty-five years. Brother W.B. London, an elder at Cornersville, helped J.R. conduct the funeral, as he had helped in the double funeral of Mary's husband and her son (*G.A.*, Aug. 5, 1920, p. 774).

1920 was really a sad year for J.R. It had been filled with funerals of friends. He had been sick for the first part of the year and not very well the last part. When J.R. was unable to help in the funeral of a dear friend it was a very sad time for him. He could only hope for better times next year.

During the New Year (1921) J.R. never sent a single report on his preaching to the *Gospel Advocate*. He did send a "rushed" or "hurry up" report that was written after the fifth Sunday of January 1922. It read as follows:

> During 1921 and beginning with the first Sunday in May; I visited the following congregations, preaching two sermons at nearly all the places, and with dinner on the ground at two or three of them: Greenwood, Odd Fellows' Hall, New Providence, Cool Springs, and New Zion, in Giles County, Tenn.; Robertson Fork, Wilson Hill, Bluff Spring, Cornersville, and Ostella, in Marshall County; State Line, and Chestnut Ridge, in Lincoln County; Richmond: Culleoka, Columbia, and Smyrna, in Maury County; Decherd and Beulah, in Franklin County; and Woodville, in Jackson County, Ala. I visit Smyrna monthly. I also preached three sermons at Elora (my home) during the past year.
>
> ...During 1922 I hope to be able to visit all of these places again. They have remembered us right well in a substantial way, as well as otherwise. I have passed the seventy-fifth milepost toward the grave and the future state but am holding up-well and right active for that age. We have a new man, a Brother Borden, just moved into Elora community, who is a fine song leader. He is a great help to our congregation. Pray for us (*G.A.*, Feb. 16, 1922, p. 162).

One can see that the report was the bare minimum of facts. He gave absolutely no statistics, which was not typical of J.R. He had changed his style of reporting totally. Maybe this had to do with old age, rather than illness, which was usually the case with J.R. He did say in this report that his health was good. That statement, however, was made in January of 1922. His actions for 1921 seem to hint of his not being so well.

His correspondence to the *Advocate* during that year was in the form of three articles, which with little effort could have been printed as one long article. In years past, when J.R. was confined to his house because of illness, he wrote articles. This leads us to believe that J.R. was sick a lot or that he had lost interest in sending full reports of his work and keeping them current in the *Advocate*. Whatever the reason, he wrote three good, yet short, articles on the subject of "Sectarianism," His first article dealt with "Paul's Attitude toward the Sects." In this article he pointed out that Paul became a Jew to the Jews, to teach and save them. He showed Paul's action in circumcising Timothy to remove a stumbling block toward the Jews, so that he might reach them. He then compared Paul's actions to his (J.R.'s) actions toward the Methodists, Baptist, and Presbyterians, and "all other sects" (*G.A.*, June 23, 1921, p. 604). It seems apparent that J.R. wrote these articles in response to the criticism he had received over his preaching in denominational houses, which evoked his lengthy question to E.A. Elam on that subject (*G.A.*, July 25, 1918, p. 708).

His second article was titled "Who are Sectarians?" In this article J.R. quotes David Lipscomb on the subject (*Queries and Answers*, by Lipscomb and Sewell, pp. 591-592). After that quote J.R. asked the question: "Now then, if I meet with, pray with, and preach with denominational churches, but always and at all times preach the truth, am I not in company with good men – Peter, John, Paul, Barnabas, and that faithful, tried, and godly man, David Lipscomb?" The article ended with that question (*G.A.* Aug.4, 1921, p. 733).

J.R.'s third article was titled: "Communing with the Sects," This is much longer than the preceding two and J.R. quotes from Lipscomb's and Sewell's (*Queries Answered*, pp. 295-296) to begin his article. He quotes: "One thing is evident, and that is that the validity of an ordinance, either baptism or the Lord's Supper, does not depend upon the administrator. If the subject is all right when immersed, his baptism is valid to him, whether the administrator is or not. The same, we think, is true of the Lord's Supper. But there are no instructions as to open or closed communion in the Bible, and we cannot undertake to give any." Bradley quotes from Larimore in *Larimore's Letters and Sermons*, vol. 1, pp. 295-296, also to show that Larimore felt that a man should examine himself in the way he took the Lord's Supper, not with whom he took it. J.R. closes the article by quoting F.D. Srygley in his *New Testament Church* pp. 67-68. "If there are no Christians in any denomination, it is the only place except hell they have kept out of." J.R. wrote:

> Now, I quote from these able men of God, for the reason that our own "church of Christ" folks, both brothers and sisters, can, and do, at some places, "outstrip" the denominational churches in acting the sect and creating factions among us. Note the "rebaptism" craze; objections to Sunday – school literature; women teachers; fighting the colleges and schools, too, who are creating factions among us by pushing the "rebaptism" hobby. This, I think, is as bad as the society and organ craze. Like the Irishman who found the turtle in the road, kicking and wriggling around, though with its head cut completely off. After studying for a time how the turtle could possibly show signs of life, he exclaimed: "Well poor thing! Him dead and don't know it!" Just so, we of the church of Christ have strong sectarians among us, and they don't know it.
>
> Well, I will close and leave this question of sectarianism among "us as a people" with more and able writers. You see, brethren Kurfees, Holt, Paisley, and others have had this job on their hands of late in their articles in the *Gospel Advocate* in a "tilt" with Brother John T. Lewis. If we must know that our baptism is "for the remission of sins" or God will not grant us remission, where was the church on earth during the "Dark Ages?" Who preached "baptism for remission of sins," between the death of the apostles and Campbell? Christ says, "The gates of hell shall not prevail against it" (Matt. 16:18). Daniel says: "It shall stand forever" (Dan. 2:44). Now if "baptism for the remission of sins" was neither preached nor practiced then, there was no kingdom nor church then and, therefore Daniel and Christ are wrong (*G.A.*, Sept. 22, 1921, pp. 916-917).

We find no response to J.R.'s final article, therefore we conclude that most everyone who read the *Advocate* agreed or did not

disagree enough to warrant a response. This was his last correspondence during 1921.

The New Year began as though it would be a good year for J.R.,
but by the end of the year his health had deteriorated very much.
He had sent a report to the *Advocate* about his work for the past
year. In that report, which he wrote at the end of January or the
first week in February 1922, he reported:

> For a start into the New Year, I have this month (January)
> preached four sermons at the following places: Smyrna, the
> third Sunday; Culleoka, fourth Sunday (two sermons); and at
> home [Elora] yesterday, fifth Sunday. During 1922 I hope to
> be able to visit all of these places again. They have remem-
> bered us right well in a substantial way, as well as otherwise. I
> have passed the seventy-fifth milepost toward the grave and
> the future state but am holding up well and right active for that
> age. We have a new man, a Brother Borden, just moved into
> the Elora community, who is a fine song leader. He is a great
> help to our congregation. Pray for us (*G.A.* Feb. 16, 1922, P.
> 162).

Due to his declining health that would be J.R.'s final report, concerning his preaching, for the *Gospel Advocate.*

He did, however, write to the Advocate two more times. He
wrote to the editors of that paper to show his appreciation for it.
He stated: "I think I appreciate the *Gospel Advocate* more now
than at any time during the fifty years I have been taking it" (*G.A.*,
Apr. 6, 1922, p. 321). Perhaps the reason that J.R. felt appreciation
for the *Advocate* "more now" was because he was already very
sick, and the *Gospel Advocate* was his main source of outside con-
tact with the brotherhood. His final correspondence with the
Gospel Advocate was dated June 7, 1922. It was a short letter about
the church at Elora. It is given in its entirety:

> Our little congregation worshipping at Elora seems to be hold-
> ing its own under the ministry of J.D. Jones, of Huntsville,

Ala., assisted by our elders. Brother Jones is certainly an able man. He rarely ever reads the Scriptures he uses while preaching but quotes them correctly. He preaches for us monthly, also at Taft monthly. Merrimac and West Huntsville are two of his monthly appointments. Brother Jones tells me that he would like to be engaged in meetings all the summer and fall but does not have the time all taken. Write J.D. Jones, Wells Avenue, Huntsville, Ala., if you need a man for your meeting" (*G.A.*, June 15, 1922, p. 561).

From this final correspondence it seems that, even though he was ill, he was able to attend services at Elora. He was still happy for good servants in the Lord's Kingdom, such as Brother Jones. 1922 was sad in the sense that it ended J.R.'s career as a preacher and a writer, even though death was still a few months away.

28

FINAL BATTLES AND DEATH

The year 1923 began the same as the last few years had begun for J.R. with sickness that restricted him very much. He was not able to leave the house very often and then only for short distances such as was necessary like going to the store or to worship with his brethren at Elora, and then there were the frequent visits to his doctor. The winter of 1921 health to continue to deteriorate very rapidly. That ended his preaching ministry. J.R.'s love had been preaching to the lost and dying world. His last two years must have been painful to him, not from the disease as much as from not being able to do what he desired most – preaching. You may have noticed that in his last report (*G.A.*, June 15, 1922, p. 561) he said that Brother Jones was assisted by the elders in his preaching at Elora; J.R. was not assisting him. That is a good indicator that he was not able to assist Jones in his preaching at Elora. J.R.'s last documented preaching was in January of 1922 (*G.A.* Feb. 16, 1922, p. 162). His last written correspondence was published as three articles, the last being published on September 22, 1921 (*G.A.*, Sept. 22, 1921, p. 916-917).

We know nothing of J.R.'s final few months, except that he suffered greatly, due to the nature of Bright's disease. It is a painful kidney disease that slowly kills its victims in an agonizing way. We know that he was probably incapacitated the last few months of his life. He was probably confined to bed most of the time with an occasional walk outdoors. By the month of August, he grew much worse and by September he was in the hospital in Fayetteville, Tennessee. Sometime during the first week of September, T.C. Little sent a report to the *Gospel Advocate*, concerning J.R. and his friend J.J. Horton, who was also in the hospital at the same time in a critical condition. This report, however, did not appear in the *Advocate* until after J.R.'s death. The article was published on September 13th and J.R. had died on September 9th. The report read as follows:

> T. C. Little, Fayetteville, Tenn., advises that two of our faithful preachers of the gospel, J. J. Horton and J.R. Bradley, both of Elora, Tenn., are in the hospital in Fayetteville, Tenn., critically ill. Brother Horton has accomplished much good in the fifteen years he has been preaching. Brother Bradley, who has passed his seventy- seventh birthday, has been a great sufferer for years, yet has been actively preaching the gospel in Lincoln County and adjoining counties for more than a third of a century and has done great good. Brother Little says: "Let the church show its appreciation of these men and their work and extend Christian sympathy" (*G.A.*, Sept. 13, 1923, p. 893).

Why the delay in printing Little's report on Bradley and Norton is unknown. It may have been received too late to get it in the September 6th issue, or Little may not have written it soon enough. You can see the respect that Little had for J.R. They had worked together many times, and especially when J.R. had lived at Fayetteville, Tennessee.

J.R. slipped into the silent deathly sleep on Sunday night, September 9, 1923, at 10:00pm (*Fayetteville Observer*, Sept. 13, 1923). Hiram Higgins of Fayetteville alerted the readers of the *Gospel Advocate* to the death of J.R. His letter was dated September 13, 1923. The announcement read as follows:

> ...I am sorry to report the death of J.R. Bradley at the hospital here on Sunday night. He was seventy-seven years of age and

had been preaching for more than forty-five years. His burial was here on Monday afternoon, after services by T.C. Little and R.A. Largen. He is survived by his wife" (*Gospel Advocate*, September 20, 1923, p. 916).

Higgins was a member of the church in Fayetteville and had been a good friend to J.R.

The *Fayetteville Observer* also reported his death on September 13, 1923. Here we insert the entire obituary, even with its few errors:

> Eld. John R. Bradley [James R. Bradley], aged 77 years, died of Bright's disease at the hospital in Fayetteville, on Sunday night, September 9, 1923, at 10 o'clock.
>
> Eld. Bradley spent forty years in the ministry of the Christian church. Educated, after his marriage, under adverse conditions at Mars Hill (sic) under Eld. T.B. Larimore. His first work was at Mission Point(s). Money was no consideration in his ministries; his activities were governed solely by his desire to do good to his fellow man. He was loved by all whom he had ever served as pastor and his long time of service added to his host of friends.
>
> The funeral services were conducted at the Christian church on Monday afternoon at 1 o'clock by Elds. Little and Largen, burial at Rose Hill cemetery. He is survived by his wife.
>
> The work of Brother Bradley, as he was universally known, extended over Northern Alabama and North Georgia, as well as Tennessee, and the esteem in which he was held was shown by the large attendance at his funeral (*Fayetteville Observer*, September 13, 1923).

Even the secular paper recognized J.R.'s worth to their community and paid an honorable tribute to him.

The final tribute came in January of 1924. R.A. Largen, who was the evangelist at Elora Church of Christ, Elora, Tennessee, wrote the tribute. He had worked with Bradley in some meetings during the last few years and had grown to love and respect J.R. very much. It is fitting that he should have written this memorial to Bradley. Largen's memorial is given in full:

> Brother J.R. Bradley, a faithful preacher of the gospel, departed this life on September 9, 1923. He was seventy-seven years of age, and for many years a true and able servant of the Lord. When quite a young man, he had an ambition to preach the gospel. So, he entered Brother Larimore's school at Mars Hill, in Alabama, and prepared himself for the ministry. He made a capable and loyal minister of the church of Christ. He was a man of fine understanding and a capable interpreter of the work, and always stood firm for the truth. As a country preacher, Brother Bradley suffered many hardships and privations, all of which he bore very patiently and charitably. He was a very kind-hearted man, and charitable to all. He was twice married to noble, self-sacrificing women, who were much help to him in his work. He spent his last then years in Elora, Tenn., where he owned a little home. His broken-hearted widow, whose privilege it was to cheer and comfort in his last days, now lives there (*Gospel Advocate*, Jan. 31, 1924, p. 120).

This was the last time J.R. was formally addressed in the *Advocate*. There were scanty indirect references to him, in a list of many other preachers who had worked in the same region of Middle-Tennessee, as J.R. had worked. Not everything concerning J.R.'s life and death had been settled with his burial. There had been a matter of settling his estate.

In 1916, when J.R. visited Wolf Creek, it appears that he had made arrangements with his brother Lafayette, to settle his affairs upon his death. When news of J.R.'s death came to his family, which lived near Iron City, Tennessee and Greenhill, Alabama, Lafayette and his younger brother A.J. (Jack) traveled to Elora, Tennessee. It was Lafayette's unpleasant duty to settle J.R.'s estate. Even though J.R.'s wife, Loula Emma, survived him, J.R. had requested Lafayette to oversee the matters of settling his estate (Carrie Danley Interview).

He organized a sale of some of J.R.'s personal items. The list still exists in the Lincoln County, Tennessee Archives. According to the list, A.J. bought a lard stand and four chairs at the cost of 35 cents. Only five persons made a purchase at the sale. A bed, a wash kettle, several glasses and chairs, and one cow were sold. The total sale brought $36.02. That sounds like such a small amount in 2019, but in 1923 that could have bought one or two acres of land, depending upon the location. There is no evidence of Lafayette having bought any of J.R.'s possessions. The money obtained through the sale would help Loula Emma survive for a while.

After J.R.'s death it was believed that Lula went and lived with her family near New Market, Madison County, Alabama. She never remarried. She died on October 14, 1929 and was buried in the Rice Cemetery near New Market, Alabama, alongside her mother Eliza Wells Sloan. She died having not made a will. In the settlement of her affairs, it was revealed that the value of her estate was $500. It was also revealed that she owned a vacant lot, located in Huntsville, Alabama, on Blunts Alley, at the time of her death. (Madison County, Alabama Petition for Administration of Estate, October 31, 1929). We are left to wonder if she had bought the lot with the intention of building a house in Huntsville.

EPILOGUE

With J.R.'s death, one of the most productive lives of any of "Larimore's Boys" came to an end. He had baptized thousands of souls into the body of Christ and had established or aided in the establishment of thirty congregations. He had revived several congregations that had been "all but dead." He helped raise money to build several meeting houses. He had performed hundreds of weddings and had comforted thousands of troubled souls. He was loved by all who personally knew him. He was respected by all and was known simply as "Brother Bradley," His accomplishments could be measured against any of the Mars Hill students and without shame. That is not bad for a "Tennessee plowboy" who, at first, could barely write his name. Larimore was proud of "boys" like J.R.

From time to time this writer drives by the Rose Hill cemetery in Fayetteville, Tennessee, and visits the grave of J.R. and thinks of all of the accomplishments that he had with minimal education and resources and wonders how he succeeded. We know that he had an unwavering faith and perseverance that many of us lack in our own time. Many lessons can be learned by studying the life of this dear old soldier of the cross. When one studies through the life of a subject such as J.R. he feels that he is in the very mind of that subject being studied. J.R. can provide the reader with an insight into the times in which he lived, along with the changes he witnessed. He listened to the battle at Shiloh from a great distance, when only a boy and rode in his first automobile only seven years before his death. He saw our country grow up into a powerful force in the world. He lived under twenty different presidents and saw the rise and fall of political parties and the demise of some ideals and the rise of others. A study of his life is a sociological study of religion. He was the force behind the establishment of more than thirty congregations of the Church of Christ in Alabama and Tennessee and helped rescue some that were in serious trouble and put them back on the right track. He raised money to help erect church buildings, when he himself needed the help in a financial way; and after more than a hundred years, some of those buildings are still standing. He battled unorthodox religious views and debated religious opponents. He wrote articles to admonish the brethren to love the Lord and serve Him. He left a legacy of hard work and patience for those who follow in the Lord's way.

INDEX

Maplewood (Giles Co., TN), 145–147, 156–157, 159

Marsh Academy, 72–74, 117

Marsh, Sheb, 70

Marshall County, TN, 12, 20, 29, 36, 43, 53–54, 56, 58–59, 65, 70, 80–81, 103–104, 107, 115, 164, 242, 250, 283, 298, 301, 306, 327

Mars Hill, 10–13, 18–21, 24, 26, 32, 43–44, 49, 54, 61, 64, 68, 94, 97, 118–119, 140, 146–147, 154, 159, 194, 221, 235, 241, 268, 288, 302–304, 335–336, 339

Mars Hill College, vii, 10, 15–17, 19, 24, 26–27, 32, 59, 95, 184, 268, 274

Martin, D.L., 216

Martin, J.C., 125

Mary (biblical character), 174

Mary (mother of Jesus), 294

Matthews, Mansell W., 224

Maury County, TN, 19, 36, 38, 43, 54–55, 61, 65, 79, 96, 104, 179, 327

Mayfield, Pamela, 110

Mayhew, Aaron, 5

Maysville (Madison Co., AL), 163*The Medical World*, 249

Merrimac, 331

Methodist(s), 23, 30–31, 40, 55, 60, 71, 73–74, 76–77, 80–82, 84, 87, 94, 114, 116, 123, 135–136, 144, 146–147, 150–151, 159, 170, 177, 184–185, 209, 240, 275, 317–319, 328

Michie, TN, 236–237, 242, 247

Miller, John A., 165

Minnow Branch (Giles Co., TN), 77

Minor Hill, TN 149, 157

Missionary Baptist Church, 102

Molino (Lincoln Co., TN), 72–77, 79, 83, 85, 118–120, 122, 124–127, 133–134, 139, 162, 173, 177–178, 180–181, 184, 218, 230–231, 235, 244–246, 253, 270–272, 285

Molloy, Sara, 216

Moody, R.N., 164

Moore County, TN, 115, 122, 139, 155, 230–231, 283

Moore, M.N. (d. 1906), 244–245

Mooresville, AL, 80

Morgan County, AL, 12–13

Morton, J.H., 67, 81, 86–87, 95, 97, 104

Morton, W.S., 54

Morton, Willie, 41–42

Moses (Israelite leader), 92

Mount Hermon (Bedford Co., TN), 254

Mulberry, 118, 120

Murfreesboro, TN, 121, 170, 197

Nance, Estelle J., 38

Nance, Martin M. (M.M.) (d. 1879), 28, 38, 146

Nance, Thomas G., 81

Nashville, TN, 67, 97, `09–110, 153, 186, 190, 205, 207, 210, 212, 229, 271, 282, 307

Nashville Bible School, 194

Neal, A.J., 27

New Hermon (Bedford Co., TN), 120, 124–126, 128–130, 132–134, 162, 180, 305–306, 308

New Hope (Lincoln Co., TN), 68

New Hope Baptist Church (Morgan Co., AL), 14

New Market (Madison Co., AL), 277, 357

New Orleans, LA, 4, 10

New Providence (Giles Co., TN), 327

New Testament Church, 329

New Union (Giles Co., TN), 102, 114

New Zion (Giles Co., TN), 327

Nichols, John H., 80–81

Nix, D.W. (d. 1919), 324

Nix, Mary E. (d. 1920), 326

Nix, R.N. (d. 1919), 324, 326

Nix, Sallie, 40

Noblit, Thomas H., 149

Noblit's Chapel (Giles Co., TN), 147–150, 159, 161

Noblitt, B.E., 259–260